THE DOCTORS ARE IN

THE DOCTORS ARE IN

The Essential and Unofficial Guide to
Doctor Who's Greatest Time Lord

Graeme Burk Robert Smith?

ecw press

For Lori Steuart and Alex Kennard.
Old friends I've just met.

— GB

For Dorothy Zaionchkovsky.
The best roommate in the world.

— RS?

Introduction

> *"When you think about it, we're all different people, all through our lives. And that's okay. You've got to keep moving. So long as you remember all the people you used to be."*
>
> — The Doctor, "The Time of the Doctor" (2013)

Over the past 50 years, no character has changed more on television than the eccentric alien known as the Doctor. From his beginnings as a crotchety, anti-heroic scientist in 1963 to his current place in British pop culture as the mad and dangerous monster-fighting saviour of the universe, the titular character of *Doctor Who* has constantly evolved. And that's not only because he can regenerate into different bodies; the character has been reshaped according to the different needs of the public over five decades.

The Doctors Are In is a guide to television's most beloved time traveller. While our previous two books (*Who Is The Doctor: The Unofficial Guide to Doctor Who the New Series* and *Who's 50: The 50 Doctor Who Stories to Watch Before You Die*, both available from this fine publisher!) were guides to the *stories* featuring the Doctor, this is a guide to the *character* of the Doctor: who he is, how he came to be, how he changed and why he's a hero to millions.

Who We Are

This book is a co-authored affair, written by two people with very different takes on the world of *Doctor Who*. This time, each co-author decided to write the biography of the other.

Graeme Burk (written by Robert Smith?) Graeme was one of the first people I met when I moved to Canada. Ever since we took a ten-hour train ride to Chicago together, we've been fast friends. Helped, no doubt, by the fact that we're very different people. He once joked that, in different ways, we were each other's id and superego. It's true: he's stepped up to the plate in areas I've been terrified to go near, while at other times become the hilarious commentary track on some of the more outrageous aspects of my life.

Graeme may be one of the smartest (and funniest) people I know. He's extremely widely read, with a love of language I admire deeply. He can mentally access obscure trivia in seconds. And he has instincts for what works and what doesn't that are honed to perfection. I learned the art of the structural edit entirely by watching what he was doing.

He also loves a good debate and can happily argue any point until the cows come home — and positively revels in the fact that I invariably disagree with him. I think that's why these books have touched people in ways more profound than you'd expect episode guides to do: because they capture all the raucous argument of a good-natured fan debate, without any of the nastiness. I take no credit for any of this, by the way; the central idea was all Graeme's, and I just went along for the ride.

Graeme has this larger-than-life thing going on that makes him a true personality, whether that be at conventions, socially (my non-*Doctor Who* friends always enjoy his party antics) or in his deep commitment to making the world a better place, thanks to having mastered a job that regularly takes him to Haiti and Namibia to help children in need. I once saw him give a speech about his ineptitude when meeting Sophie Aldred that had the audience in hysterics — and had Sophie Aldred grinning like a fool backstage, because he didn't know she was listening in and about to run out and hug him. (I was at the same meeting — it was at the original Chicago convention that Graeme and I took the train ride to, in fact — and just as inept, but Ace never hugged me. I'm not bitter. Really.)

Incidentally, this also makes him the perfect radio show host. I'm not even an audio person, and yet I adore his magazine-style *Doctor Who* podcast, *Reality Bomb*, with a deep and abiding passion. As do many others in the podcasting world. And rightly so, because it's brilliant. You should download it. Have I mentioned how brilliant it is? Oh right, I see that I have . . .

Robert Smith? (written by Graeme Burk) First of all, the question mark is part of his name. (The *New York Times* and the BBC have had no problem with printing the question mark too! The only dissenter . . . *Doctor Who Magazine.*) I'm quite convinced that alone says practically everything about Robert Smith? Really.

He came up with a funny paper where he took his full-time job as a professor of mathematically modelling disease outbreaks and used it on zombie invasions. This resulted in him being interviewed by virtually every news agency on the planet and having a Discovery Channel documentary made about him, narrated by Morgan Freeman. Robert now loves slow news months more than any man alive. The only problem I have with this interest in the undead side of things is that people sometimes miss the point of his work: Robert *actually uses math* to model diseases like Ebola and HIV, to determine their potential spread depending on disease-specific factors. You don't need zombies for that to be an awesome job.

He became a fan of *Doctor Who* watching "The Green Death" as a cute five-year-old. (Name an episode, and he'll tell you the date he first watched it.) He's edited some brilliant books reviewing *Doctor Who* called *Outside In*, which you should read.

Smith? claims to have no favourite Doctor, but he spends an awful lot of time lingering around shrines he's created for Christopher Eccleston and Matt Smith. I think in 2074, long after he's died in an autoerotic asphyxiation episode that will scandalize *Doctor Who* fandom, we'll discover he has a notebook full of fan fiction about the tenth Doctor.

As he notes above, we've known each other for two decades. (We've spent much of that time as roommates at various conventions.) As he also notes above, we're id and superego. But we get along, I think, because we both try hard to make allowances for the other and we have a way of making compromises that's mostly a byproduct of his utter decency.

It's hard to believe, given how much we love arguing about *Doctor Who*, that the biggest argument we ever had was actually about the capitalization of the word "internet." (He won.) The second biggest was over the inclusion of cast lists in our episode guides. (I won that, mostly.)

By the way, he's a genius. And he didn't pay me to say that. Yet.

What We're Doing

The Doctors Are In is all about the Doctor. What made him the way he is? What motivates him? What does he care about? We try to guess at the some of the deeper psychological reasons and connect the behaviours across multiple episodes in the hope that we can see what makes the Time Lord tick. In 13 chapters, we outline each Doctor (and the one incarnation who didn't call himself that) using the following categories:

Basic Data The Doctor's first and last stories.

The Changing Face of *Doctor Who* A potted history of how *Doctor Who*, and British television and culture, changed during the tenure of each particular Doctor.

Who is [the Actor]? A look at the actor playing the Doctor, highlighting why he was chosen for the part and what happened while he was in the role.

Top Companion Every Doctor travels with a number of assistants, each revealing new and different facets of the Doctor's character. We name the one we think is chief among them.

Classic Foe Each Doctor has faced enemies that have defined his tenure. We identify the most important one.

Who is the Doctor? Our main character study, where we talk about each incarnation in depth, exploring who they are, how they interact with people and what motivates them.

Three Great Moments We isolate each Doctor's three greatest moments that are worth tracking down on DVD or Netflix.

Two Embarrassing Moments We mention the two moments with each Doctor that make us laugh or shake our heads.

Hmm?/Oh My Giddy Aunt?/Hai!?/What?/Brave Heart?/Unstable? Unstable?! UNSTABLE?!?/Wicked?/Yes, Yes, Yes?/Oh, for God's Sake?/Fantastic?/Brilliant?/Cool?/Don't Be Stupid? The bottom-line critique of each Doctor by one of the authors.
Second Opinion The co-author also gets his say. Sometimes the two authors agree. Sometimes we don't. Sometimes we *really* don't. And then the fun begins . . .

Index Files

Appended to each chapter are mini-reviews of the five stories (for the most part) we feel are essential to each Doctor. They aren't necessarily that character's best stories (though many are), but the stories central to understanding or appreciating that incarnation of the Doctor or good examples of the era they come from. As with our guide entries, sometimes both authors agree about this. Other times they profoundly differ.

Once More with Feeling, It's the Unbelievably Geeky Part

If you're not a hardcore fan, you can skip to the end of this introduction. If you are, stick around: we need to talk about the stuff we know you're dying to argue over.

First of all, we're only talking about the Doctor's appearances on television. There have been a lot of fab adventures with the Doctor in books, audios, webcasts, comics and even on the back of cereal packages. We feel it best to draw on stories that have been broadcast on television by the BBC. We do make an exception for the webisode "The Night of the Doctor," because of its significance for the character of the eighth Doctor.

In reviewing stories for the Index Files, we did allow for incomplete stories this time, and so there are stories with animated episodes. We didn't, however, include any of the stories completely missing from the BBC Archives and only available on audio. We try to give those stories some credit elsewhere, though.

We use the same episode titles as the DVD releases, so "An Unearthly Child," not "100,000 BC." For a similar reason, we consider the Modern Series that began in 2005 to be effectively a new

TV series, albeit one linked by continuity and heritage with the original or what we call the Classic Series of *Doctor Who*. As a result, we talk about Series One of the Modern Series, not Season 27. Also, we're deliberately moving away from calling the post-2005 show the "New Series"; it's been around for a decade now, so it's not really new. We've elected to call it the "Modern Series." Perhaps fan consensus will come up with a new term (or keep the same old one in place), but, hey, we're trying it out.

Lastly . . .

Hey, thanks for sticking around!

Our manifesto in doing all these books is that they should be fun. And if there's any lead character from any television show ever made that deserves the title of "fun," it's the Doctor. He's eccentric, charming, weird, angry, excitable, funny, unworldly, romantic and much more. And sometimes much less.

But he's the most compelling character ever. That's why we love him. And that's why we're interested in exploring who he is behind the often-colourful costume.

So are you ready? When we say run . . . *run!*

The First Doctor

Wanderer in the Fourth Dimension

(1963–1966)

Basic Data

First story: "An Unearthly Child" (1963)

Final story: "The Tenth Planet" (1966)

Final appearances: "The Three Doctors" (1972, played by William Hartnell) and "The Five Doctors" (1983, played by Richard Hurndall)

The Changing Face of *Doctor Who* In June 1963, Verity Lambert was hired by Sydney Newman, the head of drama of the British Broadcasting Corporation, to become producer of a new family science-fiction series. Lambert had never produced a television series. She had previously been an assistant to Newman, who had been brought in from Canada by one of the independent networks that was part of the private network ITV.

At ITV, Newman had created a string of hits, including *Armchair Theatre* and *The Avengers*, before being poached by the BBC. One of his first problems to solve was the gap between the sports results and the family entertainment programming later in the evening. Newman's solution was *Doctor Who*, a program that evolved from a tortuous process that began as a committee-led investigation into how the BBC should do science-fiction serials. After much discussion and a few dead ends, Newman shepherded the development — which was mostly conceptualized by writer C.E. Webber — until it took shape as the show Newman envisaged: an older time traveller, a young girl and her two schoolteachers who have adventures in space and time. Newman wanted it to painlessly educate about history and science while avoiding bug-eyed monsters.

Newman felt that Lambert was the person to make this new series happen. She brought the program together, often through sheer force of will, struggling with scripts that weren't quite right, abandoning many of them (the first story originally called for the time travellers to be shrunk to a few inches tall) and casting the main roles. In September 1963, she produced a first episode from a script by Anthony Coburn, which adapted C.E. Webber's ideas . . . and had to remake it when Newman objected to, among other things, the harsh characterization of the older time traveller known as the Doctor.

The first episode was remounted with more polished direction, some tweaked dialogue and a softer Doctor. Lambert then had to fight the BBC upper echelons, who perceived the series to be too expensive. She managed to get a second broadcast of the first episode when the debut was overshadowed by the assassination of President Kennedy, which occurred the day before the series' original airing. And somehow, over the objections of her boss, she managed to make the second serial, which featured mutants from a post-atomic world (and definitely not bug-eyed monsters) known as the Daleks.

By January 1964, six weeks after its debut, *Doctor Who* was more than just a schedule-filler on BBC Television. It was a hit.

Who is William Hartnell? Though he couldn't have known it at the time, 1963 was the best year of William Hartnell's career.

The 55-year-old veteran actor had played his fill of heavies (most notably in 1949's *Brighton Rock*), police inspectors and army sergeants (most famously in the first Carry On film and the 1957–1961 comedy series *The Army Game*). But in 1963, everything changed.

January saw the release of *This Sporting Life*, Lindsay Anderson's unflinching look at the life of a professional rugby player, portrayed by Richard Harris. Hartnell played a talent scout — an older, slightly unworldly relic of a bygone age of amateur sport. It was a beautiful, sensitive performance, what would now be considered a breakout role for the actor, in a hugely acclaimed film. Hartnell's performance was noticed by Lambert, who thought he could play the character of the Doctor with the same quality that Frank Morgan played the Wizard of Oz in the eponymous 1939 film. Hartnell wasn't as convinced, but liked the departure it offered from his usual roles.

The Doctor was originally envisioned as an anti-heroic figure who was quite harsh and almost villainous. The harshness was toned down when the first episode was re-made, and it gradually softened over the initial episodes. Hartnell ultimately settled on playing the Doctor as a grandfather figure and loved the positive public attention he received as a result.

But Hartnell was not well. As a heavy smoker, he suffered from arteriosclerosis, a hardening of the arteries that made it difficult for him to remember lines and made him irritable on set. After the original cast and production team moved on, and the rigours of producing a show 48 weeks a year took its toll, Hartnell became even more difficult; he was proprietorial about the role and outright hostile to anyone who challenged him. Production staff used code phrases to deal with Hartnell: "We should talk to the designer" meant "Get a producer to the studio floor, now." Hartnell could often be placated, but not without considerable tension.

Eventually, this led to one of the bravest decisions ever made in *Doctor Who*'s history: that the show would continue without its lead actor. While this meant the end of William Hartnell's association with the part, his portrayal was still hugely influential: he is the original Doctor.

Top Companion Initially, the Doctor is deeply mistrustful of his human companions, kidnapping them and going head to head with them on more than one occasion. But through history teacher Barbara Wright, that dynamic shifts. The Doctor becomes particularly affectionate towards her, while she in turn challenges him to be less cynical and mean. The Doctor becomes more humane, and human, in his attitudes thanks to Barbara's influence.

Classic Foe *Doctor Who* would have been a fondly remembered, briefly run 1960s series — a minor curiosity for British TV geeks — were it not for the Daleks. Writer Terry Nation's idea that these robotic creatures glide instead of walk, brilliantly realized by designer Raymond Cusick, was a game changer for the nascent series. Science-fiction television and film had lots of Robby the Robot–type lumbering men in suits, but the way the Daleks moved, and even spoke, made them seen genuinely alien. Nation's further innovation — that they were mutants inside a robotic casing, not machines — gave them the xenophobic characterization that has made them so compelling over 50 years. The Daleks turned *Doctor Who* into an overnight sensation and defined the direction of the series, changing it from a program with forays into history and futuristic parables to a show with *monsters*.

Who is the Doctor? We know almost nothing about the Doctor when we first meet him. He says he's from another time and world and lets out occasional hints about his past. (He says he can't go back to his home planet in 1966's "The Massacre.") There's no backstory; he's just an old man with an impossible time machine.

Even so, when we first encounter the Doctor, he is not the hero he later becomes. The first glimpse of him in 1963's "An Unearthly Child" finds him suspicious, bordering on paranoid, supercilious and even malicious. In his very first adventure, he contemplates killing a wounded caveman simply because he's slowing them down. The following adventure, 1963's "The Daleks," is predicated on the Doctor manipulating his companions into believing they need to go to the Dalek city for mercury for a fluid link that is actually working — and he nearly kills his party from radiation poisoning as a result of that ruse.

In short, the Doctor is an absolute bastard. But this doesn't remain the status quo.

The Doctor changes mostly through his relationships with Ian and Barbara. The Doctor at first is clearly not happy with having others question his decisions (he never quite gets over that in 50 years). After he almost forcibly ejects them from the ship because he believes they've caused a fault in the TARDIS, Barbara confronts the

Doctor, insisting that their presence has helped him survive. Shamed by this, the Doctor comes to realize the value of having human friends. Barbara, in particular, becomes a confidante, and he trusts Ian with his life repeatedly. Perhaps it is the building of these friendships, and the softening of the Doctor as a result, that allows him to let his granddaughter, Susan, leave.

His enemies define him too. While his first encounter with the Daleks is something of an ordeal, by the time he meets them again, when they're occupiers of the Earth in the 22nd century, he is ready to take them on as enemies, decrying their claim to be masters of Earth and immediately resisting them. As time goes on, the enemies he faces are not so much obstacles to getting back to the TARDIS as they are foes that need to be defeated.

The Doctor becomes less of an anti-heroic autocrat and more of a grandfather figure, not just to Susan but to everyone he travels with. He's less malicious and more mischievous, giggling with delight when he's outwitted an enemy. He's charming to the string of companions he takes on after Ian and Barbara, though he still has moments of grouchiness. It's as though travelling with humans has helped him define himself and his values. By the time of 1966's "The Savages," the Doctor is seen as a very moral figure — so much so that his sense of justice is actually transplanted into another person. That's a far cry from the man who contemplated murder in the first story.

Even so, the Doctor remains alien. There's no greater reminder of this than the final episode of 1966's "The Tenth Planet" when the Doctor becomes mysteriously infirm and, at the end of the story, he falls to the floor of the TARDIS . . . and transforms.

Three Great Moments In 1964's "The Aztecs," Barbara has impersonated a god and is attempting to change history so that the Aztec people will survive the Spanish conquest. The Doctor gives her an impassioned speech, saying, "You can't rewrite history. Not one line." He then goes on to say that what she is doing is utterly impossible and adds, for emphasis, "I know. Believe me, I know." Hartnell's acting here is superb, hinting at a wealth of past pain solely through these two lines of dialogue.

"The Romans" (1965) finds the Doctor, through a chain of comic circumstances, mistaken for a popular lyre player who has to perform in the court of Emperor Nero. The Doctor borrows a page from Hans Christian Andersen and claims he's playing the lyre so quietly it can only be heard by the most discerning ear. He then proceeds to entirely mime his "recital." It's performed exceptionally well by Hartnell, who excelled at comedic scenes like this.

A copy of the end of "The Massacre" doesn't exist, but we still have the soundtrack, and it contains one of the most wonderful moments in the first Doctor's era. Having fallen out with his companion Steven, the Doctor is left alone in the TARDIS, musing about his life: "Even after all this time he cannot understand. I dare not change the course of history . . . Now they're all gone. All gone. None of them could understand. Not even my little Susan, or Vicki. And as for Barbara and Chatterton . . . Chesterton. They were all too impatient to get back to their own time. And now, Steven. Perhaps I should go home, back to my own planet. But I can't. I can't." Don't believe the docudrama *An Adventure in Space and Time*, which portrays William Hartnell doing this scene in a fog of near-dementia. In actuality, Hartnell was totally on form and captured the Doctor at his most world-weary and sad. Unforgettable.

Two Embarrassing Moments In 1965's "The Chase," the Daleks are pursuing the Doctor through time. At one point, the TARDIS lands on the Empire State Building, where they meet Morton Dill, a "Well, gol-l-l-eee!" stereotype of a dense American from Alabama. WATCH as he can't pronounce complicated words! MARVEL as he says "hot diggety" and "Gol darn it"! GASP as he even gives the story its title, saying "Y'all is in a chase"! SHUDDER as he confronts a Dalek by putting his face in its weapon! Neither of us is even from the U.S. (it's a smaller country, on our southern border), but this is not just offensive, it's downright dumb. The only redeeming thing about Morton Dill is actor Peter Purves, whom they re-hired to play companion Steven Taylor a few episodes later. Though thankfully with no resemblance to his American doppelgänger.

We're pretty sure we want one of the embarrassing moments from 1965's "The Web Planet." We're just not sure which one. So let's put it to the vote and see what you think. Is it "What if the power's that's got hold of the TARDIS has taken your pen?" Is it the Zarbi running full-force into the camera? Is it the slow-motion sky-dancing by men dressed as butterflies hanging on Kirby wires? Is it the awkward shuffling of the Optera as they hop along while wearing obvious foam extensions? Or is it the entire six-episode story? Answers to whoisthedoctor@gemgeekorrarebug.com please.

Hmm? (GB) We're here today writing this book, and you're probably here reading it, because in 1963 this goofy show designed to fill a need for family programming on Saturday nights caught the imagination of the British public. And the curmudgeonly, mischievous titular grandfather was a big part of that.

Or was he?

The thing about *Doctor Who* that's hard to get now is that, while the Doctor was the catalyst of many adventures (he did drive the time machine after all), he wasn't necessarily the hero. The Doctor was part of a character ensemble that included a brainy history teacher and a no-nonsense action man of a science teacher. Plots unfolded as much around Ian and Barbara as they did the Doctor.

Perhaps that's why the first Doctor seems so different to modern viewers. Because he's not the proactive let's-go-adventuring-and-take-down-monsters central character we all know today. But that's one of the reasons I find this era of *Doctor Who* so fascinating: watching a series take the first three years or so to develop its lead.

When the Doctor does take centre stage, it's in little moments. Like standing up to the Daleks in their second appearance. ("Conquered the Earth? You poor, pathetic creatures. Don't you realize? Before you attempt to conquer the Earth, you will have to destroy all living matter.") Or sparring with the Animus in "The Web Planet." Or out-witting the Meddling Monk in "The Time Meddler." By "The War Machines," at the close of *Doctor Who*'s third season, it's the Doctor, not Ben (the younger male lead), taking on the monsters directly.

Through it all, we have William Hartnell, an actor vastly under-rated by history. In 2013, the BBC unearthed interview footage of Hartnell from 1967 and it became instantly apparent how much a creation of the actor his Doctor was. The Doctor's manner and inflections of speech — even his accent — are distinct from Hartnell's own; they're all part of the role. (Roles, even: the character he plays in the broadcast version of "An Unearthly Child" is quieter, more thoughtful and devious than the one he settled on, and that's ignoring the unbroadcast version of the first episode.)

Here I need to make a confession: I never liked William Hartnell's Doctor when I was growing up. Troughton charmed me; Pertwee was lovely; Tom Baker was my unofficial god. But William Hartnell was . . . of his time, I concluded. My co-author once quipped that William Hartnell was his favourite Doctor and I accused him of lying. (Alcohol might have been involved.) Before the restoration processes that made those early episodes more accessible, almost no one would have said that Hartnell was a favourite.

But it's thanks to those stories being released on DVD in a more watchable form that I looked on Hartnell's Doctor in a new light. I realized how talented Hartnell was as an actor. He knew how to make a closeup say everything. He could play the hell out of a comedic scene. He did pathos equally beautifully. He fluffed lines, but he also acted the pants off most people in a scene with him. I began to realize that, even when the Doctor is taking a back seat, he's often the most compelling character in the story.

I gradually came to realize an amazing truth: the key to understanding the Doctor is that he's many men in one man (for the moment anyway), even with the first Doctor. He is sullen, grumpy, manipulative, mischievous, amused, affectionate, paternal, a joker and a sad old man. William Hartnell made all these qualities seamlessly part of the same man. And that man was the Doctor.

Second Opinion (RS?) In 2013, as part of the fiftieth anniversary mega-celebration of *Doctor Who*, Mark Gatiss produced an historical drama based on the genesis of the show, *An Adventure in Space and Time*. This was something of an oddity: it showed the behind-the-scenes story of the people involved in the very beginning of *Doctor Who*: Sydney Newman, Verity Lambert, Waris Hussein. But the star of the show is very clearly William Hartnell.

The idea that anyone other than hardcore geeks would be remotely interested in a dramatization of bureaucratic meetings, set design and science-fiction-as-designed-by-committee is astonishing. And yet *An Adventure in Space and Time* was the sixth-most-watched show on BBC2 that week. It's not merely wonderful; it's arguably the best thing that was made for the fiftieth anniversary.

Because what *Adventure* does is capture something at the core of *Doctor Who*. People struggling with something bigger than they were, facing overwhelming odds and pulling a massive success out of the fire exactly mirrors the wonder of the show itself. And by the time Hartnell himself appears, in footage from his farewell to Susan in "The Dalek Invasion of Earth," you'll be weeping buckets of tears.

As Graeme says, I loved William Hartnell's Doctor long before it was cool to do so. I think his Doctor is a fascinating one, the era he spans is a creative potpourri that was continually pushing the envelope, and the various cul-de-sacs that they didn't quite go down make for fascinating insights into where the show might have gone before it found its feet. Hartnell himself is a superb actor, playing to the back row of some other theatre, but in such a way that balances the strength of the character's personality without making him over the top.

One of the things I love most about the Hartnell years is the boundary busting. Even in the '60s, they're simultaneously discovering and trying to invert *Doctor Who*'s format. The TARDIS lands in two time zones, millions of years apart, in "The Ark," providing one hell of a shock cliffhanger. There's the 12-episode-long epic battle that is "The Daleks' Master Plan," including a comedy Christmas episode in the middle. "The Rescue" is a quiet two-parter that is there solely to introduce a new companion, on the grounds that we've never had that happen before. There's a story populated entirely by aliens ("The Web Planet"). Another story, "The War Machines," anticipated the worldwide dominance of the internet by 35 years. If you look at just about any Hartnell story, you can see the attempts to prod and poke the series, to see what's possible. It's about the only era of *Doctor Who* that doesn't have a house style, and I love it for that.

I used to have to explain to sceptics (like my co-author) that the Hartnell era didn't survive the transition to the video age very well because it was never designed that way. You're supposed to watch it one episode a week, not marathon a seven-episode story in one sitting. But I'm not sure I need to do that any more, because there's been something of a sea change.

When the Modern Series appeared, I figured its fanbase would only rarely check out the Classic Series. I thought it was too old, too creaky and too monochrome for viewers raised on modern television. You also had the immediate problem of so many missing episodes in the early years. Surely all these factors would put people off? Happily, I was entirely wrong about this. Entirely. What's more, those new fans really surprised me. I've seen teenage fangirls ship Ian and Barbara, cosplay Vicki and live-tweet their way through a telesnap reconstruction.

However, the reason all this is possible is because back then *Doctor Who* wasn't being made as throwaway weekly television. Instead, as *An Adventure in Space and Time* shows, it was being made as though it were high art. That's because those who worked on the series, who made the magic happen, weren't the staid professional men of the old BBC. Instead, you had the first female producer at the BBC, a gay Anglo-Indian director and an eccentric Canadian who came from a background in kitchen-sink dramas. And it all pivoted around a larger-than-life film actor who was at once cantankerous, bullying and loveable. Misfits, outsiders and oddballs, every one of them. People who didn't fit in, but who were driven by a passion for something greater than they were and who were determined to use their creative energies for all they were worth, no matter what anyone thought.

In short, they were just like us, the generations of fans who followed behind them. And that's one hell of an adventure.

An Unearthly Child (1963)

Written by Anthony Coburn

Directed by Waris Hussein

The Big Idea Schoolteachers Ian Chesterton and Barbara Wright are puzzled by their pupil Susan Foreman. They follow her home to a junkyard containing a police box — and wind up in the Stone Age.

Hmm? (RS?) Everyone knows how amazing that first episode is. It's a landmark piece of television, it's slick and polished, and it introduces the concept of the series to viewers in a sensational way. It's a bit of a cliché to say that the first story consists of one brilliant introductory episode and three episodes of dull running around caves, trying to make fire. I want to take a moment to point out the joys of the other three episodes.

For one thing, the story plunges right into the alienness. All of Ian's protests about the abilities of the TARDIS are swept away in seconds, because he's standing in a forest at the dawn of time, where 15 minutes earlier he was in a twentieth-century junkyard. Add to that a beautiful speech by the Doctor — "If you could touch the alien sand and hear the cries of strange birds and watch them wheel in another sky, would that satisfy you?" — just moments before he opens the TARDIS doors to let Ian see for himself, and you have a second episode that's worth it for that moment alone.

For another, you've got the moment when the TARDIS crew are trying to escape, but the caveman Za is wounded and slowing them down. And the nascent Doctor, this crotchety old alien we don't yet know, *picks up a rock and hovers over him with it*. It's only when Ian grabs his arm and asks what he is doing that he stops. The implication is clear: the Doctor was about to kill an innocent man simply for being in the way. There's another broader implication too: that the Doctor doesn't yet have the moral centre that he'll come to, suggesting that he gains it from his human companions. That right there is an awesome reason to love the third episode.

Finally, you've got the Doctor masterfully playing the crowd in the fourth episode, as the tribe discovers the old woman's death and accuses Za of killing her. Whereupon the Doctor steps up, pointing out that Za's knife has no blood on it; when Kal challenges that point, the Doctor boasts about what an incredible knife Za has, whereupon Kal's pride forces him to pull out his own knife . . . thereby revealing the blood on it. It's like courtroom drama with flickering torches, and it's the first moment we see the Doctor becoming the triumphant Doctor we know, standing up for what's right by being smarter than anyone else in the room.

It's not just those isolated moments either. This three-part story has a punishing tone to it, one that makes a bunch of humans on Earth as dangerous, unpredictable and alien as any monster story to follow. Yes, the entire tale is a disjointed melding of two very different stories. But the second of those stories has much to offer and, arguably, has as much to say about what's to follow as its predecessor does.

Second Opinion (GB) There are television shows where the first episode serves as a template of how things will go from then on. Then there are television shows where the first episode is nothing like what it becomes. *Doctor Who* is in the latter category. There's no monster; the Doctor is harsh, mean, unheroic and downright cold-blooded (he isn't even called "the Doctor" until the second episode); the adventure they're on isn't an adventure — it's an ordeal shown in terrifying detail; and the focus of the first episode is on a schoolgirl and her teachers.

However, while it's definitely not what *Doctor Who* would later become, in many ways you can see early glimmers of that later program in this story. When Barbara steps through the doors of the police box, we finally see the full-blooded imagination behind the show, and things transform from mundane to quite remarkable. The Doctor isn't the Doctor as we'll know him, but William Hartnell puts so much into the part that he's still compelling. The mystery of Susan and how it's shown (through flashbacks, something *Doctor Who* wouldn't do much of for the next 26 years), as well as its subsequent resolution, is why that first episode has eclipsed the remaining three for decades.

"An Unearthly Child" is *Doctor Who* both becoming and not quite becoming the show we know and love. And it's utterly enthralling as a result.

The Edge of Destruction (1964)

Written by David Whitaker

Directed by Richard Martin and Frank Cox

The Big Idea The Doctor and his companions are trapped within a malfunctioning TARDIS that seems to be trying to kill them.

Hmm? (GB) In the language of television, "bottle episodes" are when, to save money, an episode takes place on a standing set, often with no additional cast. They're a common occurrence in most dramas, but *Doctor Who* has only done it twice in 50 years. The first, and major, occurrence was a two-part serial featuring only the regular cast on the TARDIS set.

For years, popular lore was that this was done as a cost-saving or logistical measure because sets weren't ready (or were too expensive) for the next story, "Marco Polo." Later research revealed that the story was always on deck as a character study, which makes a lot of sense. The first two serials found the human companions mistrustful of the Doctor, and vice versa, but this arrangement probably wasn't sustainable in the long term. This story sought to clear the air and establish a new status quo.

However, what I haven't said about "The Edge of Destruction" yet is that . . . it's totally and completely *whacked*.

The basic plot involves a faulty switch on the TARDIS that's hurtling the time machine back to the creation of the universe. Rather than simply display an error message, the TARDIS instead attempts to drive its occupants mad — the story opens with Susan attempting to stab Ian with a pair of scissors — while dropping oblique clues. The result sees the series regulars performing a play Harold Pinter might have written had he been interested in science fiction or drunk a lot of absinthe.

It's totally strange and bewildering, but it's actually kind of cool too. The Doctor's paranoia is off the charts, while Ian and Barbara have to get him to trust them. The drama is gripping and unforgettable. Jacqueline Hill has the best scene as Barbara gets in the Doctor's face about his selfishness and ingratitude over the past two stories, while William Russell is brilliant at getting the Doctor to move past his suspicion and see the actual problem that's occurring with the TARDIS.

William Hartnell gives an incredible performance that takes in distrust, outrage, murderous intent and deviousness before getting to a brilliant monologue wherein he solves the problem.

All this takes him to the final point — that Ian and Barbara are his friends — and he has this lovely, touching rapprochement with Barbara, and it all feels, surprisingly, earned.

There probably isn't a more bizarre story in *Doctor Who* than "The Edge of Destruction," but that bizarreness creates intense and highly watchable drama. It's an experiment never repeated but fascinating nonetheless.

Second Opinion (RS?) This is the story that creates the Doctor as we know him. Previously we'd seen him as a crotchety anti-hero who kidnapped humans and was prepared to brain innocent cavemen or put everyone at risk to satisfy his curiosity. This story amps that up to 11 as the Doctor threatens to put Ian and Barbara off the ship. But it also comes full circle as the Doctor comes to realize not only that what's happening isn't their fault but just how damaging his accusations have been.

This comes to a head at the end of the first episode when Barbara, full of righteous anger, steps up and directly calls the Doctor on his crap. She tells him he's a stupid old man. She reminds him that she and Ian saved him from both the Daleks and from the cavemen. She tells him he should get down on his hands and knees and thank them. It's a brilliant speech. And what does he do in response? He immediately drugs everyone (including his granddaughter) with a sleeping draught.

Then, in the second episode, after things have gone from bad to worse, they're forced to work together to solve the problem. And when it turns out to be a tiny fault in the machinery, not only does the Doctor apologize in the moment, he goes back for it later. When Barbara asks why he cares what she thinks, he tells her, "As we learn about each other, so we learn about ourselves."

It's a pivotal line. Because it changes the Doctor from a selfish old man who only cares about himself and his granddaughter to one who cares about others. From this moment on, the TARDIS crew works as a team, never having the same internal conflict. And the Doctor becomes the embodiment of morality, looking out for the underdog and championing the oppressed. All thanks to Barbara and the lesson he learned in this little two-part bottle story.

The Dalek Invasion of Earth (1964)

Written by Terry Nation

Directed by Richard Martin

The Big Idea The TARDIS lands in London in the 22nd century — and Daleks are now the masters of Earth.

Hmm? (GB) Throughout these index files, we're going to be presenting you with some key moments when *Doctor Who* changed, for good or for ill. "The Dalek Invasion of Earth" is one such moment.

This is the story in which the Daleks transform from one-off monsters to a recurring foe. To do that, a lot of handwaving is performed: the pepperpots' first story saw them trapped in a single city; now they're a planet-conquering race with spaceships and the means to turn humans into robotic slaves.

This changes the Doctor as well, because he suddenly goes from this dotty scientist who randomly travels through time and space to the sort of man who has arch enemies. To his credit, the Doctor wears this change rather well; in "The Daleks," he was often as terrified as everyone else; here he's standing up to the Daleks from the get-go.

"The Dalek Invasion of Earth" works partially because of the visuals: the extended location sequences (previously unheard of on *Doctor Who*) of the Daleks occupying future London (albeit a barely disguised future) are surprisingly effective. The Second World War was just in the rear-view mirror of Britain, so the landscape of instructional posters — "It is forbidden to dump bodies in the river" — deserted streets, rations, black marketeers and a scared populace had a real punch in 1964, and it still works today.

It's a tricky story: it opens with high stakes as soon as the Dalek emerges from the Thames at the end of episode one, while the final episodes have a lot of tension as the four time travellers try to avert the Daleks' plan to destroy the Earth's core. In between those two points is a lot of stalling in order to get all the pieces from the outskirts to the centre of the Daleks' operations — and keep them alive. Fortunately, Terry Nation excels at writing tiny set pieces that are surprisingly effective: Dortmun's sacrifice is poignant, in part because of the way Nation thoughtfully built up the character over several episodes. And there are several great moments like that, most of them with Barbara, who is the perfect gateway character for these glimpses of life under occupation.

It's a good swansong for Carole Ann Ford, who, as an actress, was better than the material given to her as Susan — and who barely had anything to work with in the first place. It's 1964, so the way to write out a female companion is to — surprise, surprise — marry her off, even though she's a teenager! And yet, Ford makes Susan's almost inexplicable pairing with David seem credible. William Hartnell has the thankless job of making the Doctor's "tough love" abandonment of Susan seem like a heartfelt, loving gesture. And he actually makes it work.

With "The Dalek Invasion of Earth," *Doctor Who* in one fell swoop becomes a series with recurring villains, a hero at the ready to take on those foes and lead characters who would depart from time to time. In short, it becomes closer to the show we know and love.

Second Opinion (RS?) My co-author is wrong. Hartnell doesn't just make that final farewell to Susan work, he knocks it out of the park. The speech that the Doctor gives at the end of this story may be one of the most powerful in all of *Doctor Who*. Rightly famous for the "one day, I shall come back" parts that were re-used in "The Five Doctors" (and *An Adventure in Space and Time*), it's worth noting that the full speech is quite magnificent. The Doctor points out that as much as he's been taking care of his granddaughter, she's been taking care of him. He notes that she would never voluntarily leave a silly old buffer like him, so he has to force her hand. And so, having overheard how much she loves David, he double-locks the doors.

What's particularly impressive about this speech is that Terry Nation had only scripted the bare bones of it, so Hartnell ad-libbed much of it. And it's utterly perfect. I can recite it over and over again, usually followed in my head by an ethereal "whoosh" as I imagine the '80s credits from "The Five Doctors" kicking in.

And yet, the Doctor never does go back for Susan. Sure, she meets him again briefly when she is time-scooped for the show's twentieth anniversary. But even when he could subsequently steer the TARDIS, he never returns. This theme of the Doctor not wanting to return for his former companions — even those he loved dearly — is one that eventually plays out in "School Reunion." (As Graeme says, "The Dalek

Invasion of Earth" establishes several of the Doctor's essential characteristics.) And I think Susan knows he won't be back for her, since she drops her TARDIS key on the ground and simply walks away. Because she knows the fundamental nature of the Doctor: he's a man who runs away. And all the speeches in the universe won't change that.

The Romans (1965)

Written by Dennis Spooner

Directed by Christopher Barry

The Big Idea The Doctor and Vicki travel to Rome to meet Nero. Unbeknownst to them, Ian and Barbara are also there. But the Doctor soon discovers that, while Rome wasn't built in a day, it burnt down in considerably less time.

Hmm? (RS?) The Hartnell era has a reputation for being slow and ponderous, with scenes that take forever and a sense that the TARDIS crew never met a wall they didn't want to investigate for five minutes to see what it was made of.

And then you have "The Romans," just about the slickest comedy imaginable. It has it all. There's the high farce of Ian and Barbara being in Rome at the same time as the Doctor and Vicki but the two groups never meeting. There's the hilariously slimy Nero, continually trying it on with Barbara and failing. There's the Doctor improvising madly, comically beating up assassins and "performing" on the lyre. And there are serious moments too, such as Ian being sold into slavery, forced into hard labour on board a galleon, shipwrecked and made to fight his friend.

There's also witty dialogue, like "Oh, the child, she travels with me. She keeps her eye on all the lyres." Or Nero's "Now close your eyes and Nero will give you a big surprise" and Barbara's brilliantly timed "Pardon?" in response. Or, when Nero wants to talk to the Doctor but is too busy chasing Barbara and so runs off, the Doctor exclaims, "What an extraordinary fellow!" Hartnell's comic timing is superb, as is Derek Francis's, making their scenes together a joy to watch.

Oh, and if you're looking to ship Ian and Barbara, there's no better episode in which to do it. They lounge around in the villa in the opening moments, Ian eating grapes and Barbara doing his hair. It's about as post-coital as *Doctor Who* ever gets; the fact that it happens in the '60s is just mindblowing.

The story prior to this was "The Rescue," which was a murder mystery with one suspect. The subsequent story is "The Web Planet," an all-alien tale at the speed of treacle, with characters standing (or flying) around for what seem like hours at a time. But in between you have "The Romans," which moves like greased lightning and is confident, postmodern and hilarious. It's head and shoulders above just about everything around it and is probably my favourite William Hartnell story. You really can't go wrong with this one.

Second Opinion (GB) There's a moment in episode three of "The Romans" when a bumbling aide to Nero, who's been underfoot the whole time, finally gets his comeuppance. The Doctor rushes in to warn Nero that his drink might have been poisoned and, after the Doctor leaves, Nero gives the drink to his aide, who promptly dies. It's a demented, disturbing and unbelievably funny payoff to a brilliant running gag. It may be one of the funniest things in 50 years of *Doctor Who*.

But that's "The Romans" all over. The first story of the regime of *Doctor Who*'s second script editor, Dennis Spooner, and it seems like nothing less than a manifesto of what *Doctor Who* can be. It's the format-busting comedy episode that all great dramatic TV shows have ("The Trouble with Tribbles," "Pine Barrens," "Jose Chung's 'From Outer Space,'" "The Zeppo," "Love & Monsters" . . .), but in this case it had huge repercussions as everyone realized that *Doctor Who* was born to do comedy. The pacing in Dennis Spooner's script is brilliant, and the gags are Monty Pythonesque — before there was a Monty Python. William Hartnell and Jacqueline Hill are revealed to be gifted comic actors. When most people think comedic performances in *Who*, they think of Tom Baker. They should be thinking of Hartnell, who is unbelievably funny and can milk a scene for all it's worth without any histrionics. And as much as Derek Francis is great with the broad comedy, there are several chilling moments when it's clear his Nero is just plain crazy scary.

I think *Doctor Who* fans should commemorate January 16 (the day the first episode was broadcast) in honour of this story and what it did for *Doctor Who*. Without this story, we wouldn't have had *Doctor Who* as we know it. We could call it — wait for it — "Romans" Holiday.

Um . . . hello? Is this thing on?

The Ark (1966)

Written by Paul Erickson and Lesley Scott

Directed by Michael Imison

The Big Idea The Doctor, Steven and Dodo travel to the far future to find humans escaping the destruction of the Earth — and nearly wipe out humanity with the common cold. Seven hundred years later, that cold causes the humans to be enslaved by their former servants.

Hmm? (GB) In 1966, a BBC director named Michael Imison was coming to the end of his initial contract. The BBC weren't overly fond of him, but Imison was determined to prove his worth to the powers that be. Assigned a middling four episodes on the lower-prestige *Doctor Who*, Imison decided to push the envelope as far as he could.

Really, it's Imison's eye-popping work on "The Ark" that stands out more than anything. Imison didn't let anything stop him: not the ridiculous costume design, the silly-looking Monoids, not even the script, which starts out full of serious intent and ends in generic sci-fi clichés. "The Ark," in spite of all these flaws and more (the budget refuses to stretch to both a jail and a kitchen, so prisoners work in the "security kitchen"!) is still a visual feast of great action sequences, cool visuals, loads of background performers, a real elephant on set, awesome camera angles and a story that looks so much better than it actually is. And Imison did this in 1966, during an era when *Doctor Who* was otherwise shot "as live" in continuous sequences like a stage play. (Unsurprisingly, Imison was the first director to employ out-of-sequence shooting in *Doctor Who*.)

In fairness, the deficiencies of the story aren't really obvious at first. "The Ark" rests on a stunningly great idea, especially for the serialized era it was made in: after a seeming two-episode story where, at the end, the Doctor and his party leave a giant space ship, they arrive . . . back on the spaceship, only hundreds of years into the future, when the ship is now under the control of the alien servants. (This was an even bigger deal back in the days when *Who* was serialized and no one knew precisely when one story ended and another began.) If that conceit wasn't brilliant enough, writer Paul Erickson doubled down by having the first two episodes deal with the fallout of the time travellers bringing the common cold with them and consequently almost wiping out the last of humanity.

But that's all Erickson had. The second half of the story has the intriguing idea of the servants becoming masters, but does nothing except make them two-dimensional *Doctor Who* baddies. By the time we get to the godlike invisible aliens, the hopes of the first two episodes are lost to the *Doctor Who* Cliché Bingo that's underway (under the B, we have the Judas figure sacrificing himself . . .). It's a good thing it's a great story for the Doctor, who is the calm at the centre of the tempests between the human Guardians, the Monoids and the Refusians.

Ultimately, though, Michael Imison's contract wasn't renewed. It's the sort of ending that doesn't seem just, but then "The Ark" is frustrating that way.

Second Opinion (RS?) *Doctor Who* fans are amazingly intelligent creatures. We're always looking into the nooks and crannies of old episodes, taking them apart to see what makes them tick. And, having examined episodes of old 1960s television in forensic detail — to a degree far greater than the original writers, story editors, directors or actors ever did — sometimes we see things that they missed.

"The Ark" is a case in point. As my co-author mentions, there's a stunning trick at its core, one of the all-time great cliffhangers: the TARDIS has landed in the same spot at a different time. But, as my friend Andy Wixon has pointed out, how much better would it have been if the timezones had been reversed?

Suddenly, everything snaps into place. The Doctor could spend the first two episodes helping free enslaved humans from Monoids and discovering that the root of all this was back in prehistory, when strange travellers came aboard the Ark and infected the humans with a cold. That sets up a mystery we don't even know is going to be solved until the mid-story cliffhanger, when the TARDIS lands back on the Ark again . . . only 700 years earlier, and we learn that it's the

Doctor's companion who transmitted the cold in the first place. Even the racist undertone of the oppressed becoming the oppressor and needing to be overthrown again would be a little more palatable this way (okay, only a little).

Just about the only set piece that wouldn't translate is the reveal of the statue with the Monoid face, but that's only there to show you how much time has passed. What "The Ark" does is display the sheer scope of possibility that time travel affords. And those possibilities are quite impressive. But, as Andy pointed out, had they just gone one step further, those possibilities would have been not merely impressive, but downright stupendous.

As Graeme says, that's "The Ark" all over. Clever, but frustrating.

The Second Doctor

Change and Renewal

(1966–1969)

Basic Data

First story: "The Tenth Planet" (1966)

Final story: "The War Games" (1969)

Final appearance: "The Two Doctors" (1985)

The Changing Face of *Doctor Who* By 1966, the behind-the-scenes production of *Doctor Who* had been in some turmoil. Verity Lambert's replacement as producer, John Wiles, didn't get along with the ailing William Hartnell at all. Wiles's attempts to fire Hartnell had failed, so the producer left the show. However, a new, stable production team had recently materialized. Producer Innes Lloyd and script editor Gerry Davis had big, bold ideas for the series. Lloyd did away with historical stories, replacing them with an onslaught of monsters. Davis favoured gritty and down-to-earth tales. For a variety of reasons, this team had more clout to determine that William Hartnell should leave the role.

This led to perhaps the most novel decision in the history of *Doctor Who*. While John Wiles was planning to recast the role with someone who looked at least reasonably like Hartnell — the way recasting a part has been done since television was invented — Innes Lloyd and Gerry Davis borrowed a page from *The Strange Case of Dr. Jekyll and Mr. Hyde* and suggested that the Doctor could physically transform himself with a different face, a different costume and even a different personality. It was called a renewal onscreen and a rejuvenation in the press (it wasn't called regeneration until 1974). And they cast Patrick Troughton to play the role in a very different way.

Changing the Doctor is commonplace now, but in 1966 it was an enormous gamble, one that almost didn't pay off. Ratings for the show had dipped alarmingly towards the end of the Hartnell era, and there were fears that the public wouldn't accept another actor as the Doctor. Especially given how different his character would be.

To ease the transition to Troughton, the Daleks were brought back for the opening story, "The Power of the Daleks." This adventure saw the Doctor's companion Ben being extremely suspicious about the "renewal," with the Doctor himself not quite allaying his fears. (He refers to himself in the third person and merely answers Ben's questions with further questions.) However, the Doctor picks up a mirror and sees his past self in it, while later a Dalek recognizes the Doctor, which seals it for Ben (and for the viewers). *Doctor Who*, and the Doctor, never looked back. There was no further mention of the Doctor's transformation until the end of Troughton's tenure.

Ratings for the series were uneven for a while but stabilized with 1967's "The Moonbase," which saw the Cybermen — the new "big bad" — return, in updated form.

Troughton's second season became known as "the monster season," because it featured an array of shambling creatures oppressing small crews on isolated bases, upping the horror content and increasing the claustrophobia. Suddenly, *Doctor Who* was scary.

Behind the scenes, the changes started coming thick and fast. Production became a revolving door, with the show going through four producers in two years. Onscreen, the final Troughton season was about as chaotic. Production delays meant episodes were being filmed as little as a week before airing. Scripts fell through, resulting in last-minute replacements and, finally, there was an epic ten-episode story to close out the era, which revealed where the Doctor came from and who his people were: the all-powerful entities known as the Time Lords. The show was never the same again.

Who is Patrick Troughton? Recasting the Doctor was a precarious move, but William Hartnell saw the way forward when he told producer Innes Lloyd, not knowing who they were going to cast, "There's only one man in England who can take over and that's Patrick Troughton." Born in 1920, Patrick Troughton was exactly the age to be called up for service when the Second World War broke out. And serve he did: his boat destroyed an enemy ship by ramming it before being destroyed by gunfire. He was awarded medals for bravery and rose to the rank of lieutenant.

However, acting was Troughton's first love, and he returned to it as soon as the war was over. He established himself as a versatile character actor and was one of the first stage performers to grasp the true potential of television. Aside from a few notable parts (he was the first to play Robin Hood on TV; in fact, you can see a still of his Robin Hood in the 2014 story "Robot of Sherwood"), he rarely played the lead but was often that supporting character who always managed to steal the scene.

When it came to replacing William Hartnell, nobody knew if the idea would work, least of all Troughton himself. Fearing that the show wouldn't last, he asked to be hidden under heavy makeup or be allowed to play the role as a tough windjammer captain. Eventually the idea of the "cosmic hobo" was settled on, with Troughton's Doctor a quirky, bumbling character whom you couldn't entirely trust to save the day. Script editor Gerry Davis based this in part on James Stewart's performance in the 1939 film *Destry Rides Again.* Troughton preferred this characterization to the autocratic style of his predecessor.

Troughton approached the part more like a character role than a lead. He largely shunned interviews and publicity, often appearing as the Doctor when he did do press. In part, this was because he maintained a very private life: he had two families to support and was perpetuating the fiction (for the benefit of his mother) that he was still married to his first wife — a sham that involved his ex-wife and even his children — while he lived common law with another woman.

Onscreen, Troughton returned to the role more often than any other Doctor, before or since. He reprised the role in both the tenth and twentieth anniversary stories and also appeared in the 1985 season with Colin Baker in "The Two Doctors." Late in life, Troughton embraced the world of *Doctor Who* fandom. He was happy to travel overseas for conventions, on the grounds that his appearances there wouldn't preclude him getting work at home. It was at one such convention, in Columbus, Georgia, that he sadly passed away at 7:25 a.m. (just after ordering breakfast from hotel staff) on March 28, 1987. The previous evening, he'd played his trademark recorder on stage for fans, for what turned out to be the final time.

Top Companion Throughout the latter part of his predecessor's era, companions came and went with disturbing regularity. But the second Doctor has one reliable companion, with whom he faces every adventure except his first. Jamie McCrimmon is a seventeenth-century Scot who wears a kilt, carries a dagger and speaks in a Scot's brogue. Though from the past, he mostly accepts the wonders of the future with grace, devoting his energies to taking on villains physically or bantering with the female companion. Actor Frazer Hines had a tremendous rapport with Patrick Troughton, and the pair often engaged in comedic ad-libs. Jamie is pragmatically cowardly when he needs to be but also suave and reckless. He is fiercely loyal to the Doctor, and his travels don't end by choice; the Time Lords return him to his own time with his memory of the Doctor erased, except for a single adventure.

Classic Foe Though the second Doctor faces a gallery of lumbering creatures, the monsters most clearly established in his reign are the Cybermen. Introduced in the first Doctor's final story, they appear no less than four times in the three years that span the second Doctor's tenure, complete with a radical overhauling in look, voice and motivation. At first, they were the organ-harvesting twins of humanity, but during the second Doctor's tenure they become metallic, robotic and relentless, lurking in the shadows and ready to strike without warning.

Who is the Doctor? The second Doctor is a mysterious traveller who can't control his TARDIS, with a past he'd rather not discuss. He's a man who makes you laugh one minute and terrifies you the next. He says random things that turn out to be a brilliant destabilization of both the narrative and of the villains' plans. And he fights monsters. A *lot* of monsters.

In short, unlike his predecessor, he's the Doctor we know and love. And yet, at the same time, he's nothing like the Doctor we know and love.

He's mercurial, in all manner of ways. He's unpredictable, whimsical and erratic, twisting in every direction each time you think you have a handle on him. Instead of answering obvious questions, he plays the recorder, even if it puts him in a stickier situation as a result. He scrambles around on the floor, stealing shoelaces, just because. He's as happy paddling around in the ocean in his long johns as he is stopping monsters. And he loves to dress up: this Doctor impersonates people all the time, whether that be a bureaucrat, a soldier, a gypsy or a global dictator.

But he's also a Doctor with a steely moral core. Despite outwardly seeming like he might crumble at any moment, he has the nerve to stand up to terrifying evil. The biggest fear you have is that he won't be able to pull off a victory — and then, when he does, the second biggest fear you have is that it was all just a happy accident.

Sometimes he does things that are downright cruel, such as manipulating the archaeologists into opening the Cybertombs in 1967's "The Tomb of the Cybermen" or playing with Jamie's emotions in a Dalek experiment in 1967's "The Evil of the Daleks." Yet somehow he presents as a loveable clown, so we tend to glide over those moments. Coincidence? We're sure that's what he'd want you to think.

The second Doctor also has a tendency to break the narrative. He has a fondness for peering out of cameras, mimicking the televisual process itself. (This process eventually consumes him as his final scene is, essentially, being sucked into a television screen.) He's playful around the character's name, adopting aliases like "Doctor von Wer," which you could probably translate from German even without a dictionary. And a lot of the jokes rely on punchlines that take the viewer out of the fictional world and right into their own. For example, when Jamie asks the Doctor if he's come up with a clever plan for dealing with the Yeti in 1967's "The Abominable Snowmen," the Doctor says, "Yes, I believe I have. Bung a rock at it."

Despite being a massive change from his predecessor, the second Doctor establishes the character as we know him today. The reason the first Doctor is an anomaly, in many ways, is because the second defined the Doctor as a comedic figure who bluffs his enemies, running rings around them by spouting apparent nonsense before pulling last-minute victories out of the fire.

In other words, the second Doctor is not who he seems. He looks like your benign old uncle, but he has a ruthless streak. He bumbles around like Charlie Chaplin, but he's a self-confessed genius. He runs in terror one moment and stares down ultimate evil the next. He's everything you think he is and also nothing like what you'd expect. And that's just the way he likes it.

Three Great Moments The first regeneration is a triumph of wrong-footing the audience. "The Power of the Daleks" (1966) is sadly unavailable in the archives, but off-air recordings — still photographs married to the soundtrack — are available. The new Doctor takes every question and turns it upside down. When Polly states that he must be the Doctor, the newcomer says, "Oh, I don't look like him." He refers to the Doctor in the third person. When his predecessor's ring doesn't fit, Ben believes that proves he isn't the Doctor, but the Doctor retorts that a butterfly wouldn't fit into its chrysalis. It's a masterful performance by Troughton, taking the most shocking development in the show's history thus far and making it unsettling and edgy.

In what is merely his fourth story, "The Moonbase," the second Doctor is confronted with a plot by the Cybermen. The moonbase crew doesn't want him there and his companion suggests they leave. Instead, the Doctor utters the following 27 words: "There are some corners of the universe which have bred the most terrible things. Things which act against everything that we believe in. They must be fought." It's a speech for the ages, one that defines not just the second Doctor, but the character we're still watching today. All in 27 words.

In "The Tomb of the Cybermen," companion Victoria has just joined the TARDIS. She's a quiet girl from Victorian England, who's just seen everyone she knows murdered, including her father. While spending the night in the Cybertombs, she and the Doctor share a quiet moment, when she asks about his family. It's a topic that's never been raised before and rarely thereafter. Gently, the Doctor says that he can remember them, but only when he really wants to. Otherwise, they sleep in his mind. He then goes on to tell Victoria that their lives are unlike anyone else's, that nobody in the universe can do what they're doing. It's a lovely moment amid the otherwise tense and action-filled story, which shows us what an incredible range Troughton has.

Two Embarrassing Moments The cliffhanger to episode four of 1967's "The Ice Warriors" sees the Doctor stubbornly refusing to admit who he is to the monsters. Consequently, they reduce the atmospheric pressure in the airlock the Doctor's trapped in, which will cause his body to explode if he doesn't tell them his name. Cue cliffhanger. See if you can guess how this one gets resolved!

The fish people of Atlantis go on strike because their dictator is spending too much time with his pet octopus. We'd explain more, such as the fact that the central plot of 1967's "The Underwater Menace" involves raising a volcano from under the sea in a bid to destroy the world while the Doctor disguises himself as a sunglasses-wearing gypsy woman . . . but we don't really need to, do we?

Oh My Giddy Aunt? (RS?) There's an enormous tragedy at the heart of the Troughton era . . . and that's the fact that we can't see most of it.

I'll confess, I was late to the party on this one. Not the Troughton era per se, but the missing episodes. I'm not an audio person, so the soundtracks aren't much help to me. And watching the telesnap reconstructions — where a still image shows onscreen for up to a minute, with the confusing soundtrack playing in the background — is like some particular Sartrean torture. Only slower.

But then BBC Video started releasing animated versions of the episodes, starting with "The Invasion," whose missing first and fourth episodes are absolutely wonderful. I don't really care whether the animations are accurate or not. What they do is give me a way into the story.

Even better, people keep finding lost episodes. In 2013, nine of them turned up, adding two entire stories to the archives. You can now almost do a Season Five marathon, which is deliriously good news to a great many of us.

And through this, I discovered something wonderful: Patrick Troughton is amazing.

One of the few things just about every *Doctor Who* fan can agree on is what a brilliant actor Troughton is. He lights up every scene he's in, whether he's the focus or not. His line readings are sometimes entirely at odds with his face, so even those people who'd memorized the audio versions of his stories were surprised to see what he was doing onscreen. He's also a generous actor, often giving lines and focus to others . . . which only makes him better, in the long run.

So it's very easy to praise the second Doctor, because he's powered by such a gifted thespian. And the character is fascinating too, being a study in opposites. Yes, he sometimes defaults to clutching his companion in fear, muttering cries of "Oh crumbs! Oh my giddy aunt!" and disappearing beneath lashings of BBC foam. But even then, he makes the dullest stories (I'm looking at you, "The Dominators") palatable.

I knew all this. And yet, I still discovered an entire version of the second Doctor I didn't know was there. There's a sense in which some of the best "new" *Who* I've watched lately has been 1960s episodes, either proper or animated, that nobody had seen in 40 years.

Watching the recently recovered "The Enemy of the World," I was astonished by just how powerful Troughton's screen presence is. Impressively, while watching the white-hot intensity of Troughton's tour de force in his double role as Salamander, I actually forgot that this was Patrick Troughton, the actor who also plays the second Doctor. He's that good.

Lead character aside, the Troughton era sparks some obvious criticisms. The monster season is all samey, with the exception of the monsterless "The Enemy of the World." The final season is the opposite: it's all over the map, from the dullness of "The Space Pirates" to the brain-melting concepts of "The Mind Robber." And almost nobody has seen Troughton's debut season, so it's difficult to judge. (All our preconceptions about "The Enemy of the World" and "The

Web of Fear" were entirely swept away when we actually got to see the things, so anyone who thinks they know what "The Macra Terror" is really like is probably wrong.) And yet, that weird mix of predictability, diversity and mystery is refreshing in its own way.

The companions are great. Jamie's the most likeable right-hand man you could ever hope for, while Victoria has some wonderfully snarky comebacks, and Zoe's both brilliant and cute as a button. But where the TARDIS crew really excels is as an ensemble. The lead actors bounce off each other incredibly well, forming a trio of likeable, bumbling and hilarious characters who keep the stories livelier than they have any right to be.

So it's a damn shame that there are still so many gaps. Not as many as there once were, but it's always going to be the toughest era to get a handle on. When it comes to the second Doctor, we're a bit like *Doctor Who* archaeologists, trying to guess at the shape of a village based on a few bits of pottery, some coins and an existing wall. Of course, every so often someone unearths an entire church and we realize we have to throw out all our assumptions and start again. However, there are two assumptions that never get questioned: that the second Doctor is incredible — and that Patrick Troughton is sensational.

Second Opinion (GB)

> *"Our lives are different to anybody else's. That's the exciting thing, that nobody in the universe can do what we're doing."*
>
> — "The Tomb of the Cybermen"

I feel that quote completely defines the second Doctor.

This is a Doctor who has realized his purpose in life and really enjoys it: going through time and space and fighting monsters. This is a Doctor who realizes that the universe is his playground, and if he has to stand up to the occasional bully to enjoy his time on the swings, he'll do it.

The irony of this scene is that he's imparting this wisdom to a companion who never fully grasps the Doctor's point of view. Victoria has been called a screamer, but, in many ways, she is just an ordinary human who falls in with the Doctor because she's lost her father. And as soon as she finds a relationship that replicates something approximating sanity, she leaves his company. She doesn't want to be doing what nobody else in the universe could do.

Jamie, on the other hand, fully understands the Doctor. He loves travelling with him. Sure, it's scary, and he faces menaces all the time, but he and his best mate are there so that good can win out. He's happy that his life is different to everyone else's. And so is Zoe, the brainy outsider who knows she has a kinship with the clever time traveller and even stows away to travel with him.

The second Doctor looks half scared out of his mind most of the time, but every so often — and this is the genius of Patrick Troughton — he flashes a smile. It's the smile of someone loving every minute of what's going on, even the parts of it that have him scared out of his mind. And that's wonderfully reassuring to younger viewers. (Troughton had young children at the time he played the Doctor, so I'm sure such considerations were on his mind.) However, it's also a sign of a character loving the hell out of what he does.

Which is why his end may be the most tragic of any Doctor. He eventually has to face the Time Lords, the authority figures running the playground. And they take everything away from him: they take away his companions and even take away all their experiences of travelling with the Doctor. They leave him on a single world with no capacity to travel, and they change his form simply to punish him.

The second Doctor, though, is right. Our lives are different to anybody else's. Whether you're sitting in a tomb on Telos or reading a book about a television show on a bus to work, we have opportunities to learn, to explore, to have fun. No Doctor understood this better than the second Doctor. The question is . . . do we?

The Moonbase (1967)

Written by Kit Pedler

Directed by Morris Barry

The Big Idea The Gravitron is being used to control the Earth's weather from a base on the moon. But the Cybermen have already infiltrated the dome.

Oh My Giddy Aunt? (RS?) This is the story that establishes the house style for the next three years: an isolated base under siege from something terrifying (often the Cybermen), run by a commander with a strong personality who goes head to head with the Doctor. We saw the prototype of such a story in William Hartnell's last tale, but there the Doctor was absent from about half the story and the regeneration overshadowed everything else.

The Cybermen perform two functions in "The Moonbase": they're both the creeping menace and the unstoppable machine. For the latter, we have an army of them, just outside the base. They launch a frontal attack on the dome, sucking out the air because they don't need to breathe, whereas humans surely do. There's even a slow-motion chase scene across the lunar surface in the third episode, which currently only exists in animated form; it's one of the missing scenes I'd most like to see.

But where the Cybermen really excel is in their insidiousness. They've already infiltrated the base when the story starts. They've poisoned the sugar and are preying on the sick, carrying some of them away for nefarious purposes. The reason this works so well is because it brings out the best in the Doctor. Sure, he can coordinate the efforts of others to deflect a frontal attack. But he's at his best when he's out-plotting the villains, running tests on the disease and scurrying around at floor level taking samples of boots, shoelaces, etc.

Best of all is the second cliffhanger, when it becomes apparent that the Cybermen are inside the base, but no one knows where. The commander, Hobson, says that his men have searched the entire base, but the Doctor, with a perfect mix of dread and knowledge, asks if they've searched the room they're standing in, the busiest in the base. Hobson says he's sure that no one could be hiding there. Whereupon the Doctor takes us to a blanket-covered figure, even as we're screaming at him to run in the other direction. And then the Cyberman sits up . . .

The base-under-siege format is thus the perfect vehicle for the second Doctor. His never-quite-sure attitude only ramps up the terror, while his cleverness is a perfect foil for the sinister nature of such an invasion. It's a format that they stuck with throughout most of the Troughton years, for the very good reason that it worked. And "The Moonbase" was its perfect launching point.

Second Opinion (GB) There's a really good version of this story. It's in a novel called *Doctor Who and the Cybermen*, which is an adaptation by co-writer Gerry Davis. It isn't even out of print: BBC Books reissued it a couple of years ago, with an introduction by Gareth Roberts. In the book, the Gravitron is gigantic, the moonbase is large and imposing and the Cybermen are a genuinely scary threat.

Unfortunately, we're talking about the TV version of "The Moonbase" (or at least half of it; two episodes of this are animation married with the off-air soundtrack), and everything that I love about *Doctor Who and the Cybermen* is absent.

Instead, we have kind of the opposite. The multicultural base is populated by a bunch of national stereotypes played mostly by Brits with outrageous accents. The Cybermen lumber around in a way that would make the insidious stealth my co-author applauded possible only if the people on the base were actually brain-dead. Which, given how Hobson behaves, might actually be true. The science is laughable, even by *Doctor Who* standards: a tea tray manages to stop a catastrophic breach in the hull of the base. And it's actually kind of dull. For every incident, there's an equal amount of standing around and talking about nothing particularly interesting to counteract it.

Robert is right: "The Moonbase" pretty much sets the stage for what *Doctor Who* did for the latter part of the 1960s. The problem is, base-under-siege is cost-effective and works well in theory. In practice, it's often more enjoyable in a novelization.

The Enemy of the World (1967)

Written by David Whitaker

Directed by Barry Letts

The Big Idea In 2018, the world is at peace, thanks to the efforts of the visionary Salamander. But something is rotten at the core of Salamander's empire. And he just happens to look exactly like the Doctor . . .

Oh My Giddy Aunt? (RS?) Prevailing wisdom had it that Season Five was so great because it was the monster season. Then there was poor old "Enemy of the World," the country cousin of Season Five, forever relegated to a footnote because it lacked monsters.

Even more damning was the James Bond structure. The idea that the story could carry off Bondian intrigue, with worldwide locations, action and helicopters — something inimical to *Doctor Who* as we understood it — was laughable. That the surviving episode was its third, starring Griffin the comedy chef and on a budget so poor that Denes has to be guarded in a corridor, only evinced this failure.

But then, in 2013, the story was returned. Whereupon we discovered something marvellous: it's one of the best *Doctor Who* stories ever made. For one thing, you have an actual budget in the first episode. They don't just have a hovercraft, they actually use it. And the helicopter both lands and then, crucially, is used for a glorious tracking shot away from the beach. The budgeting decisions become clear: if you were going to make an expensive episode and a cheap one, where would you rather spend the money? Any producer worth his salt would be spending it on the first episode. It's just happenstance that vastly more people ended up seeing the cheap one.

What's more, Griffin is a superb character. He adds verisimilitude to the story, contributing nothing to the plot, but everything to the sense of the world he's living in. Everyone else in the story is one of its moving parts, but Griffin exists solely to suggest a much larger world beyond the one they can afford to film.

The casting is also cosmopolitan: Fariah is the first black woman to appear in *Doctor Who* in a speaking role. And she's a complex character who doesn't fall victim to stereotype. Yes, she's a food-taster, but she's bitter and gutsy, giving as good as she gets to all concerned.

Even more impressively, nobody bats an eyelid in her presence. Let's not forget Astrid, who is ten times of awesome.

And then there's Patrick Troughton. He plays two roles in the story — the Doctor and the villain Salamander — but each role has multiple variations. There's the Doctor pretending to be Salamander, Salamander pretending to be a wearied survivor of a global disaster to the underground society he's duped and, finally, Salamander pretending to be the Doctor. Each has different shadings and nuances, but the result is that Salamander is one of the most effective villains ever seen in *Doctor Who*.

Another thing to note is that the story follows a curious structure. It's made very clear that Salamander must have something to do with the volcanoes, yet he can't be acting alone. So the obvious conclusion, based on the rest of the season, is that he's the puppet of some enormous crabs, intent on destroying humanity. Probably operating from a secret underground base. Except that's almost the complete opposite of what's going on. Even better, where the cast is pleasingly cosmopolitan, the underground inhabitants are all very British. So it's clear: the monsters are here after all — and they're us.

So do we need monsters to make a *Doctor Who* story great? Oh, hell no. Unless they're us.

Second Opinion (GB) What he said. Twice over.

The Web of Fear (1968)

Written by Mervyn Haisman and Henry Lincoln

Directed by Douglas Camfield

The Big Idea The Yeti have taken over the London Underground. A military force led by Colonel Lethbridge-Stewart has been assembled to fight them. But there's a traitor in their midst.

Oh My Giddy Aunt? (RS?) "The Web of Fear," as shown in 1968, no longer exists. Oh sure, we now have five of the six episodes, thanks to the efforts of missing-episode hunters who found most of the story sitting in old film canisters in Jos, Nigeria. Look it up on a map sometime: it's just about one of the most remote places in the world.

This means that those film cans sat on a shelf, suffering heat, indifference and the threat of disposal for almost 40 years. It took the dedication of one fan, Philip Morris, to locate them, and then it took the BBC to manage their return and then distribution in a manner that would have been unthinkable to Douglas Camfield or Patrick Troughton: they were released simultaneously on iTunes and made the top 10 most downloaded television that week.

As a result, we can now enjoy seeing the Yeti in the underground, far scarier when confined to dark tunnels than they were in their last appearance. We can meet Colonel Lethbridge-Stewart, soon to become the Doctor's best friend (and still appearing, sort of, with the twelfth Doctor in "Death in Heaven"). We can watch the Yeti sphere roll its way inexorably across the floor as the Doctor desperately tries to seize control of it. And we can see the entirety of episode four, perhaps the tensest all-action single episode in *Doctor Who*'s history, showcasing Lethbridge-Stewart's sheer desperation as his men are ruthlessly cut down by the Yeti.

However, what we can't see is the mystery story where you suspect Lethbridge-Stewart of being the traitor, because we all know he goes on to be the loveable Brigadier, stalwart of much of the rest of the Classic Series. And without that, there's a huge sagging hole in the centre of the story.

"The Web of Fear" that we can see is a good story. There are times when it's even a great one. However, it's not the story that aired in 1968. But don't take my word for it. See it for yourself. Thanks to a man named Philip Morris, a restoration team that kept its secret for years and the decision of the BBC to release the story on iTunes for everyone to enjoy, the entire world can once again enjoy "The Web of Fear." Just not quite in the same way they once did.

Second Opinion (GB) I disagree with my co-author. Even with the problem of knowing that Colonel Lethbridge-Stewart can't be a suspect, the solution to the mystery is . . . well saying *Scooby-Doo*-esque would be an insult to cartoon dogs. There is a problem with "The Web of Fear" in that it tends to take the easy road for storytelling. A lot of the characters are unflattering stereotypes, starting with the Jewish museum owner, Silverstein, and ending with the Welsh army driver, Evans. The outdoor battles with the Yeti use up all the goodwill that keeping them in shadow in the tunnels of the London Underground bought. The climax is a pantomime. Even missing an episode, it seems a bit long.

The thing is, we sort of knew this was coming. I remember a perceptive critic in *Doctor Who Magazine* pointing out in 1998 that it probably wouldn't make the top 10 of the magazine's poll for the series' 35th anniversary if we had the sixth episode — with too much of comedy character Evans and the runaround petering out — rather than the extremely strong first episode. And he was right. The result is almost the exact opposite situation to "The Enemy of the World": esteem lowers rather than rises.

It's not that there aren't good parts. The direction is superb, and there are some great moments, including Colonel Lethbridge-Stewart returning to the base of operations after all his men have been wiped out by the Yeti. It's a great scene that works because, at the time, Lethbridge-Stewart was still a one-off character allowed to be a little bit terrified and shell-shocked. Nicholas Courtney is superlative here too.

I'm thrilled "The Web of Fear" came back from oblivion. We get to see the first appearance of *Doctor Who*'s longest-running recurring character. But we also discover a story that has a lot of flaws.

The Invasion (1968)

Written by Derrick Sherwin

Directed by Douglas Camfield

The Big Idea At International Electromatics, we've revolutionized technology. You'll want all our products! Our micro-monolithic circuits are present in almost every piece of technology. Why, we're in just about every home across the globe . . .

Oh My Giddy Aunt? (GB) "The Invasion" is a sort of back-door pilot, if you will, for the Pertwee era, with the Doctor working with the newly formed United Nations Intelligence Taskforce to handle alien invasions. And, like so many back-door pilots, there are plenty of ideas here that never quite make it into the series proper.

First, there's UNIT itself, with the Brigadier's mobile HQ in a Hercules transport jet. It's unsustainable in the long term, but wouldn't it have been cool for the Doctor to have flown with UNIT to take on alien incursions instead of hanging out in a lab somewhere in the Home Counties? There's the Brig himself, who is just, well, badass, heading an agency that dabbles in espionage operations, battling monsters and rarely seeming fazed by anything. A lot of that remained in the final version, but perhaps not with the same . . . flair. I found myself watching Nicholas Courtney's amazing portrayal of a confident, smart leader and sighing, "It's all downhill from here."

As you might have noticed, "The Invasion" is one of those stories with a couple of episodes missing; gaps are filled with animation. Now, animation is an amazing way to provide rudimentary visuals without being boring, but it's still problematic. With the missing episodes, everything is tailored to the off-air audio of the episode, which was recorded in someone's living room in the 1960s. Meaning that the tail is wagging the dog: in any other universe but one where *Doctor Who* fans live, these animated episodes would have been 10 to 15 minutes long, all extraneous action cut. But we live in a world of obsessive fans, which is why, in the animated episodes of "The Invasion," you have lots of reaction shots of a character standing around blinking while another talks.

What's frustrating, though, is that animation is used for a story where so little happens for so long. "The Invasion" has eight episodes and the first four (which include the two animated episodes) have virtually the same plot: escape from Tobias Vaughn and International Electromatics; meet up with UNIT; go back into the IE compound and get captured again. Rinse, repeat.

But once the Cybermen show up, "The Invasion" becomes the quintessential Earth-invasion story: take out the planet by stealth and wander around famous landmarks in the eerie quiet. (The sequence of the silver giants marching around St. Paul's Cathedral became so iconic that it was lifted wholesale for the 2014 Series Eight finale, "Dark Water"/"Death in Heaven.") Then battle the army while intrigue with the Doctor and a villain goes on in the background. They also have an amazing villain in Kevin Stoney's Tobias Vaughn. Vaughn isn't the wittiest or cleverest of adversaries, but, rather like the production, what he has is a sense of flair. It's glorious to watch.

And episode eight, when UNIT finally battles the Cybermen, is a great, budget-busting conflagration full of explosions and some good moments for Troughton's Doctor. In fact, it sums up why "The

Invasion" works in spite of the torpor of the initial episodes: it simply has so much style and action that the fact it's taken four episodes to get anywhere interesting doesn't matter so much once you're there.

Second Opinion (RS?) Oh Graeme, Graeme, Graeme. You're so wrong it hurts.

I love the whole-episode animation! The first time I saw what they'd done with the two missing episodes of "The Invasion," I was blown away. I love the fourth episode, with its tense helicopter rescue and the stealth approach by canoe. And the first episode is particularly fantastic, with so much moody and spooky atmosphere that you forget you're watching an animated second Doctor.

I'll say that again: you forget that this isn't the original episode. It's that good. People have criticized the animated episodes for having zooms and cuts that weren't possible in the '60s; neither was the ability to animate missing episodes and release them on DVD, so I'm not really sure there's a coherent argument there.

For me, the animations are a godsend, giving me new access to old *Doctor Who*. And tying the animation to an existing 24-minute episode soundtrack is a strength, not a weakness. The 12-minute version of the first episode that my co-author is imagining would have been a cool cartoon. But it wouldn't have captured the essence of *Doctor Who*.

And part of the joy of "The Invasion" is the sheer lengthy buildup of the thing. Yes, it takes four episodes to meet the Cybermen. But with four episodes that are this good, who's complaining? Besides, the story isn't about the Cybermen invading London, it's about the machinations that Vaughn uses to set up that invasion, putting all his pieces into place. The actual invasion is incidental.

I love all eight episodes of "The Invasion." Even the 24-minute animated ones.

The War Games (1969)

Written by Terrance Dicks and Malcolm Hulke

Directed by David Maloney

The Big Idea When the TARDIS lands in the trenches of the First World War, things don't seem to be going very well. When one of the generals has access to sophisticated technology, well, how could it get any worse? But it's going to.

Oh My Giddy Aunt? (GB) In episode six of "The War Games," two characters have a conversation that changes the very nature of *Doctor Who* itself. The security chief of a massive scheme to kidnap human soldiers from history is talking to a scientist. Up until this point, the only notable thing about these two men is that the scientist has the funniest voice ever heard on *Doctor Who*.

The conversation turns to the Doctor. Earlier, the War Chief, the man who engineered this scheme, clearly recognized the Doctor. The Security Chief thinks the Doctor is from the same race as the War Chief. The scientist says, "Are you suggesting he's bringing in his own people, the Time Lords?"

And with that casual conversation between two characters who have nothing to do with the Doctor, we suddenly learn about his race.

The great thing about *Doctor Who* is that it doesn't start with an origin story. It's expected of any new television show nowadays; in fact, every script for a revival of *Doctor Who* with an American TV network in the 1990s started with the Doctor's past on Gallifrey, which is predictable and boring. *Doctor Who*, wisely, has shunned many glimpses into the past of its lead character. When we first encounter the Doctor in "An Unearthly Child," he's already travelling in a TARDIS that he doesn't really know how to operate, but we don't know much more than that. In 1965, viewers met the Meddling Monk, a fellow member of the Doctor's race with his own TARDIS, but nothing was said about the Doctor's people or why he left them.

Here, when the Doctor admits he's a Time Lord, the story of his origin isn't one of an intergalactic superhero coming into being to avenge his dead mother or search for his lost father. The Doctor explains that the Time Lords are an immensely civilized race who can live forever, barring accidents; who have the secret of space-time travel; and who are content merely to observe. And so, with a whole galaxy to explore, he ran away from his people in a stolen TARDIS . . . because he was bored.

At once, the Doctor's origins are so relatable and so extraordinary. He came from a race of gods, and he was bored with that, so he struck out on his own. Fighting wrongs. Facing monsters. Righting injustice.

Until it comes to a crashing end, in this story. And it's all marked by an offhand remark in a conversation between two minor characters.

Second Opinion (RS?) There's a funny thing going on in "The War Games": we see so much of a day in the life of a villainous operation. And so much of it is humdrum.

You've got the inter-office squabbles between the War Chief and the Security Chief ("No, what a stupid fool YOU are!"), surely caused by one of them using the other's milk from the department fridge. You've got the quotidian machinations of the Chief Scientist, giving demonstrations for colleagues and experimenting on humans as though he's clocked into the lab that morning and is looking forward to unwinding in front of the TV with his wife and kids later that evening.

And then the War Lord arrives, and everyone behaves exactly as if the CEO suddenly appeared on your floor. He's terrifying and is great at spinning out arch putdowns, but he's scary in exactly the way your boss is.

What I love about this is that you get the sense of a villainous corporation blandly going about its business. It even allows the Doctor to infiltrate, as he claims that all the fuss was about the girl (his companion Zoe), not him, so the Chief Scientist essentially shrugs, clearly thinking he'll take it up with the PR department later, and lets the Doctor wander around freely because it's not his department.

Oh sure, eventually the IRS arrives in the form of the Time Lords and audits the whole operation. But until then, you've got just about the best insight into large-scale villainy you're ever likely to see on television. Yet another reason why *Doctor Who* is so awesome.

The Third Doctor

Rank Has Its Privileges

(1970–1974)

Basic Data

First story: "Spearhead From Space" (1970)

Final story: "Planet of the Spiders" (1974)

Final appearance: "Dimensions in Time" (1993)

The Changing Face of *Doctor Who* The Patrick Troughton era ended on something of an ebb. The show's punishing schedule, which saw *Doctor Who* running 42 weeks a year, had exhausted the actors. The producers, Peter Bryant and Derrick Sherwin, also wanted out and felt the format of spacey adventures with monsters had run its course. They were also tired of the meagre resources they had for producing a series with futuristic sets and props. The BBC, for its part, was concerned the program might not survive into the 1970s but in the end elected to let it continue.

Bryant and Sherwin felt a radical course correction was needed. Emboldened by the 1968 story "The Web of Fear," which saw the Doctor battling monsters in near-contemporary Earth with the British military, they decided to reformat the show with the Doctor exiled to Earth by his people, the Time Lords. The Doctor now worked for the paramilitary organization UNIT (set up in the 1968 follow-up to "The Web of Fear," "The Invasion"), fighting alien invasions and home-grown monsters in an occasionally futuristic version of contemporary Britain. Bryant and Sherwin cast Jon Pertwee as the Doctor . . . and then left.

This new chapter in *Doctor Who* was shepherded in by new producer Barry Letts, who, along with script editor Terrance Dicks, had his own ideas about *Doctor Who*. Letts and Dicks went along with the format change for a season or two, even refining it by adding a regular supporting cast and a regular villain in the Master. Gradually, though, they lifted the Doctor's exile and brought him back into time and space.

Letts was a populist who wanted to get the biggest audience possible, largely by making the show accessible and down to earth. He pioneered techniques like greenscreen, shortened the number of episodes in serials and changed production methods to make it more fast-paced, more spectacle-driven and less like the theatrical as-live productions of old. The series dramatically rose in popularity during this time: during the third Doctor's era, *Doctor Who* went from a series on the edge of cancellation to a well-loved part of the BBC Saturday evening lineup.

Who is Jon Pertwee? Jon Pertwee was an unlikely choice to follow Patrick Troughton. Pertwee was, at the time, mostly known as a comedian and probably best associated with his role on the BBC Radio comedy *The Navy Lark*. He was known as a man of a thousand voices, who could pull off any comedic accent or performance with aplomb. Indeed, he was cast by producers Peter Bryant and Derrick Sherwin (who left after Pertwee's first serial) precisely because they wanted to go in an even more comic direction after Patrick Troughton.

Pertwee, though, had other ideas. Rather like Peter Sellers, who signed on to the 1967 version of *Casino Royale* because he honest-to-goodness wanted to play James Bond, Pertwee wanted to play the Doctor straight, and was encouraged to do this by Letts. Pertwee nonetheless struggled to figure out how to play his Doctor. His friend Shaun Sutton, then BBC head of serials, apparently told him to do it "as Jon Pertwee." Pertwee later claimed this prompted a personal crisis for him, as he didn't know who he really was! But he figured it out and imbued his Doctor with many of his own interests. He loved vehicles and gadgets and physical activity (where possible, as Pertwee had a very bad back), and all these featured in plentiful amounts during Pertwee's tenure on the program. Pertwee also influenced his costume, choosing to wear his grandfather's old formal wear to an early photo call, which formed the basis of his Doctor's clothes.

Probably the crucial aspect about Jon Pertwee that showed most in his version of the Doctor was his own self-confidence. He possessed a variety performer's ability to command a room, and he brought that showman's bravado to the Time Lord. Lacking Troughton's aversion to publicity, Pertwee embraced the role and was continually mobbed at fêtes. In 1972, at the height of his popularity, he even released a spoken-word single (yes, really!) that encompassed the way he so thoroughly embraced the role. Its key repeated line? "I am the Doctor."

Top Companion In spite of a host of companions and recurring characters that form part of UNIT, there's only one choice for the third Doctor's top companion. Jo Grant is sweet, a bit scatterbrained but plucky and courageous and good-hearted. It's easy to dismiss Jo for her ditziness, but she and the Doctor become close in a way that his collegial relationship with Liz never matches. The Doctor is avuncular towards Jo, chiding her when she doesn't measure up to his (admittedly ridiculously) high standards, but he's also fiercely protective of her. Jo is loyal to a fault, ignoring his more arrogant tics and putting herself in harm's way to protect him. Jo leaves the Doctor when she falls in love with the environmentalist and scientist Clifford Jones — a man she describes to the Doctor as "a younger you." This implies that Jo's own feelings for the Doctor might be more complex than they first appear. Certainly, the Doctor's own crestfallen reaction to her engagement indicates he might have some deeper feelings himself. Long before the Modern Series set up the Doctor-companion relationship as one with potentially romantic feelings, the third Doctor and Jo show how it's done.

Classic Foe Unlike the previous two monster-based eras, this one is largely dominated by a singular villain: the Master. Designed as a Moriarty to the Doctor's Sherlock, the Master is a rival Time Lord as devoted to evil as the Doctor is to good. The Master and the third Doctor bear interesting similarities too: both love gadgets and tend towards the finer things while exiled on Earth. The Master fights the third Doctor nine times over a three-year period, firmly establishing the character in the public consciousness as the definitive *Doctor Who* villain. Played by Roger Delgado, who brings an immense charm to the character, the Master is the perfect mirror to the third Doctor. Sadly, Delgado's tragic death in a car accident scuppered plans for a final confrontation between the two iconic characters, leaving the Master's fate up in the air.

Who is the Doctor? The Doctor's third persona is a man of action: unlike previous incarnations, he engages in physical combat ranging from martial arts (he is particularly adept at a Venusian form of aikido — appropriately a defensive martial art) to fencing to boxing (he was apparently taught by John L. Sullivan) to gladiatorial games. He drives a wide array of vehicles ranging from his yellow touring car, Bessie, and hovercraft to jet skis and even a miniature helicopter.

He's also a man of sartorial elegance. His costume had a contemporary cut (for the 1970s) as opposed the first Doctor's Edwardian look or the second Doctor's rumpled clothes. He positively dressed up, wearing tuxedos, dinner jackets, frills, cravats and Inverness capes. Such taste didn't stop with clothes: if any Doctor would have found himself at that very 1970s event — the wine and cheese party — it would have been the third Doctor.

It's as though, having been exiled to Earth, the Doctor decides to embrace the finer parts of living on his adoptive planet. And yet, in many ways, it's only a surface adaptation to life on Earth. The first moment he gets the TARDIS key in "Spearhead From Space" (1970), and the first time he gets his hands on the Master's TARDIS dematerialization circuit in 1971's "Terror of the Autons," he immediately tries to take off and abandon everyone in UNIT to their impending threats by the Nestene and the Master. After his exile is lifted, when given the opportunity to go with Jo to Wales in 1973's "The Green Death," he decides instead to take the TARDIS to Metebelis III. The Doctor's loyalty, for all the friendships he has built with UNIT, is to the TARDIS and travelling through time and space. During his exile, the Doctor is sent on many missions for the Time Lords, and he rarely complains as it gets him away from Earth. Is it any wonder that in the four seasons we see the Doctor working for UNIT, we never see him actually have a home? There's just the TARDIS parked in his lab.

This incarnation of the Doctor is much more of a scientist. Perhaps that's just the result of his job — and, as the eleventh Doctor pointed out in 2013's "The Day of the Doctor," he *did* have a job — but this Doctor rigs up gadgets ranging from a remote control for Bessie to a device that views people's thoughts. More than that, though, he's concerned with the scientific explanations for phenomena (even if they tend towards the pseudoscientific, like "reverse the polarity of the neutron flow," a phrase that became associated with him despite his using it only twice).

The third Doctor is a character with a strong moral compass. There are rights and wrongs for him, and he frequently jumps in to be the arbiter of which is which. Like any good scientist, the Doctor is obsessed with knowledge, and that forms his biggest blind spot. His need to understand things often puts people in danger. And he refuses to tolerate the fact that others cannot, or will not, understand or agree with his view on things. This intolerance regularly manifests itself as a supreme form of arrogance, where he's rude and cutting. (He tells Jo, "Don't tell me you failed Latin as well as science?") Name-dropping goes from being a quaint trait to a full-on Olympic sport. (Even Hitler is called a "bounder"!)

One could speculate that this Doctor might have some form of Time Lord Asperger's syndrome. There's an easy case to be made: the Doctor has little empathy, seems not to understand non-verbal cues and generally tends to speak without any filters whatsoever. Certainly, the Doctor's friends make allowances for his behaviour: Jo just ignores him and defends him to others, while the Brigadier opts for an array of increasingly wry smiles.

Given the Doctor's arrogance and morality, it's odd that he would be paired with a secret paramilitary organization like UNIT. *Doctor*

Who's first producer, Verity Lambert, in fact, criticized this era, feeling that the character of the Doctor had become part of the establishment he had previously eschewed. The ambiguity is somewhat uncomfortable. On the one hand, during this era, the Doctor often stands up for a greater good the establishment finds inconvenient. On the other hand, he's comfortable with people whose first instinct is to kill. For his part, the Doctor is happy to rely on UNIT as the blunt instrument to battle monsters.

Regardless, this is also a Doctor who is willing to humble himself. He acknowledges when Jo is engaged that she's grown up and doesn't need to be impressed by him any more. In his last story, he discovers his greed for knowledge has led to a disastrous chain of events that could enslave humanity. He atones for this the only way he can: by facing his fear and sacrificing his life.

Three Great Moments The Doctor's outrage at the end of 1970's "Doctor Who and the Silurians" when he discovers the Brigadier has lied to him and is blowing up the Silurians' caves speaks as much to the Doctor's moral surety as to the streak of compassion that runs deep beneath his bravado. The way he says "But that's murder!" will always haunt us.

In "The Green Death," the Doctor faces a crowd of toughs who want to take him down, calling him "Gramps." "I'm quite spry for my age, actually," the Doctor says with a smile . . . and then gives them the mother of all beatdowns.

In 1972's "The Time Monster," the Doctor and Jo are imprisoned. Rather than focus on an escape attempt (like 98% of all *Doctor Who*), a wearied Doctor decides to tell Jo a story of his youth on his blackest day. He tells of how a hermit who lived behind his house taught him to see the world a different way. The Doctor talks about then seeing a flower: "One of those little weeds. Just like a daisy it was. I looked at it for a moment and suddenly I saw it through [the hermit's] eyes. It was simply glowing with life, like a perfectly cut jewel, and the colours were deeper and richer than you could possibly imagine. It was the daisiest daisy I'd ever seen." It's a beautiful Buddhist koan smack dab in the middle of a strange science-fantasy tale, and one of the loveliest scenes in all of *Doctor Who*.

Two Embarrassing Moments The Doctor spends much of "Doctor Who and the Silurians" burning away what little goodwill UNIT has built up with the entire staff of the Wenley Moor complex by insulting them all over the course of the story. He's really a people person, isn't he?

In "The Time Monster," the Doctor fends off the Master's time-eating machine, powered by an Atlantean demigod, with a device made from — and we swear we're not making this up — a wine bottle, a corkscrew, forks, knives and key rings. And then the Doctor tells his friends that it will work because he used it for *school pranks*. No, really.

Hai!? (GB) With three, *Doctor Who* suddenly became really interesting.

A first transformation . . . that was a curious quirk. The Doctor could have simply rejuvenated, as the press in 1966 occasionally claimed: the shambolic tramp could have been a younger, shabbier version of the old man (if you squinted hard enough). Even when it became clear this new Doctor was a different person, it was more a study of contrasts: quiet instead of crotchety, subversive instead of autocratic, dark Beatle cut instead of white long hair.

But three! Three is the number when it becomes clear the Doctor can be *anyone*. And this Doctor isn't an old man or a cosmic hobo . . . he's an action hero. He's a larger-than-life personality. He's a completely different leading man from the two who preceded him.

Which is lucky for me, because I'm rather fond of this Doctor.

I would argue that the third Doctor's era is easily the most influential of the show. I think, when reviving the series, that Russell T Davies was hugely mindful of Barry Letts's populist, make-it-a-spectacle-that-can-put-bums-on-seats-during-Saturday-teatime vision for the program. And yet, while *Doctor Who* karate-chopped and exploded and greenscreened its way into the public's affection in the 1970s (to the point where Her Majesty the Queen allegedly recognized the name Brian Hodgson during a tour of the BBC Radiophonic Workshop because it was in *Doctor Who*'s end credits), the Doctor of this era has since been ignored somewhat.

In fact, when I was a fan in the 1990s, it was fashionable to hate Jon Pertwee's Doctor because he was straightforward and establishment and rude and . . . oh, just go read my co-author's review, okay? Things are less antagonistic these days, but that's mostly because everyone has kind of forgotten about Jon Pertwee, which is a damn shame.

Because there's something surprising about the third Doctor — something delightful, in fact. I think it's precisely that he's such a straightforward adventure hero. Don't get me wrong, I love Doctors with eccentricities to spare, but Jon Pertwee's portrayal works for me because it's stripped down to its basics, but it's never, ever bland. The third Doctor has a big personality. He's charming. He's a hero. A clear, unambiguous hero who takes us to breathtaking places to fight terrifying monsters and be in the moral right, always. You would think that would be boring, but it's not. There's a remarkable comfort, an amazing sense of safety that this kind of a character elicits.

It's not like all the corners are sanded away, either. The third Doctor is, frankly, a rude little shit. He's the guy who gets saved by the Brigadier and tells him, "Next time could you get here *before* the nick of time?" He's snide to all his companions. He creates an atmosphere of instant hostility everywhere he goes. He's pompous and arrogant.

And I love him for that.

First of all, a lot of the things he's rude about, and a lot of the people he's rude to, are stupid. Secondly, I love the contrast between a man who will stand up to tyranny and injustice in a heartbeat and yet chide Jo pedantically for not realizing that Magister is Latin for Master. He has flaws. And the nice thing is that his pomposity is repeatedly pricked by Jo and the Brigadier, and even the Time Lords take a shot or two at him (reminding him that the Master actually received a better degree in school). I get why the third Doctor's rudeness irritates some (I'm only spending time on it because someone with an overly punctuated name is about to have a go) but most of the time, I don't mind; I'm enjoying the ride with him.

The fact that the third Doctor is stuck on Earth with a recurring cast of characters makes him all the more interesting. This kind of Doctor works well as the lead of an ensemble. His arrogance also gives him an authority to lead. It's another interesting study in contrasts.

When we wrote *Who's 50*, the biggest surprise I had was how much I enjoyed watching the third Doctor's stories. (I wasn't alone; our editor, Jen Hale, became a huge fan too!) I often compare the third Doctor's era to eating well-prepared comfort food. It makes me happy watching it. And, in many ways, my enjoyment of the third Doctor is a comfort thing. There are more complex interpretations of the Doctor (there's one coming up in a few pages), but in this world, there's also a place for enjoying something for what it is.

Make no doubt about it. Three is a game-changer. Suddenly, the Doctor becomes radically different and yet stays the same. And best of all, *Doctor Who* becomes different as a show too. What started as a curious one-off is now something regular: change.

Second Opinion (RS?) There's so much to like about the third Doctor's era. I love the exiled-to-Earth idea. That's a stroke of brilliance that brought the series to the audience, allowing it to survive the threat of cancellation and become immensely popular. The Modern Series should absolutely embrace that as a story arc (and it's probably only a matter of time until it does). I think the hit rate of companions is just about the best we've ever had: Liz Shaw, Jo Grant and Sarah Jane Smith are all fabulous characters, in quite different ways, all played by brilliant actresses. Even the recurring characters are great: the Brigadier is rock solid, hitting it out of the park every time; the Master as played by Roger Delgado is a stupendous villain, and the character has never been bettered since; and Sergeant Benton is a likeable everyman. (The only dud is Mike Yates, but even he gets an actual character arc, long before television did that kind of thing, turning traitor in one of the show's most impressive twists.)

The only thing about the third Doctor's era I don't like is the third Doctor himself.

Yes, yes, my co-author warned you this was coming. I'm firmly in that '90s camp that derided the Pertwee years (Season Seven aside), that found the nuance and eccentricities of almost every other Doctor infinitely preferable. The thing is, though, those '90s fans had it right: the third Doctor isn't really up to scratch.

The problem is twofold: Jon Pertwee isn't very good, and his Doctor isn't very likeable.

I'll deal with the acting first. Pertwee, like David Tennant later, is amazing when he's pushed into a corner. So when he's outside his comfort zone, like the alternate world of "Inferno" or when the Doctor is forced to confront his prejudices about the Ice Warriors in "The Curse of Peladon," he's incredible. But, rather like David Tennant, the show became far too successful for him to be pushed very often. So Pertwee settles into playing it on autopilot, being patronizing and rude because that gets him cheap laughs, and generally being Jon-Pertwee-the-actor-starring-in-this-show rather than bothering to do much acting. Sadly, the word that most often comes to mind is "wooden" — and that's not a word I'd use to describe any other Doctor.

Then there's the character. In every other era, the Doctor is an iconoclast, tearing down governments and corrupt institutions for the greater good. In this era, he's the voice of the establishment, with a couple of moments of (very) mild rebellion. I think it's telling that those who defend this Doctor often focus on those moments of rebellion, rather than embracing the other 95% of the character. This is a man who chooses to work alongside the military, even after they've committed an act of genocide. He accepts their resources and hospitality, living a life of comfort and stability. He picks up a gun and shoots down Ogrons in cold blood, shortly after enjoying wine and cheese in a country mansion. In short, he sells out — and, to me, that's just not who the Doctor fundamentally is.

In fact, the third Doctor is exactly the sort of character that Tom Baker's Doctor would roundly condemn in the next era: a misguided scientist, working with the establishment to further his own curiosity while remaining deliberately ignorant of the wrongdoing around him.

The fact that he's rude to friends and villains alike is almost incidental. Almost. When he does it to prick the pomposity of those in authority, it works. But the third Doctor doesn't know how to control his power. He's as rude to those trying to help him as he is to those who need a gentler touch, often actively making the problem worse. ("Doctor Who and the Silurians" would be about three episodes shorter if the Doctor wasn't so bullying towards Dr. Quinn.) As we posit above, the Doctor appears to have no filters whatsoever. While that might explain his actions, it doesn't make him any less unpleasant.

More than that, though, my biggest problem with this Doctor is the sheer lack of nuance. He's simplistic as a character. It's a shame, because so many of the fundamentals in his era are just about perfect. But, at the end of the day, well-prepared comfort food can only feed you for so long.

Spearhead From Space (1970)

Written by Robert Holmes

Directed by Derek Martinus

The Big Idea UNIT is called in when a swarm of meteorites crashes in an Epping forest . . . along with a police box. Can this new Doctor help the Brigadier in the fight against the Nestene and its army of Autons?

Hai!? (RS?) One of the most interesting things about this episode is the way they delay giving us a look at the new Doctor for almost the entire first episode. It's a shame his face is in the credits, actually, as we start with a psychedelic visage of Jon Pertwee . . . but thereafter we see him fall out of the TARDIS in long shot, we see him face-down in hospital, we only glimpse his grey hair under the covers and so on. It's not until the moment the Brigadier meets him, fully expecting to see Patrick Troughton, that we get our first proper look at this new Doctor.

For anyone oblivious to the media (which wasn't overwhelming in 1970), this would have been their first look as well. We didn't see the face the second Doctor was given at the end of "The War Games," so "Spearhead From Space" provides the perfect opportunity to build up the secondary characters who will be crucial in this new format.

Even better, the dialogue between the Brigadier and Liz is endlessly quotable. ("We've drawn attention to ourselves, Miss Shaw.") When the Brigadier is told that a police box was found in the woods, *Doctor Who* starts to become defined by its iconography. Nicholas Courtney's shocked reaction and subsequent decisive action is the perfect one-two sucker punch. At this point, we're halfway through the first episode and still don't have the foggiest idea who this new Doctor is . . . and it doesn't matter in the slightest, because the plot has us by the throat and isn't going to let go.

By delaying the revelation of exactly what the new Doctor looks like, "Spearhead" makes the regeneration feel earned, a crucial step for a process that was still novel, and gets the story — and the entire

1970s — up and running. If only he hadn't been in those darn opening credits.

Second Opinion (GB) It's funny. I realize that I've owned, at one time or another, "Spearhead From Space" in just about every possible format. I owned it on VHS, where they cut the story into a giant movie. I owned it on DVD, where on the minus side they deleted the Fleetwood Mac song used as background music, but oh, wow! Look at how vibrant the colours are thanks to newfangled digital scanning. Then I owned it in a special edition, which is even more stunning and has decent special features. And then I owned it on Blu-ray, where the Fleetwood Mac song was restored and oh, wow! Look at how incredible the resolution is thanks to it being in 1080p. (I can see all the signage and shops on Ealing High Street when the Autons invade . . .)

I've owned this story in just about every conceivable home video format except Betamax. I'll probably own it in the future as a holo-projection or a neurotransmission. But you know what? Every time, it's still going to be stunning from beginning to end. And it's still going to influence how *Doctor Who* stories are told in that neurotransmitting, holo-projecting future.

Doctor Who and the Silurians (1970)

Written by Malcolm Hulke

Directed by Timothy Combe

The Big Idea The Doctor and Liz investigate strange goings-on at a new nuclear power station. In the caves below, the creatures that were once the dominant species on Earth are waking up . . . and are not happy about the rise of *Homo sapiens*.

Hai!? (GB) Seven great things that happen in seven episodes of "Doctor Who and the Silurians":

Episode One: The man reduced to drawing cave paintings on the hospital wall, which is a powerful visual touch and such a brilliant way of bringing people into the themes of the story.

Episode Two: The journey of the wounded Silurian, which is beautifully directed by Timothy Combe and features a wonderful blend of point-of-view footage, cunning use of location (I love the magic-hour light on the Silurian in the distance) and a really scary cliffhanger when Liz encounters the creature.

Episode Three: The cat-and-mouse game played by the Doctor and Quinn that leads to the revelation that Quinn isn't as lovely as he first seemed, followed by his shocking death.

Episode Four: The fact that the Doctor's undoing is Miss Dawson's love for Dr. Quinn. He really didn't see that coming.

Episode Five: The struggle between the Old Silurian and the Young Silurian, which somehow transcends the silly rubber costumes and underlines the fact that, as much as the Doctor wants peace, the Silurians are no more ready for it than the humans (as represented by Masters and Miss Dawson) are.

Episode Six: The deeply creepy scenes of the plague spreading throughout London. This is what *Doctor Who* in the contemporary era should be.

Episode Seven: The ending, as we see the Doctor's heartbreak and betrayal encapsulated in the statement, "It's murder." Heartbreak, because the effort for securing peace is categorically destroyed. Betrayal, because the Brigadier outright lies to the Doctor and does his job. But it's also something else, something not explicitly said in "Doctor Who and the Silurians." It's the point where the Doctor's hubris is exposed. The belief that he could bring one side — which has shown nothing but fear and lack of understanding — and the other side — which has shown similar lack of understanding as well as genocidal intent — to peaceful co-existence. That hubris isn't necessarily bad; it may be, in the final analysis, one of the reasons the Doctor is a force for good. But here it's a limitation that is laid bare.

Second Opinion (RS?) One incredible thing that happens in "Doctor Who and the Silurians":

The entire bloody story. Seriously, this might be one of the greatest *Doctor Who* stories of all time. It has it all: UNIT, ethical dilemmas, humans as villains, sympathetic monsters, monsters as villains, sympathetic humans, Bessie, dinosaurs, actual science, a vicious plague, greenscreen, Geoffrey Palmer as a bureaucrat, bizarre-but-catchy incidental music, potholing, helicopter shots, cliffhangers to die for, the Doctor being so rude that he delays the plot resolution by several episodes, Paul Darrow playing the Brigadier's 2IC, who should have been a series regular, a nuclear facility in the countryside that's trying to solve the U.K.'s energy problems and just about the most perfect kick in the gut for an ending ever.

Okay, that's 20 things. But who cares when it's this good? Just watch it, okay?

Day of the Daleks (1972)

Written by Louis Marks

Directed by Paul Bernard

The Big Idea Guerrillas from the future are trying to destroy a peace conference to prevent a future where the Daleks rule the Earth.

Hai!? (GB) Here's a funny fact: *Doctor Who* only explored the mechanics of time travel and its effects once or twice a decade during the Classic Series. Crazy, right? These days, we're ready to complain the very moment a character says, "Time can be rewritten" . . .

"Day of the Daleks" is one of the 1970s contributions to this rare oeuvre in Classic *Doctor Who.* It even has a mind-paralyzing paradox at the centre of it: if the guerrillas blowing up the conference created the future, then who put the bomb there in the first place? (I bet a lot of kids pondered that sombrely in 1972, before moving on to read the third Doctor's adventures in the *Countdown* comic book.) But, as with later dalliances with time travel in the Modern Series, this isn't what's important. The key moment is the shock when we discover the guerrillas are at the heart of the paradox that created their world.

Even without the brain-cramping ending, "Day of the Daleks" is pretty cool in how it develops its ideas. It starts with the Doctor investigating ghosts and ends with UNIT fending off the pepperpots from a future where they rule. Any story with a throughline like that needs to be seen.

The story is populated, Daleks aside, by three-dimensional characters who have genuine, if flawed, motivations. Perhaps the most tragic is Aubrey Woods's Controller, who thinks he's doing the right thing and saving lives by collaborating with the Daleks to keep humanity alive. However, his thoroughly articulated conviction is utterly demolished by the Doctor in what must be Jon Pertwee's finest scene in the role. It's astonishing to watch Pertwee's Doctor use charm, sarcasm and finally blunt wit to cut to the heart of things. The guerrillas are similarly flawed and motivated, which makes the near tragedy of the paradoxical ending palpable. All sides just want to find a better future; some compromise while others reach for extremes. It's a fascinating cross-section of a world under occupation.

"Day of the Daleks" is really let down by the production values. (If you have the DVD, watch the special edition, which corrects the paltry numbers in the final battle and the Dalek voices.) And when the Doctor is being chased around on a motorized trike with balloon tires, you have no doubt this was made in the 1970s, even though they say it's the future. "Day of the Daleks" is one of the first stories to really be about time travel, but it also knows that gimmicks and paradoxes are mere pyrotechnics; any such story needs to have intriguing drama at the heart of it. Fortunately, "Day of the Daleks" does.

Second Opinion (RS?) This is the story that shows the third Doctor at his best and his worst.

At his best, he's as incredible in his scene with the Controller as my co-author says. And he's powerful in revealing that the guerrillas did it to themselves. These two scenes illustrate the third Doctor at his peak: in the first, it's because the odds are against him, so he's forced to rise to the situation. In the second, it's because he's the dominant force in the room, making deductions no one else can and lecturing those around him from on high.

But then there's the scene where he spends the night in Sir Reginald Styles's house, raiding his wine cellar and dining on fine cheeses like the aristocrat he so desperately wants to be. And when unknown attackers burst in, he fights them one-handed, *pausing mid-fight to take a sip of wine*. Oh please. This is just snobbish showing off, making it clear to the audience that the sophisticated upper-class gentleman is superior to the dirty working man in every way. That and all the name-dropping. Is he actively trying to make us dislike him? If so, mission accomplished. Oh, and then he later picks up a gun and shoots an Ogron. Not in self-defence, but simply because he has no other ideas.

I take it back. It's not just the peaks that illustrate the third Doctor's character, it's the troughs as well. You can see them both here . . . but you might not like them so much.

The Curse of Peladon (1972)

Written by Brian Hayles

Directed by Lennie Mayne

The Big Idea The Time Lords bring the TARDIS to the planet Peladon during a conference to admit it to the Galactic Federation. But the conference is being sabotaged by an unknown party. Could it be the Doctor's old enemies, the Ice Warriors?

Hai!? (RS?) We interrupt our regularly scheduled program to bring you "The Curse of Peladon." After two and a half years, there's no Brigadier, no Master, no earthbound setting, no UNIT HQ. Instead, the TARDIS travels to an alien planet. What's more, if you're going to go to an alien planet, you might as well go all out. *Doctor Who* as we knew it is back, bigger and bolder than ever, for four nights only.

"The Curse of Peladon" is an astonishing story that's decades ahead of its time. You could make this an episode of *Babylon 5* and it would feel right at home. The delegates are the most alien of alien races since the Hartnell years, yet, with the exception of Aggedor, they're all intelligent characters with clear motivation. There's a timely allegory to Britain joining the European Union. It features about four times as many monsters as any story in the previous seven years, with designs ranging from a shrivelled head in a tank to a huge hairy beast. One of which, if you're watching carefully, looks a little bit rude.

Of course, the sheer brilliance of "The Curse of Peladon" isn't its *Star Wars* Cantina delegates or its political allegory, it's the Ice Warriors. Because what the Ice Warriors do is make this all about the Doctor: they show up his prejudices, and that's just awesome. They not only turn out to be the good guys, they do so without fundamentally altering their own nature. And it throws the Doctor for an incredible loop that forces him to rise above the usual action-adventure fare. This is the side of the third Doctor I adore: when his back's to the wall, out of his comfort zone, he soars.

We now return you to our regularly scheduled program.

Second Opinion (GB) Except my co-author is wrong. It's not *Doctor Who* as we knew it.

"The Curse of Peladon" does feature a story on an alien planet without UNIT and all that, but that's where the similarities with 1960s

Doctor Who end. It's not the monster-filled travelogues of the Hartnell years and it's not the monster-filled base-under-siege thrillers of the Troughton era. "The Curse of Peladon" is a bold restatement of what future space stories can be.

Here it's a mystery crossed with a political allegory crossed with a romance. I can't believe they managed to do all that genre-melding in four episodes, but they did. That's what makes it so beautiful: it moves fluidly from tense, intriguing set piece to tense, intriguing set piece while playing with the tone and genre. And it's willing to take real risks, such as making the Ice Warriors the good guys.

Many of the trends that we see in modern-day *Doctor Who* have their origins in the 1970s. The modern space story with ambition, clever ideas and a sense of fun? It starts right here.

Planet of the Spiders (1974)

Written by Robert Sloman (and Barry Letts)

Directed by Barry Letts

The Big Idea Earlier, the Doctor stole a blue crystal from the planet Metebelis III. Now the Doctor must face his greatest failing and his greatest fear as the planet's rulers — a race of giant spiders — want that crystal back.

Hai!? (GB) Jon Pertwee's last story is a celebration of everything that's good and bad about his era of *Doctor Who*. The house style is now a fast-paced drama, but it's padded to the gills. The greenscreen makes the Doctor's car fly but also makes Metebelis III look cheap and nasty. The idea of a planet run by giant spiders is quite cool. The puppets used to create it aren't bad either. It's more let down by the design, where the eight-legs' dwellings are a set in Adam West's *Batman*, with raised platforms that have spiderwebs painted on, rather than, well, actual spiderwebs.

The other problem with the story is its length. Really, it would be underrunning as a four-parter. Stretching it out to six parts is ridiculous. The episode-long chase sequence, obvious padding though it is, isn't the problem (it seems rather sweet and appropriate for Pertwee's last hurrah). It's the fact that every episode is so short that it has to take a scene from the start of the following episode and add it to the end. The deficit financing of its length leads to some very odd episode endings, including a suspenseful, "Will Tommy the supporting character survive till next week?" cliffhanger.

And yet, for all these faults, there's a lot to love too. Barry Letts and Robert Sloman make this a grand end-of-an-era epic, tying together all sorts of disparate strands of Pertwee's tenure: past companion Jo Grant, the Blue Crystal from 1973's "The Green Death," UNIT, the Doctor's vehicles, the Doctor's mentor from 1972's "The Time Monster." It even epitomizes the progression of the past five years as it starts out earthbound with UNIT and ends on another planet.

Best of all, it gives a great send-off to Jon Pertwee's Doctor, as he sacrifices himself to face his own fear and arrogance — an actual character arc. The Sloman/Letts-written stories in the Pertwee era are part of a rare breed of personal stories in *Doctor Who*, as Letts shares his Buddhist beliefs in a non-doctrinaire way: the Doctor transforms into a new man, personally and literally. In spite of all its best efforts to undo itself, "Planet of the Spiders" manages to succeed, though only just.

Second Opinion (RS?) I have to disagree with my co-author. I freaking love this story.

Yes, it's long. Yes, it's padded. Yes, it takes greenscreen to ridiculous levels. Yes, it sets several episodes in the Village of Bad Actors. Yes, it has a white guy with tape over his eyes pretending to be Asian. None of this matters a damn. (Okay, that last one matters.)

Graeme's also dead wrong about the Tommy cliffhanger. Tommy is one of the most sensitive and stand-up-and-cheer guest characters in the whole of *Doctor Who*. His *Flowers for Algernon* arc is superb, so we genuinely care about what happens to him. I absolutely adore Tommy, especially in the moment when Sarah wondrously comments that he's just like everybody else and he replies, "I sincerely hope not."

Despite all of its obvious flaws (it opens with a lazy shot of cows in a field, not exactly the most exciting opening ever devised), I love "Planet of the Spiders" with a fiery zeal. Because it is, quite simply, the perfect ending for the third Doctor.

That the most confident and arrogant of Doctors turns out to be riddled with fear is an awesome character revelation. The same man whose hubris killed a psychic at the opening of the story is forced to face the consequences of his actions and accept that his greed for knowledge was as much a sin as Lupton's greed for power. And so the old man must die and the man will discover, to his inexpressible joy, that he has never existed. Cue regeneration.

The Fourth Doctor, Part 1

Monster Chiller Horror Theatre

(1974–1977)

Basic Data

First story: "Robot" (1974)

Final story (of this half): "The Talons of Weng-Chiang" (1977)

We've split Tom Baker's era in two, partly because there's so much of it, but partly because it's neatly bisected into very different halves. So this first half covers the producership of Philip Hinchcliffe, which is characterized by its gothic horror storylines, sumptuous design and Tom Baker wearing a cravat.

The Changing Face of *Doctor Who* The UNIT era had been gradually dying. Launched as a way to shake up the format, the earthbound adventures of the third Doctor were incredibly popular in their heyday. But with the death of Roger Delgado and the departure of Katy Manning, the era was coming to a close. Almost simultaneously, key players decided to leave: actor Jon Pertwee, producer Barry Letts and script editor Terrance Dicks. Only the Brigadier, Sergeant

Benton and new companion Sarah Jane Smith were continuing into the next phase of the show.

However, there was one major task that Barry Letts had to perform before he bowed out: finding a new Doctor. Letts auditioned a number of different actors, mostly older males (he very nearly cast Fulton MacKay, who guest-starred in 1970's "Doctor Who and the Silurians") before settling on what was, at the time, the youngest actor to be cast in the part, a 39-year-old named Tom Baker.

Incoming producer Philip Hinchcliffe, together with new script editor Robert Holmes (who was by now a veteran writer on the series) decided to completely dispense with UNIT and return the show to its time-travel roots. Despite a large age gap between them — Hinchcliffe was merely 29 when he took over, whereas Holmes was almost two decades older — Holmes and Hinchcliffe found themselves on the same page with respect to the direction to take the show: one that was decidedly adult, with creeping horror, gothic sensibilities and a series of homages to classic books and movies (everything from *King Kong* with a robot to Jekyll and Hyde reimagined as a planet, as well as *The Mummy*, *Frankenstein* and *The Beast with Five Fingers* along the way).

Everything came together. With an intensely charismatic leading man, a script editor who was the master of his craft and award-winning designers ensuring the show had never looked so good (or, due to subsequent inflation, ever would again), *Doctor Who* of the mid-'70s hit the ground running and never looked back. The series built on the ratings success of the Pertwee era and took it to the next level. Hinchcliffe and Holmes began to skew to an older sensibility with increased realism, horror and fantastic violence.

The show was hugely popular, but it also brought with it critics, in particular the right-wing pressure group the National Viewers' and Listeners' Association and its head, Mary Whitehouse. The NVLA had always complained about *Doctor Who*, but it brought down its wrath over the show's increased violence and horror, culminating in a complaint about the cliffhanger ending to the 1976 story "The Deadly Assassin" (showing the Doctor being drowned), which forced an apology from the Director General of the BBC. This resulted in a radical change to the series, as we will eventually see . . .

Who is Tom Baker? Ironically, for the actor who has become indelibly associated with the role of the Doctor even to this day, Tom Baker was a relatively nobody when he was cast. He had owed his career up to that point to his portrayal of a dog on stage. His canine performance caught the eye of Sir Laurence Olivier, who gave him helpful career advice as well as a berth in the National Theatre company. Baker had found some promising theatre and film roles, playing Rasputin in the lavish 1971 historical film *Nicholas and Alexandra* and the villain in *The Golden Voyage of Sinbad* in 1973 (a role that Christopher Lee had been up for). However, work was so scarce that the actor was working as a labourer on a construction site in 1974.

Baker had complained about his plight in a letter to his friend Bill Slater, the head of serials at the BBC, who had directed Baker in a television adaptation of *The Millionairess* a couple of years before. The timing was extremely fortuitous: Slater was talking at the end of the day with his wife, Mary Webster — also a friend of Baker — about Baker's desperate letter and the troubles he was having casting the new Doctor. It was Webster who suggested that her husband had the solution to both his problems.

Slater immediately called Baker and arranged a meeting at Television Centre the next day. Slater suggested departing producer Barry Letts, with his script editor, Terrance Dicks, go see *The Golden Voyage of Sinbad.* With that, everyone knew they'd found their star.

While Tom Baker was grateful for the steady work, he was unsure of the part. It was a conversation with new producer Philip Hinchcliffe that set the direction for the character. Hinchcliffe suggested that a key part of playing the Doctor was "Olympian detachment." Hinchcliffe would later joke that this wasn't a good note for an actor, but Baker ran with it. In contrast to Pertwee's Doctor, Baker took the role in a much more alien direction, just as the scripts were simultaneously liberating the character from his earthbound roots.

Once he started playing the Doctor, Baker seized the role of both actor and performer. Being single, he was available to do even more promotional events than his predecessor, often signing for hours on end. He believed very strongly in the idea of the Doctor as a children's hero and was careful not to be seen drinking or smoking in public.

The primary quality Baker brought to the role was his genuine eccentricity. When filming 1975's "The Android Invasion" in Oxfordshire, Baker traipsed through fields, collecting flowers and seeds, because Notting Hill Gate, where he lived in London, was a bit drab and he wanted to liven it up. Likewise, he'd often travel with just a toothbrush, as he never knew where he might bed down for the night (a reference to which made its way into 1976's "The Seeds of Doom"). As seen in interviews, he's intelligent, articulate and odd, not just for the sake of being strange, but because that throws people off their game and forces them to engage with him without preconceptions. Much like the fourth Doctor himself.

Top Companion For Tom Baker's first three seasons, there's only one defining companion: the inimitable Sarah Jane Smith. Smart, sassy and independent, she gave as good as she got, breaking the mould of previous companions. Sarah was introduced during Jon Pertwee's final season, but it was her easy rapport with the fourth Doctor that made her so beloved at the time. She and the fourth Doctor are best friends backpacking across the universe, sometimes teasing each other, sometimes arguing, but always having each other's backs. And it's largely thanks to Elisabeth Sladen's superb acting that Sarah came to life, as she imbued the character with little touches (such as her quiet confidence about firing a rifle in 1975's "Pyramids of Mars") that took the character beyond her original outline. She was the rare companion who came back after she left, returning in the Modern Series alongside David Tennant. She even starred in not one but two spinoffs: the 1981 Christmas special *K9 and Company* (which didn't get picked up as a series) and the BBC children's series *The Sarah Jane Adventures* (which did, from 2008 to 2011). When Elizabeth Sladen died in 2011, we bade farewell to her turn as Sarah Jane Smith at the same place where she was established: starring in a highly rated science-fiction show, adored by children and adults alike.

Classic Foe Twelve years into the series and the show does something that TV at the time hadn't done much of: it gives us an origin story. Not for the Doctor, but for the Daleks. Using *Doctor Who*'s greatest asset (time travel), our heroes are sent back to witness the birth of the Daleks . . . and they discover that the creatures had a creator. Crippled and barely alive, Davros is nevertheless a genius, both scientifically and politically. He engineers mutants so that his people can survive — and then ruthlessly wipes out those same people when they threaten his scientific work. He manipulates those around him, making a deal with his greatest enemies — and then destroys their race in the first flexing of Dalek muscle. And he even holds his own when debating the Doctor on moral issues, contemplating the consequences of releasing a virus that would destroy everything. Although Davros returns in several subsequent stories, he's never better than in his first appearance, thanks to a superlative performance by Michael Wisher and a brilliant design.

Who is the Doctor? The early fourth Doctor is mercurial, moody, sombre and funny. He's a wanderer in time and space, embodying the original concept of the Doctor in such a fundamental way that he becomes the uber-Doctor. And he's a genius with circuitry. But you can sum up this Doctor in one word: rude.

He's rude to almost everyone he meets, from companions to compatriots to villains. And he's egotistical to a fault, insulting his companions even when they show initiative. Those who can stand up to him, like Sarah, earn the status of equals, but those who can't (the Brigadier, Harry Sullivan) are blithely dismissed.

And yet this rudeness comes from a different place than his predecessor's. This Doctor is genuinely alien and more detached from humanity, something that occasionally bewilders his companion: in "Pyramids of Mars," Sarah doesn't understand why the Doctor makes quips after someone has been killed. The Doctor's response is that he's paying attention to the greater threat being faced. It's a dynamic that plays again and again.

He channels that alien rudeness into witty insults to his opponents ("You're a classic example of the inverse ratio between the size of the mouth and the size of the brain"), which puts him on an equal footing — a marked difference to his predecessor's method of dressing people down. These comments can be disarming, making the increased horror more palatable for children, or they can be hilarious, making the episodes endlessly rewatchable.

This detachment gives the fourth Doctor an alien quality quite unlike the Doctors who preceded him (who had their moments of eccentricity but were otherwise very human in all the ways that mattered). He's uninterested in being UNIT's scientific advisor and would prefer to walk in eternity. It's in this era that he frequently self-identifies as being merely as a traveller.

He has a code of ethics, but it isn't necessarily ours. As a result, he's a series of contradictions. In 1977's "The Face of Evil," he comically threatens to kill someone with a jelly baby as a bluff, but later in the story he kicks a carnivorous predator into someone for slapping a woman. In "The Seeds of Doom," he threatens people with a gun — while admitting that he'd never use it — and punches a chauffeur unconscious. These contradictions are there even with the bigger menaces. While the Doctor speaks on behalf of all nature in decrying Sutekh as a twisted abhorrence in "Pyramids of Mars," he refuses to commit genocide, even when battling the universe's greatest evil in 1975's "Genesis of the Daleks."

Despite being less of an outright action man than his predecessor, he's not afraid to get his hands dirty. His Doctor isn't into dignified martial arts; he's a brawler who takes on his opponents through any means necessary, from jungle warfare to mental combat. And yet, he can just as easily sit down with villains, chatting about galactic events with the likes of Davros or Magnus Greel as though he's at a particularly lively dinner party, debating some arcane point of philosophy with a fellow academic.

In short, the early fourth Doctor has so many shades of personality that he almost defies description. He strides through the gothic horror of this era with confidence and arrogance; he seems larger than life and yet has moments of vulnerability that allow us to connect with him. He's an absolutely riveting character, one who lights up the screen and almost single-handedly proves, decades on, why this was the unquestioned golden age of *Doctor Who*.

Three Great Moments In "Genesis of the Daleks," the Doctor is given three choices: avert the Daleks' creation, alter them so they evolve into a less aggressive species or find some weakness that can be used against them. By the final episode, only one choice remains open to the Doctor: genocide. He rigs up explosives in their incubator room and then prepares to wipe them from the universe before they begin. And . . . he hesitates. Asking a crucial question ("Do I have the right?"), he ponders the morality of this act, comparing it to murdering a child and wondering whether it makes him any better than the Daleks. Rightly held up as one of the greatest moments of the series, this scene gives pause to the action-adventure, showing that *Doctor Who* isn't just about fighting evil and running down corridors, but about deep, fundamental questions. And it invites the same from us, the viewers: faced with the same situation, what would you do?

In 1975's "Planet of Evil," the Doctor discovers a scientist, Professor Sorenson, who has messed with the forces of creation. Sorenson's meddling has infected him so that he's slowly changing into a creature of anti-matter. The Doctor lectures the man from a place of ethical scientific responsibility, saying, "You and I are scientists, Professor. We buy our privilege to experiment at the cost of total responsibility." Sorenson understands exactly what this responsibility is: he promptly goes to a mortuary tray in order to eject himself into space. (The anti-matter creature reasserts itself at the last minute.) It's a shocking scene, because Sorenson isn't a villain; he's a respected scientist gone slightly awry. And yet the Doctor essentially talks the man into committing suicide.

Aboard the Zygon ship in 1975's "Terror of the Zygons," their leader, Broton, pays the Doctor a visit in his cell, whereupon the fourth Doctor proceeds to talk smack like nobody's business. Wearing his enormous trademark grin, he asks if the monster is paying him a social call. Upon learning that the Zygons plan to terraform Earth, the Doctor asks if it isn't a bit large for just the six of them (a sly comment on the show's limited budget). Later, when he escapes from the cell, the Doctor fondles the phallic Zygon controls in about the most suggestive manner imaginable. So he's making the adults in the audience laugh while nevertheless reassuring children that the Doctor is not afraid of the monsters, simultaneously moving the plot along and turning expository dialogue into something extraordinary. Ladies and gentlemen, we present Tom Baker at the height of his powers.

Two Embarrassing Moments In 1975's "Revenge of the Cybermen," the Vogans have launched a rocket at Nerva Beacon, the space station whose nose cone the Cybermen have stuffed with bombs. The Cybermen evacuate, leaving the Doctor and Sarah on board. Faced with serious disaster, they utter the double entendre "We're headed for the biggest bang in history" not once but twice (and it wasn't funny the first time). The subsequent special effect of the Beacon just missing the planet, achieved by obviously rolling a vaguely planet-like cylinder in front of the camera, is almost as risible.

The climactic scene of the otherwise wonderful "Terror of the Zygons" involves a 50-foot monster rising from the Thames to tower over London. It looks about as bad as you'd imagine it possibly could if you tried to convey a 50-foot monster towering over London on a 1975 budget.

What? (RS?) Say whatever you want, there's never been a Doctor like this — and there never will be again.

The Hinchcliffe era, as this period has become known, is marked by almost nonstop quality. It looks gorgeous. It's written like a dream. It has top-notch directors, auditioning for the gig of their careers. Design, costume and makeup all work in synchronicity with barely a ball dropped among them. Decisions from the top demonstrated that there were grownups in charge. Scripts were edited by the undisputed master of *Doctor Who*. And it was all fronted by a leading man so eclectic that we're still trying to get a handle on him, 40 years later.

I knew a guy once who, having seen the effect that Pertwee-bashing was having in the '90s, tried to start his own bandwagon with the (only half-serious) argument that Tom Baker's first season was the worst season of *Doctor Who* ever produced. He was demolished in about 30 seconds.

You simply can't find any serious detractors of this era. The best people can do is to argue that there's one substandard story per season, which overlooks the fact that a) "Revenge of the Cybermen" is an underrated classic and b) "The Hand of Fear" is simply great, with excellent characters and a stunning departure for Sarah. Which leaves only "The Android Invasion" as subpar. Every other story in the era is stupendous. A list of its classics — "The Ark in Space," "Genesis of the Daleks," "Pyramids of Mars," "The Deadly Assassin," "The Talons of Weng-Chiang" — includes those stories that routinely find themselves topping every fan poll of the series ever taken. Even the also-rans are superb: "Terror of the Zygons," "The Seeds of Doom," "The Masque of Mandragora," "The Face of Evil," "The Robots of Death."

Beat for beat, this is easily the best run of quality the series has ever had. You can defend other eras for doing some absolutely lovely things and having some wonderful moments . . . but no other era of *Doctor Who*, before or since, can touch the Hinchcliffe era for sheer quality.

And yet, amid so many reasons to celebrate, it's the fourth Doctor himself who stands head and shoulders above everything else. Quite simply, he's just intensely watchable. Never before has someone so lit up the screen both as a performer and as a person. I dare you to find the dividing line between the fictional character of the Doctor and Tom Baker, the actor. You can't. And that's what makes his Doctor, especially in the early years, so mesmerizing.

With some eras, you simply had to be there. People who watched William Hartnell at the time adored his Doctor, but later generations struggled to see the magic. The Troughton era was largely wiped after first transmission, leaving us guessing as to its contents. Jon Pertwee was perfectly suited to his environment, but the era hasn't aged well. But with Tom Baker, the hero of your childhood becomes the witty postmodernist of adulthood without skipping a beat. And that's why we'll never see the likes of this period again, despite many, many attempts to emulate it: Tom Baker was one of a kind. They simply don't make actors like him any more — and they didn't before he came along either.

The thing I love perhaps more than anything else is how Baker takes the most arrogant man in the universe . . . and makes you love him. He should be an awful boor. And yet, there's a childlike charm to the character that makes you smile when he tells Harry Sullivan not to take any credit for having a breakthrough, because it must have been entirely his influence, or look past the sexism of his rant about girls like Sarah being all talk, because he's doing it to make her angry enough to overcome her fears. Or that has you cheering along when he pricks the Brigadier's pomposity about anyone not in England being a foreigner.

Looking forward slightly from this era, when I was nine years old and I saw the fourth Doctor fall from a radio tower and die, I don't think I've ever cried so hard in my life. That moment is etched into my childhood as one I found more tragic and more real than my grandmother dying at around the same time. For seven long years, Tom Baker simply was the Doctor, and I couldn't have imagined life without him. I love this man with an unholy passion.

There's a reason that Tom Baker was the Classic Series Doctor chosen to appear with Matt Smith in the conclusion to "The Day of the Doctor." He's the one everyone remembers — and with good reason. For seven years, he infected the childhoods of anyone who was young enough to appreciate him and made everybody else smile. Is it because of Tom Baker the actor or Tom Baker the person — or the fact that there isn't a dividing line between the two? Who knows? Who. Knows.

Second Opinion (GB) When I was growing up, my childhood best friend and I used to joke about the "Tom Baker pain expression." Watch any story during this era, usually around about the cliffhanger of episode three, and you'll see it. The Doctor appears to be not simply in discomfort but in horrible, writhing, unendurable agony. His face is contorted, his teeth are showing and his eyes are screwed shut.

It's glorious.

For me, the "Tom Baker pain expression" pretty much says everything about why I love this era of *Doctor Who* so much. The central character is played by a man who just goes for it, every single time. That pain the Doctor is going through? It's real. It's horrible. It's terrifying. I think the word I'm searching for is . . . *visceral.*

And Tom Baker doesn't just stop with the pain expression. He commits to everything in a real, physical way. I would disagree with my co-author. I think his first three seasons of *Doctor Who* are where we see Tom Baker the actor. It may be filtered through an eccentric sensibility, but watch the scene where the Doctor and Davros are talking and the Doctor is trying to convince Davros not to create the Daleks. Baker is staggering in his intensity and subtlety.

Steven Moffat once argued that if he had done this on contemporary television, Tom Baker would have been snatched up after those first few seasons and put on a fast track to stardom in the U.K. and abroad — rather like David Tennant and Matt Smith or *Sherlock*'s Benedict Cumberbatch. And you can see something of Cumberbatch and Smith in the younger Tom Baker: an actor hungry to prove himself, who's been given a huge role in which to do just that.

If Tom Baker had stopped playing the role in 1977, we probably would think differently of him. His Doctor would be called "gothic" and "Byronic" and even "romantic" (and he'd be compared to Mr. Rochester and Darcy as well as Sherlock Holmes). He's a witty character, but he's also one who broods, smoulders and is difficult. He's looking at the bigger picture all the time, whether that be what happens if he kills the Daleks in infancy or what happens if he picks up and leaves while an Egyptian demigod is still around (or takes the time to mourn the death of a friend during that crisis).

Those aspects largely get forgotten after 1977 because Tom Baker went in a different direction, but those were the things I loved about him when I first watched *Doctor Who*. I loved that the Doctor was strange and alien and aloof but also occasionally funny. I loved the way Tom Baker gave the Doctor a sense of gravitas just through his voice. I loved the chemistry with Elisabeth Sladen that made the Doctor and a companion actual friends.

I loved everything about Tom Baker. Especially the "Tom Baker pain expression."

Robot (1974)

Written by Terrance Dicks

Directed by Christopher Barry

The Big Idea A breakaway scientific elite is using a sentient robot to build a new world order. UNIT needs the Doctor's help, but the Doctor isn't the man he used to be.

What? (RS?) Three is a magic number. When you remember Classic *Doctor Who*, you think of three things: UNIT soldiers shooting things in the countryside; a mysterious something that's only revealed by an arm until the first cliffhanger; and an examination of what it means to be human, refracted through the monster. "Robot" has all of these in, perhaps, the most quintessential *Doctor Who* story of all time.

But then Tom Baker drops into the story and everything changes. He skips out of the gate laughing, with a manic performance that has you falling in love from the first moment. Effortlessly establishing the costume-change scene as a new trope for the show, he sweeps you up in his whirlwind of comedy outfits, hilarious putdowns and brilliant deductions, delivered eccentrically, but no less impressively.

"Robot" might look like the quintessential *Doctor Who* story, but the sideways slide resulting from the change in leading man makes it simultaneously every story of your childhood and unlike anything else. When you remember Classic *Doctor Who*, you think of four things: UNIT soldiers shooting things in the countryside; a mysterious something that's only revealed by an arm until the first cliffhanger; an examination of what it means to be human, refracted through the monster; and an eccentric Tom Baker, lighting up the screen through sheer personality. Four is a magic number.

Second Opinion (GB) Robot is a late '60s episode of *The Avengers*, with Sarah as Tara King, the Brigadier as Mother and the Doctor as Steed ("Well, obviously; the rest are all foreigners"), and not just because the Nazi-like baddies — the Scientific Reform Society — are a direct steal from Terrance Dicks's own 1963 *Avengers* episode "The

Mauritius Penny." Steed and Ta— er, the Doctor and Sarah investigate different lines of inquiry featuring colourful and outlandish characters (take a bow, Professor Kettlewell!), all leading to the reveal of the true menace. The only thing that's missing is the elaborate fight sequence set to jazzy music.

But that doesn't really matter because Tom Baker's debut as the Doctor is the televisual equivalent of witnessing a thermonuclear detonation; Baker just explodes onto the scene. His performance is a complete about-face from Jon Pertwee's: the Doctor is bolder, braver and madder than ever. Every scene he's in is worth watching, because Baker throws everything into his performance. Without him, this story is so slight it wouldn't have passed muster as a comic strip, much less a television story; with him, it's absolutely riveting.

The Ark in Space (1975)

Written by Robert Holmes

Directed by Rodney Bennett

The Big Idea In the far future, humanity stands at the brink of extinction, its last survivors cryogenically frozen aboard a space station. But an alien infestation threatens to destroy everything — and forces the survivors to confront their own humanity.

What? (GB) The Doctor stands in a room with what's left of the human race sitting frozen. And he says this: "Homo sapiens. What an inventive, invincible species. It's only a few million years since they've crawled up out of the mud and learned to walk. Puny, defenceless bipeds. They've survived flood, famine and plague. They've survived cosmic wars and holocausts. And now, here they are, out amongst the stars, waiting to begin a new life, ready to outsit eternity. They're indomitable. Indomitable!"

Honestly, it's the greatest speech in the history of *Doctor Who*. It was written by Robert Holmes with such a Shakespearean rhythm and sense of metre that I hope people perform it 300 years in the future. And Tom Baker performs it as though he were doing the Bard — and doing him justice. It's a spontaneous love letter from an alien to us that says beautiful things not only about the human race but about why the Doctor enjoys the company of this fragile and yet incredible species.

And that's what "The Ark in Space" is all about. It's about the struggle to save what's left of humanity, from both the insect-like race that's preying on it and the soulless, insect-like race that *Homo sapiens* is in danger of becoming. The Doctor is never smarter, never more desperate and, at the same time, never more romantic than he is here. It's magic.

Second Opinion (RS?) This new show, starring William Hartnell as the Doctor, with William Russell and Jacqueline Hill as companions Ian and Barbara, gets off to a magnificent second serial with "The Ark in Space." Some might criticize the first episode for its slowness, featuring the ship's crew wandering around corridors and investigating an apparently empty ark, but closer examination proves that it's paced to perfection. Hartnell delivers a speech for the ages, Barbara is cleverly transported into the inner workings of the space station and Ian performs his usual amusing bumbling.

The subsequent peril plays perfectly to the cast's strengths, with William Russell's action-man scientist/teacher a perfect foil to the soulless humans and Jacqueline Hill magnificent in her laborious (but tension-filled) crawl through the ducting. Clever effects, such as the monster in the cupboard at the first cliffhanger, give the impression of much more movement than the 1960s cameras were capable of.

The only letdown are the adult Wirrn, with legs too spindly to hold themselves up and played by puppets in the final effects sequence, but that's to be expected of television in its early days. And the story lends itself perfectly to the staginess of the era's filming, with conceits such as the human race in one room and the central theme being a ponderance of what it means to be human. Oh, and that it was made in black and white is just perfect. I wouldn't change a thing!

Genesis of the Daleks (1975)

Written by Terry Nation

Directed by David Maloney

The Big Idea The Time Lords send the Doctor on a desperate mission to stop the Daleks from being created. But when he learns of their true origins, the Doctor finds more than he bargained for.

What? (RS?) No, Graeme, you're just wrong. As I keep saying, "Genesis of the Daleks" is a fantastic story, from beginning to end. Yes, even the beginning! Those first three episodes are wonderful, with a brilliant establishment of the Nazi-like Kaleds, the Doctor and Harry being the only splashes of colour among the black-and-white costumed bunker and there's some clever establishment of Davros as —

Oh, I'm sorry. I know this is a whole new book and everything, but my co-author was so snippy about this fantastic story in our last book that I really need to state my piece. And it's true that if one of us wrote the main entry last time, then we've swapped this time, to keep things fresh. But I just can't sit back idly while he trashes something that's sheer perfection itself!

Point to anything that's great about *Doctor Who* and it's in "Genesis" somewhere. You've got utterly superb direction, from — quite literally — the first moment. The script is outstanding, layering the tension brilliantly and upping the stakes with every episode. The pacing is extremely solid, throwing in complications for the companions and even making us care about characters who were bullies at the outset.

And, oh yes, the Doctor is utterly superb. Watch him in any lengthy conversation he has with Davros and marvel at what this talented actor is doing. Watch how he swings effortlessly from humour and snark to misery and depression. Watch how he makes philosophical debates seem like the most riveting thing on television. In fact, just watch it. And pay no attention to the man in the second opinion.

Second Opinion (GB) Meh.

"Genesis of the Daleks" is an overrated story where the set pieces used in clip shows are better than everything around it. It cheats its biggest moral dilemmas. It screws up established Dalek history completely. It's not even particularly interesting (just exceptionally well directed and acted). But you can read *Who's 50* to see my full opinions in their apoplexy-inducing glory. All that said, even I can't argue with the fact that the Doctor is magnificent here and that every scene with Tom Baker is like watching a breakout star in his finest moment. Shame it had to be in this.

The Deadly Assassin (1976)

Written by Robert Holmes

Directed by David Maloney

The Big Idea The Doctor is summoned back to the place he swore he'd never return: his home planet, Gallifrey. But waiting for him is an old and deadly enemy who plans to use the Doctor as a pawn in a much larger game.

What? (GB) In an era when *Doctor Who* filched from genre stories with wild abandon, the ones most people attach to "The Deadly Assassin" are *The Manchurian Candidate* (which also involves a political assassination, although neither the writer nor the producer had seen it) and *The Most Dangerous Game* (because the entire third episode rips it off). But really, it's directly lifting from film noir. The Doctor is an outsider figure who is framed for a crime he didn't commit and has to prove his innocence. And if getting out of that wasn't hard enough, he mentally puts himself in a nightmare world where he's being ruthlessly hunted down.

We see the Doctor truly vulnerable in a way we've never seen before — which makes the drama all the more compelling. We also meet the Time Lords and discover that they're brilliant, narrow-minded and indolent to the point of being corrupt. And suddenly the Doctor's moral stance is thrown into sharp relief. People define themselves in relation to their home. It's no wonder the Doctor rejected Time Lord society.

Two of the great charms in this story are the companion-surrogates the Doctor is given: a grizzled Gallifreyan police inspector and a superannuated archivist. It sounds like it could never work, but it does beautifully. That there's even space for this to happen along with everything else says something about how special this story actually is.

Second Opinion (RS?) What? Are you insane? Have you even watched the thing? At a recent convention, I conducted an informal poll, and the entire audience voted "Genesis of the Daleks" the single greatest story of all —

Ahem.

Speaking of things that all right-thinking individuals should absolutely adore, the first episode of "The Deadly Assassin" has to be seen to be believed. It's like nothing you've ever experienced in *Doctor Who* before. The plot runs like clockwork: the Doctor has a premonition of himself shooting the Time Lord president dead; he evades capture cleverly, whereupon a mysterious hooded creature we've never seen before says, "Predictable as ever, Doctor"; the Doctor infiltrates the presidential ceremony; then, up on a catwalk, he picks up a sniper rifle . . . and (apparently) shoots the Time Lord president dead.

It's about as perfect a construction as you can get, giving us exactly what it said it would and simultaneously shocking us to the core when it does. And the best thing about it is that it throws the Doctor out of his comfort zone: with no companion, he's forced to improvise massively, out-think his peers and get his hands dirty. That first episode is an utterly brilliant story in its own right. Almost as good as "Genesis of the Daleks," in fact . . .

The Robots of Death (1977)

Written by Chris Boucher

Directed by Michael E. Briant

The Big Idea Aboard a futuristic sandminer, the decadent crew have their every whim catered to by subservient robots. But there's a murderer aboard, and the implications could destroy a whole society.

What? (RS?) One of *Doctor Who*'s greatest strengths as a series is its ability to blend genres. Not just to steal from them, but to take the best bits of something, use them for all they're worth and then transform into something else. "The Robots of Death" does something quite mind-boggling: it crashes together Agatha Christie mysteries, horror movies and Asimov-inspired hard science fiction. All with a luxurious art deco backdrop.

It really shouldn't work. Agatha Christie mysteries are sedate drawing-room affairs. There's a murderer afoot, yes, but rarely is Miss

Marple stalked through the claustrophobic confines of a submarine, with the villain's severed hand caught in a door. In Asimov's high-concept sci-fi, robotic societies aren't usually so comfortable with a leotard-wearing huntress pushing back against all the technology. And the sheer terror of violent, creeping horror doesn't usually stalk people with such ludicrous hats.

And yet . . . it works. It really works. There's a reason "The Robots of Death" is one of the standout stories of Classic *Who*: it's because of the fourth Doctor.

No, really. Without him, it'd be a hodgepodge of random ideas stuck together. But the Doctor strides through the narrative, wittily insulting the small-minded, effortlessly taking charge when the sand-miner is sabotaged and thinking outside the box when it comes to voice commands. He does all this by sheer power of deduction, from proposing the idea of the robots as murderers from the outset and recognizing Poul's deteriorating condition to determining D84's true nature and discovering the identity of the killer. By standing apart from the narrative, the Doctor allows that narrative to come together in a way that's at once bizarre and beautiful. Rather like art deco, in fact.

Second Opinion (GB) As my co-author says, it's not just the genre-bending that makes "The Robots of Death" such a superior story. But I actually disagree that the story wouldn't work without the Doctor. I will grant that the Doctor is a superior detective because of his lateral thinking, but, honestly, "The Robots of Death" is about as perfectly constructed a world as you're liable to get in *Doctor Who*.

Writer Chris Boucher is great at complex characters with mixed motives, perfect for a mystery where it's death by robot. (And the mystery is sublime: the clues are there right from the killer's very first scene. It's a brilliant bit of writing and acting.) Commander Uvanov may be one of *Doctor Who*'s all-time great characters: abrasive, sarcastic on the surface but with a lot of hidden depths. (And credit to Russell Hunter; he realizes Uvanov brilliantly.) Every character has a hidden agenda, which they mask with brittle dialogue. Even the robots, who are constantly placid, are creepy killers precisely because their actions are so at variance with their well-spoken servile nature.

Doctor Who has never looked better than it does in "The Robots of Death." And, in many ways, it's never been better, either.

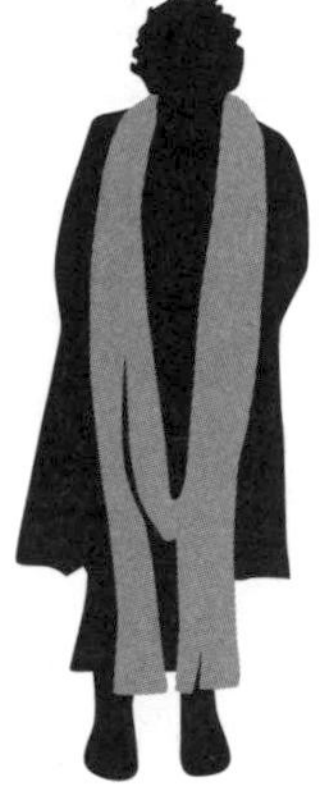

The Fourth Doctor, Part 2

The Tom Baker Comedy Half-Hour

(1977–1981)

Basic Data

First story (of this half): "Horror of Fang Rock" (1977)

Final story: "Logopolis" (1981)

Final appearance: "The Day of the Doctor" (2013)

The second half of the Tom Baker era was characterized by an increasingly larger-than-life Doctor, a plethora of jokes and wild science-fiction ideas, realized on a tiny budget. The exception is the final season, which took a different tack, but we've put them together because they're still all fundamentally about Tom Baker, the personality.

The Changing Face of *Doctor Who* In 1977, incoming producer Graham Williams was given a remit to tone down the horror (and its attendant violence) that had become a signature of the series by this point. Consequently, Williams faced a difficult question: with what do you fill that void? Williams decided to look to the series' best asset, Tom Baker, who was already injecting significant amounts of humour into the show. More comedic elements were added to scripts, and Tom Baker was given a wider berth to be funny — elements that hit their apogee two seasons later when Douglas Adams became script editor.

And yet, enhancing the comedic aspect of the series was one of Williams's more minor achievements. With script editor Anthony Read, Williams added more genuine literary science-fiction concepts into *Doctor Who*. Williams also attempted a season-long story arc, years before such things were fashionable, as the Doctor was sent on a quest to find the six segments of the Key to Time. He also added one of the most child-friendly elements to the show in the form of the now-iconic robotic companion K9.

However, Williams's tenure on the series was turbulent. Inflation spiralled in the late 1970s in the U.K., leaving the production of *Doctor Who* cash-strapped all the time. (Most of the popular assumptions that Classic *Doctor Who* is a cheap-looking show with wobbly sets come from this production era.) In one instance, Williams was out of money for scenery and was forced to invent the virtual set decades ahead of time, with the cast performing almost the entirety of a story in front of a crude greenscreen. Compounding the problems, Williams tended to use directors who were experienced in other facets of television, but not in making a show with the complexity of *Doctor Who*. And one of his biggest problems was the show's star, who became increasingly difficult as time wore on.

But onscreen, none of this mattered. *Doctor Who* was now a Saturday-night institution, part of a lineup of BBC television that was a ratings behemoth. This was only destabilized during Baker's final season when the regional television networks that comprised competitor ITV finally started coordinating their programming and showed the flashy American series *Buck Rogers in the 25th Century* opposite *Doctor Who*.

Williams eventually left at the start of 1980. (His final story, the Douglas Adams–scripted "Shada," was unfinished, due to the perennial labour problems the BBC experienced in the late '70s.) His replacement was his production unit manager (effectively a line producer in today's television), John Nathan-Turner. Nathan-Turner had worked in television since the late '60s (one of his first jobs was as a floor assistant on a Patrick Troughton story, 1969's "The Space

Pirates") and saw *Doctor Who* as his big break. He immediately found more budgetary resources, brought in new directors and writers, dumped composer Dudley Simpson (who had been primarily scoring the series since the Pertwee era), rearranged the theme song with synthesizers — and eventually got rid of Tom Baker. John Nathan-Turner went on to produce *Doctor Who* for the entirety of the 1980s.

Who is Tom Baker? (continued) With producer Graham Williams, Tom Baker was granted more freedom than ever before. The Doctor became grander, more eccentric and had funnier lines. In many ways, he became more like Tom Baker, who at the time was becoming increasingly larger than life.

Always full of boundless energy and willing to offer ideas to improve scripts — he was fond of telling people that he pushed to have a talking cabbage for a companion — Baker began to do this even more. But where Philip Hinchcliffe and Robert Holmes had been capable of constraining the star to production practicalities, Graham Williams was less successful. Dialogue was often rewritten in rehearsal by the cast, led by the star.

As time progressed, Baker became more proprietorial over the part. He openly derided scripts in table reads and frequently clashed with directors, at one point telling Alan Bromly, the director of "Nightmare of Eden" (1979), "Are you a director or a fucking commentator?" (Bromly left the production before it was completed.) A year prior to that, Baker had threatened to leave the show if he didn't have script and cast approval, and Williams had threatened to walk if Baker wasn't fired. In the end, both sides were convinced to stay.

In 1980, new producer John Nathan-Turner came in intending to shake up *Doctor Who*. The tone between the producer and star was set early: Tom Baker had avoided wearing theatrical makeup on camera for the past several years; Nathan-Turner insisted he wear it. Nathan-Turner and his new script editor, Christopher H. Bidmead, believed that the humour of the past several years had been juvenile, so it was removed in favour of a harder science-fiction slant. When Baker turned in his resignation this time, it was accepted.

In spite of the behind-the-scenes turmoil, by the time Tom Baker completed his record seven years as the Doctor, he had cemented his reputation in the public's mind as the definitive Doctor. *Doctor Who* would be forever associated with long scarves, jelly babies and saying funny things to monsters. When the fiftieth anniversary special "The Day of the Doctor" was made in 2013, there was no question which Classic Series actor would appear in a surprise cameo at the end. It was a 79-year-old Tom Baker, still indomitable.

Top Companion The second incarnation of Romana (or Romanadvoratrelundar, to give her full name) gives rise to what may be the wittiest relationship between a Doctor and a companion ever. (Witness this exchange from 1979's "City of Death" when Romana first sees the *Mona Lisa* and declares it "quite good": "'Quite good'? This is one of the great treasures of the universe and you say 'quite good'?" "The *world*, Doctor, the world." "What are you talking about?" "Not 'the *universe*' in public. You'll attract attention.") A Time Lady from Gallifrey who was forced on the Doctor by the White Guardian, by the time she regenerated (for no apparent reason except vanity) she had begun to emulate the Doctor, dressing in eccentric but stylish fashions, making perfectly flippant remarks and out-thinking everyone except (but often including) the Doctor. There was a real frisson of energy between her and the Doctor that spilled over to real life: actress Lalla Ward and Tom Baker were briefly married.

Classic Foe The Black Guardian is only onscreen for about five minutes, but he makes an indelible impression during that time. A barely explained super-being who oversees chaos and darkness, he's the presence that opposes the White Guardian, who has sent the Doctor and Romana on a quest for the Key to Time that will restore balance to the universe. He only appears at the very end of the season finale, but he's played by the fearsome-sounding Valentine Dyall (in a rare bit of stunt casting for the series back then; Dyall had played Mephistophelean figure "The Man in Black" on radio in Britain). It was enough to have the Doctor attempting to elude him the following season (and to come back for a rematch in the fifth Doctor's era).

Who is the Doctor? The later fourth Doctor is funny, mad and exuberant. He's still a wanderer in time and space, but he's even larger than larger than life. And you can sum up this Doctor in one word: outrageous.

In "City of Death," the Doctor faces down interrogation with a series of ridiculous retorts. The villain's mistress says, "My dear, I don't think he's as stupid as he seems." To which the villain, Count Scarlioni, replies, "My dear, nobody could be as stupid as *he* seems." And yet, it seems to be a winning strategy for this Doctor. Other Doctors have counted on his enemies to underestimate him. The fourth Doctor does it one better by just seeming like he's barking mad.

He might well have been. But he was also quite, quite brilliant as well.

The Doctor at this juncture is wildly contradictory like that. On the one hand, during this era, it's clear he's a brilliant technician and scientist, figuring out hyperspatial riddles and planet-swallowing mass conundrums and causality-loop concerns as though they were mere trifles. On the other, he seems to take nothing seriously and routinely sends up his opponents. (This is the Doctor who told the Daleks, "If you're supposed to be the superior race of the universe, why don't you try climbing after us? Bye-bye.")

It could be the company he keeps. Aside from the savage Leela and the Australian air hostess Tegan Jovanka, all his companions are veritable brainiacs: two incarnations of Romana, the mathematical genius Adric, the aristocratic scientist Nyssa and, of course, a mobile computer that looks like a dog. Travelling in the TARDIS is like some timey-wimey version of Mensa. It's almost as if hanging out with above-average intellects caused the Doctor to decide he wanted to enjoy witty repartee and a bit of a laugh.

The Doctor becomes a man of many passions during this time. It's the first era where it's stated on record that Earth is the Doctor's favourite planet (confirming what many viewers already knew). There's a series of running gags in the TARDIS as the Doctor takes up painting, plays chess against K9 (he's a sore loser) and even declares a day off to go fishing in the middle of the quest for the Key to Time. He's essentially a man of leisure who keeps having his holiday plans interrupted to fight monsters. With his costume becoming ever more bohemian, he really is the backpacking student of Doctors.

And yet, he does treat some things quite seriously. He remains ferociously moral. In 1978's "The Pirate Planet," he's unequivocal in his revulsion for the Pirate Captain's plan that destroys whole planets. He's similarly repulsed by the drug dealing in 1979's "Nightmare of Eden" or the slave trading in 1981's "Warriors' Gate."

In his final season, the fourth Doctor becomes more sombre and less outrageous, revelling more in wordplay than actual jokes. He seems older, more universe-wearied. Given how unfazed he is by the ghostly presence known as the Watcher — the shadow of his future self who is a portent of doom in his final story, 1981's "Logopolis" — it's easy to speculate that perhaps this Doctor had become aware of his fate. Or, as he says in his last words, "It's the end, but the moment has been prepared for . . ."

Three Great Moments In *Who's 50*, we assert that "City of Death" episode two is the funniest, wittiest, smartest 24 minutes and 33 seconds of *Doctor Who*, ever. We still hold firm in this view. If you haven't seen it, put this book down and go watch it right now. We'll wait.

While Tom Baker is widely known for his scenery chewing during this era, one of his best moments is at the end of "Nightmare of Eden," when the Doctor is confronting a man he knows to be dealing drugs. Baker completely dials it down and simply whispers, "Go away." It's chilling.

The fourth Doctor's final scenes in "Logopolis" are astounding as the Doctor sacrifices himself and falls from a radio telescope to stop the Master from holding the universe to ransom. In those final moments, the Doctor sees the faces of both the menaces he fought and the companions he travelled with. Never before on television had a montage of clips reinforced the impending sadness of the departure of a beloved character.

Two Embarrassing Moments During 1979's "The Creature From the Pit," the Doctor faces a giant blob with a rather large . . . appendage protruding from it. What does the Doctor do when faced with a phallic-looking monster? Let's just say that it makes the ending of 2006's "Love & Monsters" look tame.

While Tom Baker was sufficiently icy with the drug dealers in the aforementioned "Nightmare of Eden," this wasn't the usual state of play in that story. Earlier on, the Doctor is being attacked by a band of monsters. At which point, he exclaims, "My arms! My legs! My everything!" It's even worse to actually hear Baker say that.

What? (GB) As I indicated in the previous chapter, I tend to think that the first three years of Tom Baker's tenure are more about Tom Baker the actor, whereas his latter years are more about Tom Baker the personality. It's less a performance piece, more a television production bowing to the superior will of a dominant lead. There isn't a lot of modulation to Tom Baker's portrayal at this point. The technique boils down to never making eye contact with anyone, staring into the middle distance and sounding vaguely amused about everything.

And you know what? I really don't care about any of that. Because Tom Baker's latter period is one of those iconic performances that defines the Doctor as a character.

Philip Hinchcliffe told Tom Baker that Olympian detachment defined the Doctor and made him alien. During his last four years in the role, Tom Baker added to that and made the Doctor delighted, fun and funny. The result is the same effect, only more bonkers. The Doctor isn't simply detached, he lives at a 45-degree angle from the rest of us. He sees the universe in a totally different way, one that mostly amuses him. And amuses viewers as well.

He seemed unfazed by anything, and that is part of the fun. It's true he is at times beaten up, tricked and outsmarted. It's that he just isn't bothered by setbacks for too long. There were some, such as the producer who ultimately showed Tom Baker the door, who felt that the vulnerability of the character was sacrificed by this behaviour.

Maybe that's true, but I think such an interpretation is shortsighted. I think something greater comes out of it. This Doctor is more like the great comedic icons, like Chaplin's Tramp or Tati's Monsieur Hulot: a character inhabiting his own universe who interacts with our own when it suits him (to brilliant effect) and who bends our world to his own purposes. The Tramp would eat his own shoe; Hulot would unknowingly bring chaos to a seaside resort; the Doctor would flash a boggling smile to a despot before undoing his plans and saying, "Bye-bye."

I immediately gravitated to that aspect of the Doctor when I was younger. I discovered a hero is so much easier to cheer for when he's funny. In the Doctor's odd disconnect with the world around him, I found not a superhero, but a smart hero. Someone who goes to the darkest corners of the universe believing that being exceptionally witty and smart is all it takes to fix things.

This Doctor is, basically, a geek. Only he's a geek who doesn't care whether that term has any negative connotations and who mostly has the moral high ground. Who is funnier than everyone else. As a geek who didn't have the Doctor's sense of detachment, it was something I loved.

It's hard to believe now how much this Doctor was hated by fans at the time. People decried the "Tom Baker Comedy Half-Hour" and despised everything about it. I remember reading one of the first academic texts about the show, the 1982 book *Doctor Who: The Unfolding Text*, and it had pages and pages of interviews with fans, the current producer and others who felt the show had gone too far, was too comedic, and that the star was out of control. A grander example of missing the point couldn't be found: the audiences were huge (granted, ITV hadn't gotten its act together as a competitor) and that version of the show has had a greater afterlife in the public's imagination than any other before it. Because it's grandly entertaining — a term that only *Doctor Who* fans have a particular problem with.

As I got older, I went along with the "it's too cheap-looking and too silly" party line for a couple of years until I watched the mostly complete first two episodes of "Shada," the story that was abandoned in 1979 due to a BBC strike. And I fell in love with that era of *Doctor Who* all over again: witty quips, really clever ideas, the Doctor being bold and mad, with funny lines all over the place.

The final season of Tom Baker's tenure kind of undoes most of those things; all the funny lines are replaced with merely witty ones. All the out-there science ideas that have visual representations of them (on a BBC budget) are replaced by conversations about scientific ideas. And the Doctor is just a scientist, not some travelling, adventuring bohemian. It's as though the fourth Doctor suddenly had to take on a proper job and pay a mortgage. Make no mistake, Baker turns in some great moments in that final season. But he seems so much . . . older.

I had the privilege to meet Tom Baker only once in my life. It was when he was signing his delightfully barmy autobiography, *Who on Earth Is Tom Baker?* (And if people want proof of how influential his Doctor was on popular culture, this book was produced during the lowest ebb in the wilderness years between the Classic and Modern Series, yet it was printed by a major publisher.) I was living in Britain at the time, and he was signing at a Waterstone's in Oxford Circus. I was asked to go in to work on Saturday to attend to some crisis. I said, "I'd love to, but I want to get Tom Baker to sign his autobiography." My employer not only offered to let me have the time off for the signing, but paid for my copy of the book for me.

I lined up for a little while — it was a sizeable queue — and then gave him my book. And I said the only thing I could think of: "Thank you for making my adolescence bearable."

I wasn't lying. I was already a fan of *Doctor Who* by the time I came to this period of the show. But in the latter half of the fourth Doctor's era, the Doctor became my hero.

Second Opinion (RS?) Eighteen jokes you won't BELIEVE made it past the censors!

1. When the Doctor can't even walk through a lighthouse door like a normal person — and it means that the new Tom Baker has arrived.
2. When the tiny clone of Leela kicks a synapse inside the Doctor's head and his tiny clone complains that it's him she's kicking.
3. When the Doctor suggests a fruitcake recipe that involves baking whole apple cores for two weeks in order to bring an old woman back from a trance — and it works.
4. When, on a planet of overtaxation, we get a zinger from Leela, who's only just heard of taxes: "Perhaps everyone runs from the tax man."
5. When the Doctor reverses the flow of a toxic gas, he brazenly announces, "Whatever blows can be made to suck."
6. When the Doctor walks down a corridor and suddenly starts to hopscotch. For *no reason whatsoever*.
7. When the Doctor insists Romanadvoratrelundar shorten her name or be known as Fred — and she chooses Fred.

8. "Hello. Are you by any chance the Mentiads? Well, it's just that you look like Mentiads to me."
9. While tied to a stone, awaiting execution, the Doctor asks if the knife the druids are holding has been properly sterilized.
10. When, trapped in the Pavilion of the Summer Winds, the Doctor is offered free passage by Count Grendel. Striding out into the open, he's immediately shot at by Grendel's men, so he dashes back inside. At which point, he pops his head out again and yells, "Liar!"
11. When the Doctor asks Romana to introduce him as a wise and wonderful person who wants to help, then tells her not to exaggerate.
12. When the Doctor pretends to be evil simply by fluttering his eyelids — and it works.
13. When the Doctor checks the scanner upon materializing and pronounces, "Oh look, rocks."
14. When the Doctor pretends to be a thief, explaining that Romana is his accomplice and Duggan a detective who's been kind enough to catch him, because their two lines of work dovetail beautifully.
15. When the Doctor is shackled but convinces a guard to scratch his itchy nose, just revelling in the sheer joy of it (before knocking the guard out).
16. Rigg: "First a collision, then a dead navigator, and now a monster roaming about my ship! It's totally inexplicable."
    Doctor: "Nothing's inexplicable."
    Rigg: "Then explain it!"
    Doctor: "It's inexplicable."
17. When the villain tells the Doctor he will be questioned, tortured and killed, and the Doctor responds that he hopes he gets it in the right order.
18. When the Doctor interrupts Romana's poem about spring to tell her that it's October, she counters that they were supposed to come for May week, and he points out that May week is in June.

The Invasion of Time (1978)

Written by David Agnew (pseudonym for Graham Williams and Anthony Read)
Directed by Gerald Blake

The Big Idea The Doctor returns to Gallifrey to assume his rightful position as president of the High Council of the Time Lords. But has he betrayed his people to the Vardans?

What? (GB) In all the annals of *Doctor Who*, there has never been anything like "The Invasion of Time." For four episodes, there is a brilliant, format-bending story that fantastically ignores everything that's safe and blasts into new territory. But then that plot ends and there's a two-part runaround.

The first four episodes are unbelievably good. They have to be: when the story begins with the Doctor agreeing to betray his own people, it's an enormous twist that purposely baffles the viewer for the first two episodes. Then, by the third installment, everything makes perfect sense as all of the Doctor's actions slowly come together to undo the invaders.

It's aided by some great performances. Tom Baker is at the apex of his transformation into an over-the-top comedic actor, but here he uses that personality to great dramatic effect to make the Doctor seem all the more bizarre and unstable. The fact that he's very funny is an added bonus. John Arnatt as Borusa balances Baker's wackiness with incredible gravitas. The story is worth watching just to see Baker and Arnatt spar together.

The first four episodes are let down only by some terrible production values; the invading extra-dimensional Vardans are nothing more than shimmering pieces of tinfoil. Fortunately, the DVD provides a CGI alternative, and they look rather more menacing now — at least until we have to see them in their humanoid form.

But then episode five happens, and the Sontarans show up. The prosthetics and costumes are awful. Leaving aside that their presence actually undermines the threat the Vardans brought, there's also the problem of how they're dispatched. The Doctor constructs the ultimate Time Lord weapon: a jumped-up disintegrator gun. Then he hunts them down. It's not the Doctor using a gun to kill that bothers me; it's the sheer unoriginality of it. It's livened up a little by a chase inside the Doctor's TARDIS but even that flight of imagination is let down by the production as they're forced to rely on very earthbound locations to convey the inside of a time machine.

If you want to see *Doctor Who* at its best, watch episodes one through four of "The Invasion of Time." If you want to see *Doctor Who* as a well-acted runaround, watch episodes five and six. The fact that it combines both is the beauty — and the curse — of *Doctor Who*.

Second Opinion (RS?) My co-author is witty, urbane and in general a charming and wonderful human being. But he does talk rubbish sometimes.

Episodes five and six of "The Invasion of Time" are wonderful! They have Tom Baker being hilarious while leading a ragtag group of people through a neverending shaggy dog story inside the TARDIS. Which is fantastic. The unstable pedestrian infrastructure. The endless attempts to reach Storeroom 23A. The Doctor's way-too-complicated directions. All brilliant.

I love the addition of the Sontarans to this story. It was one of the genuine shock moments of my childhood, a genuine "Oh crap!" bombshell of a cliffhanger. Even more impressively, if you don't know how long the story is supposed to be, it comes magnificently out of left field. And then the ensuing politics are great, with the excellent running gag that the Sontarans only know the Doctor as "the President" and keep interrupting Castellan Kelner whenever he tries to explain. Comedy gold.

I also love the TARDIS interior. I love it. Complaining about the fact that it looks like the hospital it was filmed in is a grand exercise in missing the point. It's the first time we get to see just how boundless the TARDIS actually is. Previous excursions have been limited to a room or two, but here we get an idea of its sheer scale. It makes perfect sense that there'd be whole rooms devoted to art or swimming, with stairwells and corridors everywhere. I even love the use of film for the locations because, as per the conventions of 1970s television, we're given the sense that being inside the TARDIS is also somehow outside.

And the D-mat gun is genuinely disturbing. Yes, it looks like a plain old laser gun. But that's irrelevant: it's the concept that's so powerful here. It's a weapon that *erases you from history*. That's the kind of thing only the Time Lords would have, and the fact that the knowledge has been forbidden only ups the ante. I adore the resolution, where the firing of the weapon actually erases its existence from the Doctor's mind. That's when *Doctor Who* becomes a fairytale. So I can only conclude that Graeme must have watched these two episodes and then fired his own D-mat gun, thus erasing their brilliance from his mind. It is the wisdom of Rassilon.

The Pirate Planet (1978)

Written by Douglas Adams

Directed by Pennant Roberts

The Big Idea The Doctor and Romana travel to the planet Calufrax to seek the second segment of the Key to Time. But Calufrax is gone, and another planet, Zanak, is in its place, led by a marauding Pirate Captain.

What? (GB) If "The Pirate Planet" were just the opening argument between the Doctor and Romana about procedures for landing the TARDIS — probably the wittiest conversation between a Doctor and a companion to date — it would be enough.

If "The Pirate Planet" were just the scene with the Doctor wandering around asking citizens if anyone has seen a planet called Calufrax, it would be enough.

If "The Pirate Planet" were the Mentiads, who start out as a menace and then become one of the most intriguing ideas for a group of characters in *Doctor Who* ever, it would be enough.

If "The Pirate Planet" were just the brilliant gag where K9 predicts the Doctor will arrive in 21.9 seconds, continues with a conversation and then, when the Doctor arrives saying, "Surprised to see us?" says, "Amazed, master," it would be enough.

If "The Pirate Planet" were just that chilling moment when it becomes clear what Zanak really does to planets, it would be enough.

If "The Pirate Planet" were the Doctor committing "Newton's revenge" on a guard — a silly gag that I tried, and failed, to explain at a convention panel to a ten-year-old who asked for my favourite funny moment — it would be enough.

If "The Pirate Planet" were just the Pirate Captain, as played by Bruce Purchase, who imbues the role with scenery-eating bluster that hides someone with real menace, it would be enough.

If "The Pirate Planet" were just the lovely Mr. Fibuli, my favourite henchman in all of *Doctor Who* (brief aside: I always thought Andrew Robertson would make a great Doctor), it would be enough.

If "The Pirate Planet" were just one line — "My biorhythms must be at an all-time low" — delivered brilliantly by Tom Baker, it would be enough.

If "The Pirate Planet" were just the start of episode four when the denouement to the cliffhanger reveals yet another level to a cork-screw of a plot, it would be enough.

If "The Pirate Planet" were just the intense "Appreciate it?!?" confrontation between the Doctor and the Pirate Captain, it would be enough.

If "The Pirate Planet" were just the ridiculous ending where everything is resolved in a two-minute conversation of technobabble that's played for laughs ("Why I thought that was perfectly obvious") and ends in K9 concluding, "Piece of cake, Master: blow them up," it would be enough.

If "The Pirate Planet" were any of these things, it would be enough to be brilliant, smart, funny and engaging. The fact that it's all these things and more is what makes it special.

Second Opinion (RS?) *The Doctors Are In* notes that "The Pirate Planet," a late 1970s adventure story from the mind of digital-watch-wearing writer Douglas Adams, is generally held to be not only the most inventive story of the Key to Time season, but, in fact, the most inventive concept of any kind at all. Regular reviewers judge that the best critical enjoyment is usually to be found while travelling through an anti-inertial particle accelerator located inside a massive engine masquerading as a bridge, whilst the episode itself is beamed into your head as your latent telepathy awakens, leading to a new golden age of prosperity for all.

The plot is on the whole very simple and mostly follows the familiar theme of boy-Gallifreyan meets girl-Gallifreyan inside a hollow planet that jumps about the galaxy critiquing capitalism's critique of Iron Curtain communism while being shouted at by a clever and dangerous blustering pirate with a subtle plan to destabilize the secret power held by a comatose elderly crone cunningly disguised as a pretty extra.

Many episode guides have now banned discussion of this episode altogether, sometimes for artistic reasons, but most commonly because the story's mental acuity contravenes local strategic arms limitations treaties.

This has not, however, stopped its reputation from pushing back the boundaries of pure hyperadulation, and its chief cosplayer has recently been appointed Professor of Neointerpretation at the University of Maximegalon, in recognition of both her General and Special Theories of "Pirate Planet" evaluation, in which she proves that the whole fabric of the review process is not merely curved, it is, in fact, totally bent.

City of Death (1979)

Written by David Agnew (pseudonym for Douglas Adams and Graham Williams, from a story by David Fisher)
Directed by Michael Hayes

The Big Idea The Doctor has to stop the Jagaroth from going back in time to prevent his ship from blowing up, which is tied to the theft of the *Mona Lisa* — all seven versions.

What? (RS?) "City of Death" is bristling with fabulous ideas, from an alien splintered through time and the human race threatened by grandfather paradox to art theft as a capitalist venture and a single punch collapsing the narrative. It has some of the wittiest dialogue ever recorded on television, gorgeous locations and a plot that's simply exquisite. And yet, nestling in among all that is something quite spectacular. Something that doesn't get talked about nearly enough. That's right, I'm talking about the definition of art.

"City of Death," when it's not distracting you with hilarious banter or brilliant ideas, is genuinely interested in asking hard questions. What is art? Can computers draw? If you hide a painting in a cellar for hundreds of years and nobody sees it, is it still art? If Leonardo painted multiple *Mona Lisa*s, does that invalidate them? If you park your vehicle in a gallery, does that give it artistic meaning?

This is where the Doctor comes in. As much as he's investigating the mystery, he's also the one character who simply appreciates what he sees. Romana interrupts her sketch, thus ruining it. Scarlioni is simply in it for the money. The Countess, for the illicit thrill. Kerensky, for the chickens. But it's the Doctor who won't let Duggan ruin a Louis XV chair, even if it means capture by the villains. It's the Doctor who recognizes the uniqueness of Leonardo's brushstrokes. And it's the Doctor who realizes that if you need to X-ray a beautiful painting to determine whether it's real, you've missed the point entirely.

There are many amazing things about "City of Death." We're talking about a story that features a brilliant character forced to concoct a clever scheme across millennia . . . because he doesn't quite have the budget to pay for his exceptional ideas. Remind you of any time-travel TV shows you may be familiar with? And yet, the art theme is the glue that holds it all together and makes you think long after you've stopped laughing. That's because "City of Death" isn't just throwaway family entertainment to amuse on a Saturday night. No, it's more than that. Much, much more. "City of Death" is art.

Second Opinion (GB) When we were editing *Who's 50*, our brilliant copy editor, Crissy Calhoun, confessed that not only had she *not* seen "City of Death," but she hadn't read Douglas Adams's classic *The Hitchhiker's Guide to the Galaxy*. The two best comedy-science-fiction writing achievements of the twentieth century, we noted. This prompted us to ask her, repeatedly, "WHY HAVEN'T YOU DONE THIS?!?" in all caps. We did this rather a lot.

So I have this to say to any of you who haven't seen "City of Death" yet: WHY HAVEN'T YOU WATCHED THIS STORY YET, FOR GOD'S SAKE?!?

That is all. Thank you.

Nightmare of Eden (1979)

Written by Bob Baker

Directed by Alan Bromly

The Big Idea The Doctor and Romana arrive at a hyperspatial crash scene to discover drug dealing and monsters. But the two are connected more closely than they realize.

What? (RS?) A comic relief character who's also a failed scientist teams up with an unlikely partner to run a drug ring predicated on the idea that they're simply smarter than everyone else, evading the bumbling authorities by flying below the radar and easing their consciences by claiming that the ends justify the means.

But that's enough about *Breaking Bad*; let's talk about "Nightmare of Eden."

"Nightmare of Eden" is the kind of story that you can love or hate, but you can't be neutral about. I love watching the Doctor and Romana ham it up around the ship, seizing easy control of every situation they encounter. When the Doctor pretends to be from Galactic Insurance and is informed they went out of business 20 years ago, he says, "I wondered why I hadn't been paid." Which is *then* followed by Rigg saying, "Now that's not good enough," and the Doctor replying, "That's what I thought." Sublime. When Romana tells the Doctor that he won't have any protection from the Mandrels, he pauses briefly and then says, "I'll have to use my wits." There's no better manifesto for *Doctor Who*. Except possibly when Romana asks for a screwdriver.

In fact, the ideas are utterly brilliant and they keep coming at you. Two ships merging because of a transporter accident? Genius. The source of drugs being the obligatory monster? Wild. Using the faulty CET machine to capture the villains in their escaping ship? A master stroke. I'll take an inventive script that's firing on all cylinders over yet another well-directed gothic horror remake any day. And the sheer genius that results in the comic-relief character being the drug kingpin is decades ahead of its time. Nobody at the time could have guessed this. Nobody.

"Nightmare of Eden" is spectacular. It's silly, dark and hilarious. Wait, no, I think I've got it . . .

It's *Doctor Who*.

Second Opinion (GB) "Nightmare of Eden" deserves far better than what it got.

It boasts a beautiful, imaginative and innovative story. The drug storyline is *Doctor Who* attempting to be relevant without being preachy, and it could have added a real bite to the episode even if done with a family audience. (And in fairness, Tom Baker tries to pull back and plays it straight. Shame no one else other than Lalla Ward is bothering.) The ideas, such as the merged ships or the drugs-are-the-monsters, are clever.

But "Nightmare of Eden" is a textbook example of what went wrong with late 1970s *Who*: terrible design, wretched casting and indifferent direction. All of the script's goodwill is blown by shooting it with all the subtlety of *On the Buses*. The Mandrels are a dreadful design, but even that could have been mitigated by using a darker set and limiting the angles in which they were shot. But . . . nah. Better not actually be creative.

The drug storyline is one key example. How much better could that storyline have been if any of the actors actually, oh, I don't know, cared about their performance? Lewis Fiander's instinct that he should send up Tryst in order to make people think he's comedy relief and not behind everything is criminally wrong. If you're doing something as serious as a drug story in a family television series, do it for real. Don't put on funny voices like you're doing an impression of Peter Sellers at a party. My co-author is clearly hopped up on blue meth: Tryst isn't Walter White; he's a bad cartoon villain.

It's true: *Doctor Who*'s reputation for being a low-budget show with ham acting came from stories like "Nightmare of Eden." But the thing is, it's so much better than its reputation. And that's a real tragedy.

Logopolis (1981)

Written by Christopher H. Bidmead

Directed by Peter Grimwade

The Big Idea On the planet Logopolis, a group of mathematicians is the only thing standing between the universe and its destruction — through a process that passed the point of no return long ago.

What? (GB?) When it comes down to it, "Logopolis" changed everything.

Finale stories for Doctors before this one were somewhat perfunctory affairs. The first time it happened, in 1966 in "The Tenth Planet," there wasn't really an adequate explanation, beyond the Doctor's infirm behaviour in the last episode and the oblique remark that "this old body of mine is wearing a bit thin." The second Doctor's departure was signposted a bit by the mention of the Doctor's origins, but really the end of the last episode of "The War Games" comes somewhat out of left field. By the third Doctor's era, there's a determination to give the lead character a truly heroic end with a personal story arc in "Planet of the Spiders," but it's business as usual until the Doctor stumbles out of the TARDIS at the end of the final episode.

"Logopolis" changed that. In terms of the actual plot, there is the Watcher, the future Doctor playing Banquo's Ghost at his predecessor's swansong. His part is minimal and somewhat oblique, but it's played for maximum value onscreen, especially in the early episodes set on Earth as he stands in the distance. It's ghostly, eerie and unsettling.

There's a sombre tone permeating everything. Peter Howell's score is full of clanging bells and minor keys and everything's sad from the first moment. And when we meet the Doctor in the Cloister Room, he's alone and brooding, which remains his emotional register for the entire story. It culminates in the Doctor's stark admission that he has never chosen the company he keeps — including an alliance with the Master to save the universe.

And then there's the Doctor's death. As he hangs by a cable, he sees flashbacks of all his main adversaries; as he lies on the ground, there are callbacks to all of his companions. This is huge: flashbacks from past episodes in a *Doctor Who* story never happened before this. Anyone watching would have been gasping with shock. I know I was.

It's with this story that the Doctor's departure becomes a capital-B, capital-D Big Deal. It took the sadness of the end of the fourth Doctor's era and made it a part of the televised story. And yet, very little of that sadness actually comes from Christopher Bidmead's script; instead it's the sombre music, Peter Grimwade's direction, Tom Baker's acting and John Nathan-Turner's production instincts. But it works. No Doctor's departure would be a low-key event again. And as an added shock, we have a final flash of Tom Baker's smile before his features boil away into . . . something totally new and unexpected.

Second Opinion (RS?) What's most painful about "Logopolis" is just how destabilized Tom Baker's Doctor actually is. His attempt to flush out the Master is thwarted by accidentally landing on a barge. He's forced into an alliance with his worst enemy. He's not only trapped inside the TARDIS, he's shrunk down to size, a shadow of his former self. His most proactive action in this story is to pilot the TARDIS to Logopolis . . . and even that he does only because his future self told him to. He can't even measure a police box without everything going to hell.

For a character who once loomed so large, it's a depressing, gloomy place to end. It's there in the opening titles: Tom Baker simply isn't as young as he was when his era started, almost a decade earlier. Where he once represented bohemian youth, swanning about the galaxy on a lark, he's now burdened by responsibility, but unable to do much of anything. The character we loved has lost his wit, his centre, his friends and his verve. In short, he's grown old. And that may be the most heartbreaking fate of all.

In the end, destabilization proves to be his salvation. It's the Master's attempt to impose order that's shown to be wrong, so the fourth Doctor's final action is to break a cable and plunge the universe back into chaos, where it belongs. And then he lies on the ground, the broken hero with only memories to comfort him, surrounded by children. With one last destabilization to come: that of *Doctor Who* itself. Because the show would never be the same again.

The Fifth Doctor

Splendid Chap

(1982–1984)

Basic Data

First story: "Castrovalva" (1982)

Final story: "The Caves of Androzani" (1984)

Final appearance: "Time Crash" (2007)

The Changing Face of *Doctor Who* In his first season (1980–1981), producer John Nathan-Turner had managed to change more about *Doctor Who* than any producer — including seeing off Tom Baker, its popular star. Nathan-Turner had some simple criteria for his new leading man: he wanted a younger actor, he wanted someone more vulnerable, and he wanted someone with straight hair.

According to Nathan-Turner, his basic checklist was fulfilled when his eyes looked over the large corkboard in his office and alighted on a picture of Peter Davison, an actor Nathan-Turner knew from when both had worked on *All Creatures Great and Small*. Nathan-Turner knew he had his Doctor. The producer still approached other actors, including Richard Griffiths and Iain Cuthbertson, but Davison was his first choice.

With the new Doctor cast, there was one last mooring of *Doctor Who* as viewers knew it to be cast off: the show left Saturday, the night the program had aired since 1963, to air on two consecutive weeknights. It was a bold gambit, done in part because, with ITV finally networking its Saturday programming, *Doctor Who* was getting beaten in the ratings by *Buck Rogers in the 25th Century*. The move also allowed the BBC to test out whether it could roll out a program across multiple nights (gearing up for the eventual arrival of an evening soap, *EastEnders,* three years later). And yet, in spite of the fact that it effectively halved the number of weeks *Doctor Who* was on the air every year, the show's ratings improved significantly.

Fandom in the U.K. had grown substantially since the official fan club, the Doctor Who Appreciation Society, had been founded by some students in 1977. Thanks to PBS broadcasting it (which began in earnest in the late '70s), the series was now hugely popular in North America as well. As *Doctor Who* moved into the 1980s, the show embraced its fanbase in a way it had not done earlier. John Nathan-Turner joined the stars of *Doctor Who* at conventions around the world and, at the time, became probably the best known television showrunner apart from *Star Trek*'s Gene Roddenberry.

With the twentieth season of *Doctor Who* approaching, John Nathan-Turner and his script editor, Eric Saward, tapped into this growing fandom, bringing back more past monsters than ever before, culminating in 1983's "The Five Doctors," a 90-minute special featuring all living Doctors. The media hype and nostalgia surrounding the twentieth anniversary was akin to what was later seen with the fiftieth anniversary. As Peter Davison departed the role, *Doctor Who* was on a high. But all that was about to change . . .

Who is Peter Davison? As an 11-year-old, Peter Moffett missed the first episode of *Doctor Who* when it aired — twice (it was repeated a week later). However, he watched the series during the Hartnell and Troughton eras from the second episode onwards. Eighteen years later, now working as an actor under the stage name Peter Davison, he was called by John Nathan-Turner and asked if he wanted to play the Doctor. Davison was dubious but said he would think about it. The 29-year-old actor felt he was too young for the part and had merely been hoping he'd guest-star on the program. Davison had another concern. While Hartnell, Troughton and Pertwee had been well-established character actors, and Tom Baker a virtual unknown, Davison was a genuine TV star, coming off the huge success of the BBC adaptation of James Herriot's Yorkshire vet books, *All Creatures Great and Small*, where Davison played the hapless younger vet Tristan Farnon. Davison worried his casting might be so against type that the audience wouldn't accept him.

At the same time, Davison worried that if he turned down the role, he would later regret it, so he took it on. He was immediately surprised by the popularity of the role; his casting was announced on the BBC's main news broadcast, *The Nine O'Clock News*, and friends who had the sound turned down thought the actor had died!

Nathan-Turner chose cricket whites as the fifth Doctor's costume based on a photo he'd seen of Davison at a charity cricket match. Davison was keen at first but later stated he wished the look had been more "off the peg." At this juncture in the series, Nathan-Turner was looking for ways of selling the show and felt it was more marketable if the characters wore consistent costumes; hence the highly coordinated costume, complete with stick of celery, which the producer thought would add some eccentricity.

Soon after being cast, Peter Davison ran into Patrick Troughton in the parking lot at the BBC. Troughton, whose Doctor Davison adored, congratulated Davison on the role but told him "Don't do it any longer than three years." Davison took Troughton's advice and left after three seasons. While maintaining a successful career after leaving the show, Davison never lost touch with the series, appearing in Big Finish audio adventures and even writing, producing and starring in a comedy spoof for the fiftieth anniversary called *The Five(ish) Doctors Reboot*, which featured a panoply of guest stars, including Peter Jackson and Sir Ian McKellan. Another of those guest stars? David Tennant, who was by then Davison's son-in-law.

Top Companion In today's era, when companions are Impossible Girls or the bringers of Bad Wolf, it's surprising to look back and realize all this started with Turlough, the first companion to be given his very own story arc. Turlough is an alien teenager living incognito at a boarding school on Earth who agrees to kill the Doctor for the Black Guardian. Over the course of three stories, Turlough struggles with his mission before ultimately rejecting the Black Guardian in favour of the Doctor. Once he leaves the Black Guardian's employ, he's given less to do, but he still plays the companion role against type: somewhat cowardly and often sarcastic.

Classic Foe There are few creatures in the *Doctor Who* universe as abstract as the Mara. It's not really a creature so much as the personification of evil thoughts. It manifests itself only through the mind of a willing host — which turns out to be the Doctor's companion Tegan Jovanka, in two instances — and can take the form of a giant snake. Both appearances of the Mara were written by Christopher Bailey, who drew from Christian and Buddhist mythology in creating it. The Mara brings chaos through knowledge and is stopped only by being forced to look at itself.

Who is the Doctor? The fifth Doctor is the youngest-looking Doctor yet. And that youthful façade often works against him. His companions are more apt to argue with him than defer to him — which makes sense, as this Doctor looks more like a peer to them. His vulnerability is enhanced by his demeanour, which tends towards the nice and pleasant.

But this Doctor isn't what he seems.

From his affectation of wearing reading glasses (as the tenth Doctor pointed out in 2007's "Time Crash," he didn't really need them) and his tendency to break into a world-weary sigh to his (often overlooked but considerable) moments of tetchiness, this is, for all his youthful attributes, an old man in a younger man's body. The fifth Doctor is someone who realizes youth is wasted on the young but is also old enough to know he's not getting much out of it besides the running around.

And the pleasant manner isn't really him either. The fifth Doctor is polite to a fault — even his testiest remarks include a "please" or a "thank you" — but there is flinty steel under his surface. When backed into a corner by colonial authorities in 1984's "Frontios," he gives them a scathing assessment of the situation. Accused of being a murderer (twice) in 1982's "Earthshock," he immediately takes charge of the situation (twice) as soon as the true threat is revealed.

With his sonic screwdriver destroyed in 1982's "The Visitation," this incarnation relies more on his intellect to solve problems. The fifth Doctor is quick to assess the assets of any particular situation and use this knowledge to save lives or defeat an enemy. His heroism is without a lot of bravado. When told he's about to fight someone who is "said to be the best swordsman in France" in 1983's "The King's Demons," he says, borrowing a line from Errol Flynn, "Fortunately, we are in England." Most of the times he uses a weapon, it's almost perfunctory, expertly used in the moment and then thrown away and forgotten immediately.

He is less alien and more human in a way. But it's not really that he's human emotionally, it's that he likes the trappings of being human, as though he's cosplaying as a human. Which makes the cricketing gear he wears even more fascinating: he's appropriating human culture in a way even the eccentric faux-Edwardian dress of his predecessors hadn't. And he plays that part to the hilt when it comes to cricket: he's not only great at the game, he's the only Doctor who has checked the sports section immediately after the TARDIS sets down on contemporary Earth. (As seen in 1982's "Time-Flight.") In "Earthshock," he's quick to tell the Cyberleader the joys of life, though his affection for humans is exploited as a weakness.

He often finds it easier to relate to strangers — like Richard Mace in "The Visitation," Todd in 1982's "Kinda," Captain Stapley in "Time-Flight" or Polly in 1984's "The Awakening" — than his actual travelling companions, around whom he is somewhat awkward. On the one hand, there's his youth working against him; on the other, there's a sort of prescience about it as all of his companions face sombre fates: Adric dies alone and ultimately unable to connect with anyone; Nyssa and Turlough face uncertain fates (she in a leper colony, he going back to the homeworld that had rejected his family); the Doctor destroys Kamelion; and Tegan effectively breaks up with him.

At the end of the day, for all his seeming sunny disposition and matching bright cricket whites, the Doctor's fifth incarnation sees a lot of darkness. He is forced to massacre Silurians and Sea Devils, sees Daleks wipe out humans on both sides of a time corridor and simply stands by as the Master dies in flames. Perhaps it's no wonder that, in his final act, the fifth Doctor sacrifices himself to save a single person (the first regeneration where he does this) and, when it comes time to regenerate, he gazes into a cruel abyss — and sees it gaze back with a new face.

Three Great Moments In "Earthshock," the Doctor has five minutes to defuse a bomb (operated, unbeknownst to him, by the Cybermen) that has the potential to blow up Earth. These five glorious minutes start quietly as the Doctor methodically works on the bomb, improvising on instinct as the Cybermen attempt to reactivate it. It's a scene where the Doctor shows panic and desperation, yet real steel as well. It's accomplished purely because of Peter Davison's stunning performance.

Few companions have left in messier circumstances than Tegan does in 1984's "Resurrection of the Daleks." The Doctor and Tegan's relationship is always complicated at best, and, at the end of that story, having seen lots of innocent people slaughtered in a Dalek war, she decides it's over and leaves. The scene plays out like a brutal break-up as the Doctor begs her to stay ("No, don't leave, not like this!") and she runs off. The Doctor stands there, babbling, "It's strange. I left Gallifrey for similar reasons. I'd grown tired of their lifestyle. It seems I must mend my ways." It's a brief glimpse into the Time Lord's own pain and insecurities.

Truthfully, we could have picked any number of moments from the fifth Doctor's swansong in 1984's "The Caves of Androzani," but we fully affirm the cliffhanger of the third episode when, even though beaten, suffering from the ravages of a disease that will ultimately kill him and imprisoned on a spaceship headed away from the planet where Peri is trapped in the clutches of a madman, the Doctor still finds a way out of his bonds and seizes control of the ship. The Doctor never makes any of this seem easy, so when he tells his captor, Stotz, that he's not going to let him stop him now, as the ship crashes into the planet, it's all the more incredible.

Two Embarrassing Moments In "Resurrection of the Daleks," the Doctor suddenly decides — for no reason related to the events unfolding — that he needs to execute Davros. And so he takes an obscenely large gun and puts it to Davros's head. Only he doesn't kill him. Normally, we would put that in a "Three Great Moments" segment to demonstrate the Doctor's occasional heroic stance against violence . . . but Davros uses it as an opportunity to insult the Doctor, saying, "You are soft, like all Time Lords. You prefer to stand and watch. Action requires courage, something you lack." There's no emphasis on why the Doctor doesn't ultimately kill Davros; no affirmation of other, better values. The Doctor just skulks out the door. Even Peter Davison can't do anything to make this scene work.

"Mawdryn Undead" (1983) gives us the scenario where the Doctor is being forced to give up one of his regenerative lives for every one of the affected crew. Eight of them, eight of him. "It would be the end of me as a Time Lord!" Which might have real gravitas if a) the Doctor didn't say it with all the dramatic impact of a teenager forced to stay home on a Saturday night and b) it didn't equate to "Oh no! I'll be stuck with having just one life, like the rest of you."

Brave Heart? (GB) One of my prized possessions is a copy of *Doctor Who: The Making of a Television Series*, a book for young adults that goes behind the scenes of *Doctor Who*. I have a tremendous connection to it, given that I checked it out of my high-school library about a million times when I was in ninth grade in 1984. (I was given a copy many years later.) It was the first book I read about how *Doctor Who* was made, and it ignited my passion for knowing how television was made generally. At that point, Davison's episodes had just started airing on my local PBS station. The cover of that book was one of the first times I had ever seen a picture of Peter Davison as the Doctor.

It's a great picture too: he's standing beside the TARDIS, wearing that gorgeous panama hat (how I've wanted one for years) and perfectly coordinated in fawn, red and white. I was so fascinated by how young he looked. There was something new to this Doctor, something utterly *vibrant*.

I was never put off by his age. When I was younger and had seen a little bit of Jon Pertwee's stories (just after his episodes were shown for the first time in Canada in 1976), I remember seeing a picture of Tom Baker in a magazine, which pointed out that he was the new Doctor Who (newspapers never called him "the Doctor"). And I remember thinking at the tender age of six that it was good they finally had someone *younger* playing the part. Davison was only a decade younger than Tom Baker had been when he started; a younger Doctor wasn't actually all that new.

And yet, for a long time — I would honestly say up until David Tennant and Matt Smith showed up — there was a fashionable attitude, particularly in British fandom, not to like the fifth Doctor. There were magazine articles, reviews, online discussions and jokes that he was too young, not brave, nicknamed the "wet vet" . . . really, a lot of the time what they meant was *not Tom Baker*. Davison didn't have the qualities people expected after Baker's Doctor: that sense of authority, that kind of invulnerability.

However, I think that kind of misses the point. Peter Davison brings a lot of wonderful qualities of his own. Subtle touches, the fact that he's acting and not performing. The way he shows moral conflict in his actions and speech patterns as opposed to giving lectures about morality. The way he created a character that felt real pain and real panic and still came out on top . . . most of the time. The fifth Doctor was a more vulnerable hero — and a more complex one.

I really began to love the fifth Doctor when I was just out of university and, perhaps, I was old enough to appreciate what the character brought to *Doctor Who*. (That's not to say that his performance didn't connect with kids; after all, one of his biggest fans at the time was an 11-year-old who later took on the stage name David Tennant.) For me, the fifth Doctor is a Doctor for grownups. He isn't a series of eccentric tics and quirks and bravado. He's a smart man who makes smart observations and choices played by a smart actor who knows how to make all that work.

What I love about the fifth Doctor's era is that it features a lot of things I'm not wild about, yet somehow makes them work in a way I didn't think possible. The companions, for instance. When I was younger, I never understood why Tegan wanted to travel with the Doctor. She seemed to downright loathe him. But I've come to realize that Tegan and the fifth Doctor are one of the most intriguing relationships in 50 years of the series. It's full of subtle touches, intimations that there's some connection under the surface that keeps these two opposites attracting. (It helps that Janet Fielding is a remarkable actress; one of the great injustices of British television is that her career didn't follow the same upward trajectory as Helen Mirren's.) I also think it's a shame Davison was saddled with so many lacklustre stories. But even then, he puts in some interesting bit of stage business — a quirky gesture, an interesting line delivery — and it's eminently watchable.

Peter Davison as the fifth Doctor did what any actor following Tom Baker would have done to survive: he made a clean break. But he also did something surprising: he enabled *Doctor Who* to not just survive, but thrive. He provided change: change that was scary but necessary and also utterly thrilling. Over 30 years after Davison departed the role, I still view his Doctor as an exciting vanguard of something different. And it taught me to welcome change in *Doctor Who* with the same anticipation and excitement as I did when I read *Doctor Who: The Making of a Television Series* in my high-school library.

Second Opinion (RS?) Hmm. I'm not so sure. My co-author is right that Peter Davison is a gifted actor. He doesn't come at you with his maniacal setting turned up to 11, and he doesn't dazzle you with his brilliant oratory or larger-than-life personality. Instead, he offers subtlety, thoughtfulness and nuance. It really shouldn't work — and it probably wouldn't have in the hands of a lesser actor. Fortunately, Davison has an enviable ability to walk the tightrope of understatement while nevertheless keeping himself the focus. This is an astonishing achievement. But while that's definitely not nothing, I'd argue that this is just about all the fifth Doctor has going for him.

Almost nothing about the fifth Doctor's era feels right. The costumes are forced. The companions are forced. There's far too much bickering in the TARDIS and way too many annoying teenagers running around. The era is too dark, with a Doctor who's continually fighting a losing battle against forces that are out of his league. The Doctor commits acts of violence and near-genocide on a fairly regular basis. And he loses ground, over and over again.

Don't get me wrong, I like the fifth Doctor himself. I can appreciate the idea of having a vulnerable hero in a complex universe . . . but that only works if the hero eventually overcomes his limitations and finds the inner strength he needs to pull out a victory. That's noticeably absent from the fifth Doctor's era. Almost everything ends badly: Adric is killed for no reason at all; the Doctor is forced to massacre the Silurians and Sea Devils when he can't negotiate with opposing sides; so many innocents are killed in the Dalek crossfire that Tegan ends up disgusted with his lifestyle; and his benign investigation of Androzani Minor results in a bloodbath, with every male character dead, himself included!

The exceptions prove the rule: just about the only story where the fifth Doctor is unambiguously heroic is "The Five Doctors" — and that came about because he was given Tom Baker's role instead! He works as a character in "The Caves of Androzani" far better than he does in other stories, largely because he throws out smack talk and cynical bravado that sounds far more like his predecessor than Davison does any other time, with the possible exception of "Frontios," episode one.

And yet, there's utility in such a flawed character. He's the perfect Doctor for something as abstract and surreal as "Kinda" (which was actually written with Baker in mind), and his major achievements — such as letting Turlough decide which side he's on — are often achieved through standing back and letting others take the lead. However, we also see the flipside of this inaction as well: when the Master's attempt to restore himself goes wrong, the fifth Doctor simply stands by and watches his old foe burn, unable to lift a finger to save his life.

Look at his conversation with the Terileptil in episode three of "The Visitation." It's a fascinating interplay, as the two aliens discuss art, beauty and war. The Doctor tries to reason with his opponent, offering him safe passage, but the Terileptil refuses. Against the Doctor's attempted debate, the Terileptil ends up shouting, "It's not supposed to be an argument! It's a statement!" The fourth Doctor would have wiped the floor with this monster, drenching him in witty putdowns and forceful intensity. The fifth simply can't.

So on the one hand, I applaud John Nathan-Turner for succeeding at what he tried to do. The fifth Doctor is almost nothing like his predecessor — and that probably ensured the survival of the series. But, in trying to see that contrast through, the fifth is so flawed and vulnerable that it's actually difficult to watch at times. Without Peter Davison, this era would be a godawful mess, with practically no redeeming features. Fortunately, they had a great actor on hand, one who almost saved the entire thing by playing it subtle. *Almost.*

Castrovalva (1982)

Written by Christopher H. Bidmead

Directed by Fiona Cumming

The Big Idea The Doctor is suffering from an acute post-regenerative crisis. Tegan and Nyssa decide to take the Doctor to the dwellings of simplicity known as Castrovalva. Unfortunately, they're taking him into a trap.

Brave Heart? (RS?)

C is for Castrovalva, a city made by the Master. A man whose traps pile up higher and faster.

A is for Adric, the awkward boy genius. Whose equations bring life in matters ingenious.

S is for Shardovan, a man created by evil. Whose freedom exists but results in upheaval.

T is for TARDIS, a home and a trap. With dizzying corridors, zero room and no map.

R is for Recursion, which powers the story. Defined by itself, it's a sort of mad glory.

O is for One, the first event of creation. Where hydrogen reigns, the stuff of formation.

V is for *V. officinalis*, the pharmacy's medication. Four approaches exist, but just one dedication.

A is for Acting, when Peter plays older Whos. Echoing Pat's, Bill's and Jon's points of views.

L is for Life; did the people really exist? Or was their fine city just one big plot twist?

V is for Viewpoint, to see through the jumble. Mathematicians escape the city's vast crumble.

A is for Architecture, constantly shifting. Like the story itself, a refreshment uplifting.

Second Opinion (GB) One of my oldest and best friends, Dennis Turner, and I have had a debate about "Castrovalva" that stretches back to quite literally the last minutes of 1995. No, really, we were arguing about this story so intently that we missed ushering in 1996.

Dennis's point was that it was a boring, meandering story where not a lot happens. My counterpoint was that people who like *Babylon 5* shouldn't throw Vorlon stones.

The thing is . . . Dennis is kind of right.

The first episode, with the Doctor in an acute post-regenerative crisis and the Master throwing the TARDIS into the explosion that started the galaxy, is really cool. The last episode, in which the Master finally springs his trap, is fascinating. The middle is . . . pastoral, to put it politely. Actually, dull would be a good word.

Even the "good" episodes leave a lot to be desired. The whole plot of "Castrovalva" hinges on the idea that Adric can create Castrovalva using block transfer computations . . . except a) there's not a single explanation of what block transfer is, so people who missed it in "Logopolis" are out of luck, b) nothing in "Logopolis" indicated it could create people and c) how does Adric — who barely shared more than a handful of scenes with the Monitor — know how to do something that took the entire Logopolitan race to accomplish, and know how to do it to the extent that he *creates an entire functioning society with its own culture and written record?!?* It's utter nonsense.

Still, kudos to my co-author. That's a cute acrostic.

Snakedance (1983)

Written by Christopher Bailey

Directed by Fiona Cumming

The Big Idea The Doctor's companion Tegan is still possessed by the Mara, which seeks to regain corporeal form during a planetary festival celebrating its defeat a century earlier.

Brave Heart? (GB) The 1982 story "Kinda" is one of the strangest — and most oblique — stories *Doctor Who* has ever done. What's surprising isn't that they made a sequel to "Kinda" in "Snakedance," but that the sequel is much more accessible. Don't get me wrong: the climax of "Snakedance" is predicated on the Doctor finding the "still point" or some sort of Buddhist/Jungian-influenced mumbo-jumbo, and it's further sabotaged by being cut for time, so they have to use part of the next story, "Mawdryn Undead," to clarify why Dojjen didn't destroy the crystal that Mara sought. But it feels less like a Buddhist fable with *Doctor Who* characters inserted into it and more like a *Doctor Who* story that appropriates Buddhist concepts. It's an important distinction: while "Kinda" lives and dies on the ambience of the piece, "Snakedance" is more fully integrated into the world of *Doctor Who*. The characters are colourful and fascinating, the settings are interesting and writer Christopher Bailey has made his peace with the fact that *Doctor Who* requires some modicum of explanation, so he creates a balance between the explicable and the mysterious. And the jeopardy conforms more to *Doctor Who*'s rules of engagement.

That said, though it's more action-packed than "Kinda," it isn't dumbed down. Paradoxically, it's a much denser story, with even more mysteries within mysteries, and it requires even more foreground on the part of the viewer. The Doctor is more than a passive observer as he uses his intellect in a concrete way, making it a great story for Peter Davison's Doctor. It inverts the format somewhat in that the Doctor appears as a bizarre madman to people he encounters, without the "home team advantage" he has with viewers, where his actions are always explicable. He's a bit of a show-off as he demonstrates the sixth face of delusion to Ambril and seems utterly mad when he tries to explain the imminent threat from the Mara.

Janet Fielding's performance, though, is on a whole other level. Given the opportunity to effectively be the villain of a *Doctor Who* story, Fielding makes you realize how brilliant an actress she was and how utterly wasted her talents were in *Doctor Who*. "Snakedance" is usually trotted out on British TV, because it's the first TV work of *Doc Martin*'s Martin Clunes, who looks like Mick Jagger in a bad dress. Honestly, it's so much better than that. "Snakedance" isn't as experimental or as intriguing as "Kinda," but it feels in many ways like the superior effort.

Second Opinion (RS?) What a load of old codswallop! How can you think that "Snakedance" is better than "Kinda"? That's crazy talk!

"Kinda" has beautiful and surreal dream sequences, colonization metaphors, academic theories made flesh, you name it. Decades later, we're still deconstructing "Kinda." And that's because it's one of the richest texts *Doctor Who* ever offered. "Snakedance" . . . isn't.

I like "Snakedance" just fine. One of my proudest moments as a fan was watching the first episode with a friend who'd never seen *Doctor Who* and hearing him exclaim, incredulously, "But I thought it was a space show!"

That's excellent. It's almost a manifesto for why *Doctor Who* is so great. However, "Snakedance" is still far more pedestrian than its predecessor. Which isn't a bad thing on its own, but it isn't the urtext that "Kinda" is. The two aren't even in the same game, let alone on the same playing field.

Mawdryn Undead (1983)

Written by Peter Grimwade

Directed by Peter Moffatt

The Big Idea The Black Guardian uses Turlough, an alien teenager stuck on Earth, to trap the Doctor on a *Flying Dutchman*–like ship piloted by a perpetually regenerating crew of renegades seeking death. And the Brigadier is here as well — in two time zones, six years apart.

Brave Heart? (RS?) There's a scene in "Mawdryn Undead" that never fails to make me cry.

When I was a kid and first saw the flashback clips, it was so overwhelming I cried, but in secret. I couldn't help myself. At the time, television was very different. We simply didn't have long-term continuity back then. So watching clips from episodes long gone was very emotional.

These days, nostalgia is a corporate exercise. We trade in it. Hollywood is hugely invested in turning familiar properties into blockbusters, then throwing sequels out after them, and there's not a single season of the decade-long Modern Series that hasn't featured old monsters or blasts from the past.

But back in the '80s, we weren't used to this sort of thing. The idea that a character (rather than a monster) who hadn't been seen for seven years would show up was pretty wild. That he'd show up as a sad old man who'd forgotten everything we loved about him was just brutal. It's the scene where the Doctor has to jog the Brigadier's memory that gets me every time. And yet the tears now aren't the same as they were then.

This is what "Mawdryn Undead" is trying to teach us. That time is a powerful thing. Memories are both fragile and overwhelming. The passage of time takes its toll on everyone, even the immortal. And, at the end, you might well be stuck in a cluttered bedsit with someone you love, desperately trying to find a spark within them that tells you this is the same person with whom you once shared great adventures and memories, but knowing at the same time that it's all passed by and is never coming back.

So when I see the vibrant and youthful fifth Doctor desperately trying to reach his once-proud best friend, there's a part of me that looks back to the time I watched this as a child and saw an entirely different version. There's a part of me that watches this episode in the present and sees myself desperately trying to connect with loved ones whose memories aren't what they were. And then I look into the future and see myself as that old man in the bedsit, with everything locked inside and only pieces emerging.

As I said, it never fails to make me cry. But the reasons have changed, as time has passed.

Second Opinion (GB) "Mawdryn Undead" is another moment where *Doctor Who* changes, for both the good and the bad.

Up until this point, past continuity in *Doctor Who* was minor ephemera, no more than a year or so old. But "Mawdryn Undead" brings back the Brigadier and makes his part in the story a major plot point (and even changes UNIT from an organization of the near-future 1980s to one from the mid-1970s).

Suddenly, the past history of the program was another ball in play, an element that could be used to please fans and longtime viewers. The Brigadier is perfect for this, both because he gives the Doctor a genuinely old friend to play opposite and because Nicholas Courtney is brilliant at conveying both the slightly burned-out retiree Brigadier of 1983 and the gung-ho just-left-UNIT version of 1977.

Moreover, using a past companion like the Brig gives an easy way into the almost-once-a-decade exploration of time travel in the Classic Series (1980s edition). With "Mawdryn Undead," we get an explanation of why the Doctor can't go back to stop himself from doing something. The mystery of the Brigadier's nervous breakdown and the inevitability of events as they close in on the two versions is really compelling, particularly when Mawdryn and his cronies show up.

"Mawdryn Undead" signals that the past of *Doctor Who* had become as valid an element as, say, horror or monsters. When it's done in an interesting way — as it is here — that opens up possibilities. But it could just as easily make *Doctor Who* a closed system, a game only fans can enjoy. The possibilities and dangers still exist three decades later.

Resurrection of the Daleks (1984)

Written by Eric Saward

Directed by Matthew Robinson

The Big Idea The TARDIS is trapped in a time corridor to 1984 and the Daleks are breaking Davros out of a prison ship in space. Not surprisingly, these events are connected . . .

Brave Heart? (GB) If, as my co-author has posited across several reviews in our various books, *Doctor Who* has always been about the acting, then this story is one of the finest examples. "Resurrection of the Daleks" finds Peter Davison and Janet Fielding eschewing the macho violence surrounding them and delivering one of their finest performances.

The final scene is one of the saddest in all of *Doctor Who*. Watching Tegan announce her departure is gut-wrenching. But it's the Doctor's reactions to it that are astounding. His plea of "Don't leave, not like this!" is heartbreaking, and his speech to Turlough afterwards is a revelation, as he babbles about his reasons for leaving Gallifrey and making amends. The sight of the Doctor so fragile is one of the most powerful 45 seconds in the history of the program, and one of the best demonstrations of how good Peter Davison is.

Nothing brings out great performances better than a tragedy, and "Resurrection of the Daleks" is one of the bleakest, grimmest tragedies *Doctor Who* has ever seen. Perhaps too bleak. Styles not only doesn't get a first name, she gets saddled with the grimmest character arc ever, as she has to perform a suicide mission (and *fails* at it). The superfluous, random killing of a shoreline scavenger on the Thames pushes it off the scale. And the Doctor suddenly deciding to execute Davros kicks it well beyond redemption.

And yet, "Resurrection of the Daleks" succeeds in spite of itself. A lot of that is down to the Daleks, who are far more ambitious and manipulative than they've been in ages. The Daleks thrive in settings where characters as nasty as them are trying to play them, and this story is no exception. There's violence, mayhem, surly macho characters by the boatload and, astonishingly, with the Daleks as a real threat, it all makes some sort of sense.

Part of the fun is watching everyone manipulate everyone else: Davros manipulates Lytton, the Daleks manipulate Davros, Davros manipulates the Daleks, the Daleks manipulate the Doctor through Stein, Lytton and the Daleks manipulate each other to their own ends and on and on. (If only that subtlety applied to Davros: I defy anyone to not scream at the TV screen at the end of episode three, "It's time to switch to decaf!")

"Resurrection of the Daleks" is unrelentingly bleak and cynical. But I think that's one of the things that makes it so fascinating. The Daleks finally fulfill their potential as killing machines, and the series embraces what it truly means to kill without remorse or compassion. I wouldn't want every story, or even every Dalek story, to be like this, but it's compelling in its own right.

Second Opinion (RS?) Pah! I won't argue with my co-author's assertion that Davison and Fielding are excellent. They are. But couldn't they have been excellent in a better story than this?

"Resurrection of the Daleks" represents everything that went wrong with the series in the '80s. It's full of violence, characters with only surnames engaging in macho posturing, pointless and brutal deaths, sequelitis, a story far too complicated for anyone to make sense of and a feeling that *Doctor Who* has lost its way.

What's worse is seeing the Doctor dragged down with it. He hunts both Daleks and Davros with a gun. (Davison at least underplays the former to take away its sting; as I said, he's excellent.) He has absolutely no refutation to Davros's accusations. He releases a devastating bioweapon against his enemies. And he tops that act of moral bankruptcy with a tasteless joke. ("Lunch has arrived.") We're just a few episodes away from the arrival of the sixth Doctor — and you can tell.

Tegan leaves for a very good reason: because the adventure has stopped being fun. Unfortunately, by this point, so has *Doctor Who*.

The Caves of Androzani (1984)

Written by Robert Holmes

Directed by Graeme Harper

The Big Idea The Doctor and Peri become embroiled in a war over a life-prolonging drug — and they're dying of a rare form of toxaemia.

Brave Heart? (GB) Robert Holmes's original title for this story was "Chain Reaction," and, honestly, it's the perfect title. If the Doctor and Peri hadn't investigated those monoskid tracks, they wouldn't have slipped into the cave, given themselves Spectrox Toxaemia, found where the mercenaries were hiding out, been captured by Chellak, been captured by Sharaz Jek . . . and so on down the line.

Everything just ripples outward. Events crash into each other, while motivations trip into other motivations. Chellak fakes a transmission to Morgus, because Salateen (freed by the Doctor and Peri) tells him his transmissions are being bugged, and starts a series of events that lead Morgus to leave Androzani Major, which allows Timmin to depose Morgus.

By the end of the adventure, the Doctor's desire to investigate a monoskid track has led to every principal character being wiped out: Sharaz Jek, the army, Chellak, Salateen, Morgus, the President. Only Krau Timmin reigns supreme.

And yet, the chain reaction isn't the only thing that's happening here. In the middle is the Doctor, struggling to save Peri from her impending death, fighting against a rising tide of circumstance and willing to do, at the end of the day, the only thing none of the other characters obsessed with power, revenge, wealth and lust are capable of doing — sacrifice himself so his friend can live.

That's why I love "The Caves of Androzani."

"The Caves of Androzani" is a story with perfect dialogue, great scenes for the Doctor, beautifully cynical characters and exquisite direction and casting. I'm sure you've read that review a thousand times. But, for me, it's really everything I love about Peter Davison's tenure as the Doctor. In the middle of a really dark place, where things spiral out of control and become uglier and uglier, there's this man who might seem outwardly pleasant but has a will of iron. And he will do whatever it takes to save just one person.

Second Opinion (RS?) Just what the world needs: another review of "The Caves of Androzani." Instead, I'm going to suggest that you try something.

Watch the Davison era in order. You'll see the soap opera–like flow of the show in the early '80s, when crucial plot resolutions get tied up in subsequent stories (such as the humans from the freighter in "Earthshock" being returned to their own time in "Time-Flight"). You'll see the pleasant diversionary stories of Season 19 meld into the continuity-obsessed stories of Season 20 and then into the edgy stories of Season 21. Along the way, you'll see some good stories, you'll see a few bad stories and you'll see way too many stories that are merely okay.

You'll finish "Planet of Fire" and you'll wonder why you're doing this. And then you'll watch "The Caves of Androzani."

Seen this way, rather than as a standalone story from the Classic Series anthology, you'll be blown away by just what a miracle they produced here. All the praise that's been heaped upon this story over the years is true — only more so when you see the ashes from which this phoenix took flight. Every once in a while, the miracle occurs: plot, acting, direction, design, camerawork and special effects come together to produce something truly astonishing.

That's "The Caves of Androzani." It's not "Genesis of the Daleks," "Blink" or "Inferno" — outstanding stories produced when the series was at the height of its powers. Instead, it stands as tall as those stories do, but on much shakier foundations. Seen in that context, it might just stand a little bit taller.

The Sixth Doctor

Whether You Like It or Not

(1984–1986)

Basic Data

First story: "The Twin Dilemma"(1984)

Final story: "The Trial of a Time Lord (The Ultimate Foe)" (1986)

Final appearance: "Dimensions in Time" (1993)

The Changing Face of *Doctor Who* It was the most turbulent time in *Doctor Who*'s history, but nobody saw it coming. In 1984, with Peter Davison leaving, the show was on a high. The twentieth anniversary had been a global phenomenon, ratings had bounced back from their unhealthy slump at the end of the Tom Baker era and goodwill was everywhere. *Doctor Who* had been on the air continuously for 21 years and Colin Baker, the incoming lead, had publicly stated he was planning on staying for at least seven years. So it was unimaginable that *Doctor Who* would ever go away.

In a move that was decades ahead of its time, producer John Nathan-Turner decided that the stability of the show meant he could develop a character arc for the new Doctor. As Colin Baker explained in a 1989 interview, "It was very frustrating because we had envisaged an overall plan over a few years of how we could learn more about this Doctor and didn't want to give too much away in the first few seasons." A year later, he elaborated, saying, "I always like to compare the idea to that of the character Darcy in *Pride and Prejudice*. For the first 35% of the book you hate him, then you grudgingly come to like him, and by the end of the book you think he's the best person in it." The aim was to take risks and present the new Doctor as initially unlikeable, allowing him to mellow over time before blossoming into greatness.

Nathan-Turner didn't stop there. He commissioned an outfit so hideous that the BBC costume designer had trouble stooping to such low standards, and the producer insisted it be continually revised to the point where it was, in his words, "totally tasteless," even picking out colours and patterns for the coat with Colin Baker. He introduced the new Doctor with a single story at the end of the season, when the money had run out. He made the Doctor so unstable from his regeneration that he attempted to strangle his companion. The new Doctor was unpleasant from his first moment and the only time when he's even remotely warm was a brief smile at the end of his fourth episode. And then, for the following season, Nathan-Turner let his script editor, Eric Saward, have free rein to immerse this violent and unpleasant Doctor in a violent and unpleasant universe.

And that was just the beginning.

Much to everyone's surprise, the show got cancelled midway through Baker's first full season. Incoming BBC controller Michael Grade was a new broom sweeping away the cobwebs, and *Doctor Who* was one of many shows consigned to the dustbin. In response, Nathan-Turner covertly used a fan proxy to orchestrate a media campaign, tying the cancellation to the potential raising of the licence fee, which got the story on the front pages of the papers. The ensuing uproar left BBC bosses unprepared. Grade wanted to cancel the show completely but was convinced by the negative publicity to bring back the series in a reduced form. A top BBC official even called the head of the Doctor Who Appreciation Society at work to inform him that the show would be back. The intervening 18-month gap — the longest the show had ever experienced — became known as "the hiatus."

But Nathan-Turner had bigger problems around the corner. Cancelling all upcoming scripts for the aborted 1986 season, he envisioned a season-long story (again, decades ahead of its time) that put the Doctor on trial in a mirror of real-world expectations. They had 18 months to plan this extravaganza . . . but the end result was confused and chaotic. At one point during production, Colin Baker was confused about a scene, so he went to both the writer and script editor separately — only to be told by each that the other had written it. Unsurprisingly, there was interference from the BBC head of drama about the stories, and Eric Saward's relationship with John Nathan-Turner began to fray.

And if that wasn't bad enough, tragedy struck: the lead writer for the season — Robert Holmes, former script editor and writer of many classic stories from the previous decade — died partway through writing the climactic finale. Eric Saward finished the story but then fell out with Nathan-Turner so badly that he quit, refused to let his work be used and gave a tell-all media interview, exposing the production team's dirty laundry for all to see. (Something that was also a decade ahead of its time, although it did his career no favours and Colin Baker never spoke to Saward again.) The actual final episode was commissioned in a room full of lawyers, with writers Pip and Jane Baker (no relation to Colin or Tom) — among the very few who were still talking to Nathan-Turner, who by this point was holding the show together almost single-handedly — penning the end of the 14-episode season without any knowledge of Holmes's or Saward's original endings.

And then, if that wasn't enough, Grade ordered Nathan-Turner to fire Colin Baker after a mere two-and-a-bit seasons in the role, the shortest tenure of any Doctor yet. Nathan-Turner asked Baker to return for a regeneration story, but the actor refused. So the Classic Series concluded its penultimate stretch with no Doctor, no lead writer, no script editor and very little optimism.

They were turbulent times, indeed. And nobody saw it coming.

Who is Colin Baker? Colin Baker originally studied to become a solicitor, but at age 23 enrolled in the London Academy of Music and Dramatic Art. As an actor, he was often cast as the bad guy. He was famous in the 1970s for being "the man you love to hate" when starring as the villain in the BBC drama *The Brothers*, and he played a memorable role as Bayban the Butcher in an episode of *Blake's 7* shortly before appearing on *Doctor Who*. He made history by being the first actor who had previously appeared on the show in a guest role to play the Doctor. In 1982, Baker had been cast as Time Lord Maxil, a guard who at one point shoots Peter Davison's Doctor in 1983's "Arc of Infinity."

Soon after making "Arc of Infinity," Colin Baker was invited to the wedding of a member of the *Doctor Who* production crew. Producer John Nathan-Turner was there, along with Peter Davison and many other members of the cast and crew. During the reception, Baker held court, recounting actorly anecdotes, performing dead-on impressions and delivering acidic remarks. Nathan-Turner was impressed by Baker's charm, wit and ability to be the captivating centre of attention. When Davison announced his departure shortly afterwards, Nathan-Turner arranged to meet with Baker immediately; he was the producer's only choice for the role of the sixth Doctor.

Peter Davison subsequently commented that Nathan-Turner's casting of Baker was "Truffaut-esque," referring to the famous French film director who often cast actors who resembled himself. Nathan-Turner was burly, known for his ego and abrasiveness, and he enjoyed wearing tasteless clothes (his Hawaiian shirts were a mainstay of conventions) — qualities that the sixth Doctor inherited.

From the outset, Colin Baker wanted to make the Doctor more alien and more physical. He saw him as someone who would mourn the passing of a butterfly while callously stepping over a dead body. By all accounts, Baker was a director's actor, working well under instruction. He remains the only Classic Series Doctor never to perform a regeneration scene.

However, Baker never left *Doctor Who* behind, reinventing his Doctor in the Big Finish audios in more likeable way that was popular with fans. He also made appearances in *Top Gear*, *Jonathan Creek* and, memorably, on *I'm a Celebrity . . . Get Me Out of Here!*

Top Companion Perpugilliam Brown (Peri, for short) joined the TARDIS just in time to see the fifth Doctor regenerate into the sixth, which was a wild ride for all concerned. He was bombastic, rude and smug; she was American, whiny and so beautiful all the monsters fell for her. Could these crazy kids make it work? Or would it all end in tears, with her head shaved, an alien brain transplanted into her body and the Doctor seemingly abandoning her? Or was it just a dream and she was actually a queen somewhere? Who knows, because even the writers didn't seem to have a clue.

Classic Foe In his first full year, the sixth Doctor faces Daleks, Cybermen, Sontarans and the Master as the series starts to feed on its own nostalgia. There are a few original monsters introduced, such as the Vervoids and Sil. But top honours go to the Valeyard, who is the prosecutor in the Doctor's trial. Intelligent, cunning and fond of the sound of his own voice, the Valeyard is revealed to be the Doctor himself — or, rather, an amalgamation of his dark side, somewhere between his twelfth and final incarnation. It's an astounding idea: the Doctor is both prosecutor and defendant at his own trial, with the Valeyard an enigma wrapped in a mystery (and who should probably stay that way, as he worked for the trial but would likely be a failure in any repeat appearance). Originally, the line was "somewhere between your twelfth and thirteenth incarnation," suggesting a shadow Doctor, like the Watcher (from 1981's "Logopolis") or Cho Je (a shadow of another Time Lord, from 1974's "Planet of the Spiders"). However, the line was changed to suggest that there might be more than 13 Doctors — something that's since proven quite prescient. This also negated the need for the Valeyard to pop up between the second David Tennant incarnation and the Matt Smith one. Which is probably quite fortunate, all things considered.

Who is the Doctor? Every Doctor is a reaction to his predecessor. With the sixth Doctor, that reaction is an extreme one. He spends most of his first episode insulting his forerunner. (When Peri describes the fifth Doctor as sweet, he responds, "Sweet? Effete.") And he hits the ground running: he's cowardly, violent, unlikeable and rude.

It isn't much better once we get to his first full season. This is a Doctor who casually fires a gun without a second thought. Who outright kills several people. When the TARDIS runs out of fuel in 1985's "Vengeance on Varos," he immediately gives up, resigning himself to an eternity of boredom, callously telling Peri that at least she'll die relatively quickly. His jokes are in poor taste, his greatest triumphs are correcting Peri's grammar, and he puts most of his energy into being an arrogant jerk. In short, he's a bully.

And yet . . . there's something strangely appealing about him as well.

If nothing else, the sixth Doctor certainly is different. The Doctor has mostly been an unambiguous moral hero until this point. He's been fairly human-seeming, with a few notable exceptions. But even those were funny and likeable, making us empathize with the character. Not so with Number Six. He actively defies you to like him or make any allowances for anyone who can't keep up. You get the sense that not only does he not suffer fools gladly, he'll actively belittle them and kick their puppies. When he confronts the Borad, a misshapen half-monster who commits crimes in the name of wanting to find love in the 1985 story "Timelash," he humiliates the guy, telling him that nobody wants him, nobody needs him and nobody cares. He might as well tell him that his mother wears army boots and he looks fat in those jeans. When the climactic confrontation with the villain has you feeling like the Doctor really went too far this time, you know we're not in the cozy confines of UNIT HQ any more.

The sixth Doctor is like Lord Byron: mad, bad and dangerous to know. He's the equivalent of that colleague you're forced to hang out with who sends out every signal to keep away, who is rude and nasty on countless occasions . . . but who would also go out of his way to help you sometimes, just because. The kind of person so many people dislike, but in whom, if you do manage to crack that nut, you can find a loyal friend. We talked earlier about the third Doctor having a dose of Time Lord Asperger's syndrome. The sixth is a full-blown psychopath.

This also makes the sixth Doctor the most masculine of all the Doctors. He's relentlessly male, embracing violence and bullying his way into situations. The person he shows the most respect to is a trained assassin (in 1985's "Revelation of the Daleks"). The only time he admits he's wrong is when a confirmed murderer turns out to have been helping a race of female aliens (in 1985's "Attack of the Cybermen"). He makes fun of Peri's weight while being quite porky himself. And he excels at investigating clues and sniffing out details, like Sherlock Holmes with no fashion sense.

The irony of this masculinity, of course, is that he's also the weakest of all the Doctors. He's almost entirely ineffectual. He can't save anyone from the Cybermen except his companion, he can only suggest a change of government practices to the people of Varos, and he does almost nothing to stop the Daleks. He only stumbles upon Earth's fate at the hands of the Time Lords when it's too late, and the evidence he presents in his own defence at his trial actually gets the charge increased to genocide. He's a Doctor who tries to confront a violent universe head-on, but who largely ends up on the sidelines, making snarky comments. It's perhaps telling that "Mindwarp" (1986) is built around the premise that you can't trust this Doctor or truly know what he's up to — and it works, better than you could possibly imagine. The last time Peri sees him, he's tied her to a rock and is interrogating her. That says it all, really.

The sixth Doctor was the experiment that failed. Had there been a longer arc, we might be reading this differently. But there wasn't. On the other hand, he's a Doctor who's different, who relentlessly goes his own way and who is unlike any other.

Three Great Moments Faced with unimaginable corruption on the part of the Time Lords in the final episodes of 1986's "The Trial of a Time Lord," the sixth Doctor gives the speech of his life. He talks of having battled evil throughout the universe, but says that Daleks, Cybermen and power-mad conspirators are in the nursery compared to what the Time Lords have done. That their ten million years of absolute power have made them truly corrupt. It's a magnificent speech and the one unambiguous moment where the sixth Doctor's morality shines through.

In contrast, the Doctor gives hints at the hidden depths he possesses in 1985's "The Two Doctors" when the Doctor posits that the universe might end in a few centuries. Peri is unconcerned but the Doctor can understand the scale of such things and quietly, and sadly, ponders the loss of sunsets, fish and butterflies. It's a brief glimpse into the Doctor's sadness, played beautifully by Colin Baker.

The rapport between the Doctor and Peri at the beginning of 1986's "The Mysterious Planet" is filled with genuine warmth and friendship. Coming after a season of bitchiness and an 18-month hiatus, it's a positive breath of fresh air to see the Doctor and his companion wandering through the woods as though they actually want to be travelling together. Our collective relief was palpable.

Two Embarrassing Moments "The Twin Dilemma" (1984) starts like any post-regeneration story: with the brand new Doctor being confused, rude and eccentric. But then, rather than showing us why this new guy is going to be so great that you'll forget the previous guy entirely, it takes a turn for the badly thought-out and has the Doctor strangling his companion, in the only instance of domestic violence in the TARDIS that the show ever perpetrated. The intention was to make the Doctor unlikeable, but this is like a children's game where somebody suddenly gets out the machete. And, in case you need to be reminded, this is the new Doctor's *first episode*.

"The tree won't hurt you." We'd give you more context for 1985's "The Mark of the Rani," like the fact that this line is the result of a landmine that turns people into plants, or the fact that Peri has stumbled into said minefield and gets gently hugged by a plastic tree branch. But we don't really need to. Because the line "The tree won't hurt you" is one of the all-time best/worst lines of dialogue.

Unstable? Unstable?! UNSTABLE?!? (RS?) Everything that's said above is true . . . and yet I still kind of like the guy.

The sixth Doctor is the only Doctor I've cosplayed repeatedly since I was 10 years old. I can watch the costume-change scene from "The Twin Dilemma" over and over again. I think the cravats in "The Trial of a Time Lord" are one of the cleverest and subtlest things Classic *Who* ever did (blue for past, red for present, yellow for future). It's hideous and godawful and so incredibly '80s . . . and I downright *love* that costume.

That's the sixth Doctor in a nutshell for me. I absolutely understand why he's the least loved of all the Doctors. I appreciate that his stories are so problematic that many people find them unwatchable. I can see why the train wreck of the behind-the-scenes politics sours what's happening onscreen. I get all of that. But it doesn't make a difference.

Because one of the things I love most about *Doctor Who* is just how willing it is to go its own way. I love that it's a show that's not afraid to keep changing, even when things are going well. Especially when things are going well. If the show had found its winning formula and stuck with it, it would have been cancelled in 1969. Or 1974. Or 1981. And it would have been remembered as a great success . . . but it wouldn't be running today. It's experiments like the Colin Baker era that prove just how amazing *Doctor Who* is: it's the show that keeps evolving, keeps changing. In short, that's what makes it immortal.

So yes, the Colin Baker era is the experiment that failed. But that's what most experiments do. If everything always goes right, then you don't learn anything. The Modern Series — hell, even the TV Movie — just fundamentally gets that the Doctor is a hero who doesn't use guns. Why is that? Because when we see that basic tenet questioned, as we do with the sixth Doctor, we learn why it was a good idea in the first place. The same goes for turning the Doctor-companion combativeness up to 11; could be a daring place to go . . . nope, let's not quite go there, because look what happened when they did.

However, it's more than that. I love the fundamental contradiction at the heart of the sixth Doctor. That the most aggressive and thuggish Doctor is also the weakest speaks volumes to me about the failure of masculinity in a violent world. As a child, the fourth Doctor inspired me to be gentler. But the sixth Doctor showed me the alternative — and boy did that hit home. (Appalling pun intended, because violence always gets bound up in those, right?) The sixth Doctor also showed me that just because you're smarter than everyone around you, you don't need to be insulting about it. Oh, and that there's a very thin line between extroversion and boorishness.

They tried to soften the sixth Doctor in "The Trial of a Time Lord." It didn't really work. They tried to soften him again in the Big Finish audios (at Colin's request). It worked perfectly fine, making him adored at last by the fanbase — and I hated that. It undid the fundamental essence of the sixth Doctor and made him just like everyone else.

There's one more thing I love about the sixth Doctor: he puts the entire character of the Doctor in (amazing technicolour) perspective. He's the Doctor, only with the gloves taken off. The sixth Doctor's actions make him look cruel, yet they're in keeping with many of the Doctor's actions we've unquestioningly accepted over the years. The fourth Doctor committing genocide with a quip in "The Horns of

Nimon"? The second Doctor sending a fleet of intelligent reptiles into the sun in "The Seeds of Death"? The third Doctor callously gunning down an Ogron in "Day of the Daleks"? The fifth Doctor attempting to murder Davros in "Resurrection of the Daleks"? The second Doctor electrifying a set of doors that will kill any innocents who pass by in "Tomb of the Cybermen"? None are fundamentally different from anything the sixth Doctor does, yet we're horrified by the sixth's actions (and bad puns) while accepting the others without question. The perspective has been skewed, yes, but only a little — and it's downright disturbing what this perspective reveals about our "hero."

Take his actions at the end of "The Two Doctors," for instance. It's the end of the climactic battle with the villain, a bloodthirsty cannibal named Shockeye. The Doctor is injured and on the run. So what does he do? Turn the enemy's weapons against him? Devise a brilliant strategy that no one had ever thought of? Rewrite the underlying principles of the game? Nope. He captures Shockeye with a butterfly net and then uses cyanide to murder him. Up close and personal. Oh, and then makes a bad pun afterwards. (Did we mention the show got cancelled around this time?) And yet, the only differences between this and the fourth Doctor using cyanide against Solon in "The Brain of Morbius" are that a) Solon wasn't posing a direct threat to the hero's life at the time and b) the sixth Doctor actually gets his hands dirty.

We're quick to reject the sixth Doctor's philosophy. His regeneration was shaky; the era was a violent one; Eric Saward was a tired script editor, over-fond of violence and shock; the Doctor was nasty. But remember that the production team was actively trying to present an unlikeable character — who was still unquestionably the Doctor. The Doctor commits violent acts and makes bad jokes, yes, but Colin's face shows us the true horror of what he's doing. When the Doctor murders Shockeye, he's bleeding and limping, desperate to stop a villain who's physically much stronger than he is and who has explicitly threatened to eat most of the human race. It's a terrible, unsavoury moment, but it's hard to argue that it's all that unreasonable.

Maybe, just maybe, the sixth Doctor is showing us the true horror of what the Doctor has to do on occasion . . . something that the confidence and parlour tricks of the other Doctors blinded us to before. It's an unsettling thought, isn't it?

Second Opinion (GB) It's a valiant effort, but at the end of the day, my co-author is just plain wrong.

It's not that I dispute his assertion that *Doctor Who*'s ability to experiment and change is what's kept it vital all these years; it's that the sixth Doctor's era is a cul-de-sac. This bit of experimentation turns out to be utterly misguided. And while I get that the whole point of experimentation is that some of it will fail, this is a failure that should have been avoided or at least better contained.

The chief problem is the casting of Colin Baker. Baker is a superb actor, and I think British television has done itself a great disservice by not using him more since *Doctor Who*. However, I think he's an actor who commits to the part as it appears on the page and not to an interpretation of what he thinks the part should be. If the page tells him to make ugly Bondian quips when people die, he's on it. Verbally abusing companions, he's all over it. Being thuggish and unpleasant or even cowardly, he's got it.

But there's nothing underneath that. It's all surface. Peter Davison takes a scene in "Resurrection of the Daleks" where the Doctor hunts a Dalek mutant with a gun and, after shooting it, hands back the gun like it's a live snake. It's a thoughtful touch from an actor who has considered how this behaviour would be regarded by the character he plays. I think if Colin Baker was given that scene, he'd just shoot the mutant and there'd be none of that extra thought; he believes his job is to transfer what's on the script onto the screen and that's it. He's doing a character performance instead of a lead role. Characters do what's scripted; leads consider how the actions reflect their understanding of the character.

It's honestly one of the reasons why fans have loved his performances in audios more than on TV. In the audios, he's still playing the character on the page, only it's being written by sympathetic fans invested in making his character more palatable. And that's my second problem with the sixth Doctor, the part that's not Colin Baker's fault at all: the Doctor is completely and deeply unpleasant.

Robert's absolutely right. Other Doctors have been as nasty, as duplicitous and as violent as the sixth Doctor. And the idea that the viewer sees this laid bare through the sixth Doctor has merit. But do we really need or want two-plus seasons of that object lesson? I respect the idea of making the Doctor more anti-heroic, but to write an anti-hero, you have to provide the means to at least care for the character. The flashes of vulnerability are all too rare. The moments of humour are so snarky that they make the problem worse. Touches of deeper sadness are all but missing.

Even dumber is the costume, which is sub-moronic. On top of the fact that the Doctor's gone from wearing eccentric dress to a full-on clown costume, it's a choice that negatively affects productions: decisions ranging from lighting to what other colours can appear in a scene become dictated by the technicolour barf bag that he's wearing.

History is usually written by the winners, but in the case of the sixth Doctor it's written by the losers — and when a near cancellation and the lead actor's firing take place on this Doctor's watch (though neither was Colin Baker's fault), we can call this era a loser. I dispute the whole notion that there was any grand plan behind any of this. I think John Nathan-Turner basically tried the same trick when they cast Peter Davison and created a character who was a contrast to his predecessor. Only where the fifth Doctor's understatement worked against the fourth Doctor's larger-than-life nature surprisingly well, that idea doesn't necessarily work in reverse: how do you contrast against a pleasant, friendly, thoughtful character in cricket whites? The strategy is flawed from the get-go.

Robert is right: without experimentation, things can't progress. But the ideas that went into this experiment were flawed, the ingredients in this experiment were misconceived and the people making it happen should have left the show by this point. The experiment was a failure and the subject nearly died in the process.

The Twin Dilemma (1984)

Written by Anthony Steven

Directed by Peter Moffatt

The Big Idea Twin mathematical geniuses have been kidnapped by the slug-like Mestor, who plans to destroy a solar system. Only the Doctor can stop him . . . but the Doctor's regeneration has gone horribly wrong.

Unstable? Unstable?! UNSTABLE?!? (RS?) This is, hands-down, the worst *Doctor Who* story of all time. It's a train wreck that almost has to be seen to be believed.

Everything that could possibly go wrong does. There's no budget. The Doctor's an arrogant jerk. The villain is a slug. The costumes are laughable, not least of which is the Doctor's. The acting is horrendous. The dialogue is worse. ("That is a direct order from the Minister. And may my bones rot for obeying it.") The science is nonsensical. The Doctor *strangles his companion*.

And yet . . . I maintain that there's something good to be found in every *Doctor Who* story. For me, it's the costume-change scene. I've watched that over and over, because it sings with verve. It takes the bitchiness between the two lead characters and shows us that they're two damaged people who barely know themselves, let alone each other, and now must share a life. And so they're self-defensive and brittle — but the dialogue shines, in its own way.

Yes, the Doctor chokes Peri, but immediately thereafter he tries to atone for what he's done. In a telling overreaction, he decides to hide from the universe for a thousand years, without a thought to Peri's lifespan. He's at once thoughtlessly arrogant and childishly penitent. It's in no way pretty, but it is the perfect illustration of a regeneration gone horribly, sadistically wrong.

We've put this story in the Index File because it illustrates something very fundamental about the sixth Doctor. If you want to watch a "nice" story with him in it, watch the next one on our list. Hell, watch the previous one in the season. But if you want to see just how far *Doctor Who* was willing to go, then strap yourself in and watch this one. If you dare.

Second Opinion (GB) The number three story in *Doctor Who Magazine*'s 2014 poll of the past 50 years of *Doctor Who* was "The Caves of Androzani." The worst, at number 244, is "The Twin Dilemma." These two stories were broadcast *one week apart*.

It's a sign of how disastrously bad "The Twin Dilemma" actually is.

As good as Colin Baker is, watching the Doctor in the first two episodes is like watching your best friend turn out to be bipolar. And not the seemingly cool, sexy bipolar (we'll get to that in a couple of chapters); no, the sixth Doctor here is the scary bipolar friend who suddenly finds himself standing outside on a bridge in the snow wearing nothing but pyjamas and crying, while scaring you half to death.

It would have been so easy to fix this. The script could have more clearly shown the jeopardy of the Doctor being out of his mind. Or they could have used an askew camera angle, even a POV shot, showing the Doctor's off-kilter perspective. Instead, the viewer is left with the job of sorting out whether the Doctor is unpleasant because of his unstable regeneration or unpleasant just because he is. And that's where we start the sixth Doctor's era: at the bottom of the heap.

The Mark of the Rani (1985)

Written by Pip and Jane Baker

Directed by Sarah Hellings

The Big Idea Three Time Lords — the Doctor, the Master and the Rani — find themselves at the dawn of the Industrial Revolution, in a village where the Rani is conducting experiments that turn humans aggressive and violent.

Unstable? Unstable?! UNSTABLE?!? (GB) "The Mark of the Rani" is a surprisingly traditional *Doctor Who* tale in an era when there aren't a lot of them to be found. The Doctor seems more familiarly "Doctor-ish" and less acidic. There's an interesting historical setting that is used to good effect (the story was made mostly on location at an historical recreation of a nineteenth-century coal-mining community), even if it gets some of the actual history wrong. Moreover, the extended episode length actually works for the first and perhaps the only time — mostly because it seems the scripts were written for the old format.

Pip and Jane Baker's writing gets a lot of criticism for its loquacious dialogue — the characters talk as if they were puerile pundits of profundity (to use a thoroughly apposite epithet) — but here it works. There's something approximating witty banter, particularly any time Kate O'Mara is in a scene as the Rani. The Rani is one of characters you wish had been used more often. I love the fact that she's not a supervillain like the Master, but simply a scientist without any interest in ethics whatsoever.

The real star of the story is director Sarah Hellings. Through a weird production fluke, Hellings was able to shoot half the story on film; consequently, it looks lusher than the average '80s *Who.* It's a shame it's wasted on what's essentially a runaround. The battle of wits between the Rani and the Doctor at the start of the Industrial Revolution is an interesting idea . . . but then the Master shows up. After that, it just becomes competitive bickering between the Doctor, Peri, the Rani and the Master.

And it features landmines that turn people into bad pantomime trees. There are no words.

Overall, the chief sin that "The Mark of the Rani" commits is that it's ordinary. In an era when most stories were either departures from form or unforgivably bad, that's actually not the worst thing to be.

Second Opinion (RS?) Would you earnestly cogitate upon the actuality that a superlative narrative of this division is indited by a duo of personages who unremittingly exercise their propensity for locution, whose predilection for synonyms is unrelenting and upon whose ears the oral communication of *Homo sapiens* has ostensibly never berthed? That such heretofore-mentioned parties could author what transpires to be the most guileless account of this annum baffles the wits. The exordium of the Rani is a sagacious postulation: a learned but amoral reprobate maiden was perspicacious in all aspects; the adhesion of the Master was the antipode. Notwithstanding, ascendency is achieved when a luminary discerns the TARDIS and interrogates the Doctor as to the proclivities to which he and Perpugilliam habitually engage therein. His droll, self-aware riposte: "Argue, mainly."

And if you understood what that was all about, then you'll really enjoy this story.

The Two Doctors (1985)

Written by Robert Holmes

Directed by Peter Moffatt

The Big Idea The Sontarans have teamed up with the bloodthirsty Androgums to steal the secrets of time travel. The Time Lords send the second Doctor on the case . . . but his apparent death brings the sixth Doctor into the action.

Unstable? Unstable?! UNSTABLE?!? (RS?) Hold on to your multi-coloured lapels, because this one's about to get personal. That's right, I'm going to talk about how I became a vegetarian.

There's a myth floating around that "The Two Doctors" is about cannibalism. It's not, because cannibalism is defined as a species eating itself. The Androgums aren't cannibals, they're meat eaters. That is, they consume lower life forms (i.e., us) for food, on the grounds that a) such simple creatures aren't highly evolved and b) they taste good. And so we see brutal depictions of food preparation for the very sensible reason that food preparation is a brutal business.

The food industry is very careful about not letting us see how the sausage gets made. Because when you do — if you *really* do — then you would probably stop eating sausages. "The Two Doctors" shows us this very clearly. The lines we draw between what's acceptable food (cows, pigs, fish) and what's not (pets, insects, Grandma) are very thin indeed. But the simple fact is that the meat industry always involves cruelty, whatever the propaganda says.

The end result is that the Doctor becomes vegetarian. And you have to ask yourself why he wasn't one before. (Or why he lapses later.) I would be terribly embarrassed if some poor animal had to die simply to satisfy my tastebuds. I like to think that the Doctor is better than that — and here, in the sixth Doctor's era of all places, for a brief time he is.

Robert Holmes wasn't even a vegetarian, but he captured the argument perfectly. "The Two Doctors" used its ostensibly violent and nasty story to show me that cruelty was something I didn't need to engage in and that there were other ways to find nutrition. "The Two Doctors" made me a vegetarian — and I love it for that.

Second Opinion (GB) The thing is, all the ingredients are there: *Doctor Who*'s best writer, Robert Holmes; the return of Patrick Troughton; Sontarans . . . and yet "The Two Doctors" is a soufflé that never quite rises. The Androgums, while conceived in satire, are completely grim. In fact, "grim" is a good adjective for this story. Lots of people and things are killed — probably no more than in any other *Doctor Who* story, but it's done with such nastiness that one feels something's gone off the boil.

There's a nifty idea of having a multiple-Doctor story where a future incarnation has to rescue a past one. Unfortunately, as the story progresses, all we have is Patrick Troughton — surely an asset to any television production — tied up and later turned into an Androgum in a sequence best thrown in the compost. And the story is an equal opportunity unemployer too: the Sontarans also have nothing to do.

What works well in this story is Colin Baker, who relishes the opportunity to perform Holmes's witty dialogue and gets a couple of nice speeches too. What a shame that this is lost amid jokes about dismembered Sontarans and an ending where the Doctor commits cold-blooded murder, concluding the grimness with . . . more grimness.

No one could accuse Robert Holmes of writing subtle satire — that's really his greatest strength when it comes down to it — but while this story successfully conveyed its veggie theme with question-mark boy, many of us tuned out before getting there.

Mindwarp (1986)

The Trial of a Time Lord, episodes 5–8

Written by Philip Martin,

Directed by Ron Jones

The Big Idea A plan to transplant the brain of Sil leader Kiv into that of others threatens the fabric of space and time. With the Doctor unreliable, can Peri be saved from a fate worse than death?

Unstable? Unstable?! UNSTABLE?!? (RS?) *My fellow Time Lords, let us look back into the past to see Robert's first impressions of "Mindwarp,"* *when it aired on Australian TV in two double-episode parts. Thanks to the wonders of time travel, which in this instance is an entry in Robert's diary of the time, we can see what impression this pivotal story made on a 14-year-old fan.*

> **Sa21/2/87** Doctor on strange blue and pink planet. Hypnotized to be stupid. Slug men are main enemies. Went to Art. Painted Desert picture. Brett came over for the night.

Wait, that's not how I remember it. I remember being amazed by the duelling narrative structure, astounded at the unreliability of the Doctor, but confident in his ability to be performing the mother of all double bluffs. And I also remember that Saturday art classes were the highlight of my week, because I was the only boy in the class, which meant I got to talk to actual girls (or shyly paint pictures while they sort of vaguely talked around me, as the case may be). And Brett, my favourite cousin, coming over for the evening was hugely fun and exciting. Could the Matrix by lying? Surely not. And yet, my memories are not all there . . .

> **Sa28/2/87** Peri killed off in Doctor Who by the Time Lords when she was changed into some weird alien. Went to art. Doing Geography assg.

That's it? That's all? But I remember so clearly the climactic rush to the finale as the Doctor races to save the day but is pulled back, in slow motion, to the TARDIS when the Time Lords seize control. I remember shouting for joy when I saw the opening special effect of the Trial ship reused in this instance, linking the past to the present. And I remember the Inquisitor, who had appeared neutral thus far, suddenly speaking with a newfound authority, saying, "We had to act," as though she'd been part of it all along. I also remember those art classes being the talk of school all week, because I was the only boy in Year 9 who actually knew any girls, so I would regale everyone with minute details. But wait, I don't remember anything about that geography assignment. Nope, not a skerrick. So clearly the Matrix invented the whole thing.

Second Opinion (GB) Or, in other words . . .

Let's put this in context. By 1986, the show had been cancelled, then uncancelled, then had its season halved. Nobody really wanted to make a show that had been as publicly humiliated as *Doctor Who* was back then. But John Nathan-Turner was a BBC staff producer and lived in hope that he'd get moved to another program (he never was), whereas Eric Saward, the script editor, was stuck in a job he hated and, for whatever reason, didn't move on.

Watching this season-long arc, "The Trial of a Time Lord," you feel deeply saddened because you can see right onscreen the broken hearts and crushed spirits of everyone involved.

Which brings us to "Mindwarp." This is the only story of the four "Trial" segments that actually pays attention to the brief given for this season: the Doctor is on trial. The trial scenes advance a genuine mystery: is the Doctor reckless (or insane) or is the evidence being tampered with? The actual story shows a typical *Doctor Who* scenario gone horribly wrong as the Doctor and Peri get embroiled with oppressors and rebels (led by a wonderfully over-the-top Brian Blessed), but the Doctor is ineffective, and Peri is killed in the process. The end result is darker than *Doctor Who* has ever been, but it's also deeply affecting.

And, regardless of the outcome of the Doctor's trial, it's interesting to note that the Valeyard's central case isn't refuted: the Doctor can create real harm to many just by bringing his companions to another planet.

"Mindwarp" is deliberately confusing because it's actually trying to do its job: to make 14 episodes of the Doctor on trial not only interesting but intriguing. It's the forgotten highlight of the sixth Doctor's era.

The Ultimate Foe (1986)

The Trial of a Time Lord, episodes 13–14

Written by Robert Holmes and Pip and Jane Baker

Directed by Chris Clough

The Big Idea The Doctor has been charged with genocide by the Time Lords. When the Master hijacks the court proceedings, it seems like things can't get any worse. But they're about to.

Unstable? Unstable?! UNSTABLE?!? (GB) These might be the most insane conditions under which a *Doctor Who* serial has ever been written: the two-part finale to a season-long story is begun by its most lauded writer during the illness that ultimately kills him. It's finished by the script editor who writes a second part that he then withdraws after a tense standoff with the producer. Completely different writers are brought in, shown the opening episode and told to complete the story — indeed, the entire season. Oh, did I mention they had one weekend in which to do this?

The story starts well. Anthony Ainley's Master shows up at his most sardonic with the revelation that launched a million fanfics: the prosecutor of the Doctor's trial, the Valeyard, turns out to be a future version of the Doctor. It's an amazing reveal that pulls the rug out from under everything and finds the Doctor facing his own worst enemy: himself.

From there, they blow the tremendous lead with a series of own goals. While the nightmarish sequences in the Matrix are stunningly realized (particularly for the 1980s, when it was all made on video), they are warmed-over retreads of "The Deadly Assassin." Michael Jayston finally gets to show what a great actor he is, with a great scene in which he outlines his plan to the Doctor . . . but the idea of an evil Doctor is completely undercut by playing him as a typical bombastic *Doctor Who* villain, with lines like "There's nothing you can do to prevent the catharsis of spurious morality."

Credit must be given to Pip and Jane Baker for at least keeping the story moving from where Robert Holmes started it, but onscreen it comes off as a

Second Opinion (RS?) desperate attempt to finish things. So we have the introduction of Mel as a regular companion taking place after her future adventure with the Doctor from the previous story, a cliffhanger ending that goes nowhere and the worst final line for a Doctor in the history of ever ("Carrot juice, carrot juice, carrot juice!"). Worse, the Valeyard needs careful explanation and clear motivation but has neither. So we're left to deduce that a future Doctor wants to kill his past self so that he can, um . . .

But the secret to this story is not to be a casual viewer. Which is fortunate, because there weren't very many of them left in 1986. If you've just tuned in for the trial, you're going to be hopelessly lost. On the other hand, if you're a rabid fan, armed with behind-the-scenes details, knowledge of the internal politics and aware of the personal lives of the producer, lead writer and script editor, then you can only marvel at the fact that anything even remotely sensible makes its way onscreen at all.

So this is a story that actually improves with age and insider knowledge. In hindsight, this story's downfall is also its saving grace: the fact that it was written under the most insane conditions imaginable.

The Seventh Doctor

From the Dawn of Time

(1987–1996)

Basic Data

First story: "Time and the Rani" (1987)

Final story: "Survival" (1989)

Final appearance: "Doctor Who" (a.k.a. the TV Movie, 1996)

The Changing Face of *Doctor Who* After the turmoil that rocked *Doctor Who* following its brief cancellation in 1985 and diminished revival in 1986, producer John Nathan-Turner was the last man standing. Nathan-Turner himself asked to be moved on, but his request was refused. He had reinvented the show when he first took over, and he'd reinvented it again with Colin Baker's Doctor. Now he was faced with the task of reinventing it a third time.

Nathan-Turner called in Pip and Jane Baker (just about the only people who were still speaking to him) to write the first script before a new Doctor had even been cast. Needing a script editor, he found Andrew Cartmel, a British-born Canadian who was just 28. Cartmel was working as a tech-industry writer but had taken the BBC's drama-writing course. Cartmel was young and ambitious: in his interview for the position, when asked what he wanted to do with *Doctor Who*, he answered, "I'd like to overthrow the government." He had an interest in contemporary comics, which were in the process of reinventing established superheroes with a darker twist. So he was an ideal candidate to take over the creative direction of the series. Cartmel recruited like-minded fresh blood, with up-and-coming writers like Ian Briggs, Ben Aaronovitch and Rona Munro brought on board.

Nathan-Turner had always tended to give his script editors considerable leeway on the development of stories. He was impressed with the enthusiasm Cartmel brought to the role, while Cartmel benefitted from Nathan-Turner's wisdom as the longest-serving producer on the series. At one point, Cartmel decided a scene needed to be jazzed up and suggested having some tentacles reach out to menace the Doctor and his companion. Nathan-Turner simply sighed and, with the tone of one who knew from bitter experience, definitively stated, "No tentacles."

Cartmel was largely disinterested in continuity with past *Doctor Who*, preferring to move forward. Feeling that the audience knew too much about the Doctor's backstory, he decided to change that. He drew up a document, in consultation with the other writers, that outlined a secret backstory that would play in the background. This subsequently became known as the "Cartmel Masterplan" and was the subject of much debate among fans. As a result, in its final three years, the Classic Series saw a creative resurgence, with the Doctor as a darker hero, a companion who wasn't a screamer and intelligent, adult themes.

However, all good things come to an end.

Doctor Who had held on for three years opposite *Coronation Street*. It received plaudits in the press that it hadn't received in years and even gained in the ratings, in spite of little promotion and unbeatable competition. With productions now being farmed out to outside companies (John Nathan-Turner was virtually the last BBC staff producer in drama) and a new regime at the BBC, it was decided, very quietly in 1989, that *Doctor Who*'s day was done. On December 6, 1989, *Doctor Who* aired its final episode of the Classic Series. Contracts weren't renewed, and Cartmel moved on to other projects.

Nathan-Turner remained employed by the BBC for a few years as a consultant, approving merchandise, creating materials for BBC video and consulting for *Doctor Who Magazine*. Without a series on the air, Virgin Publishing launched a series of original novels starring the seventh Doctor and Ace that continued the adventures in print.

Doctor Who as we knew it was over.

Who is Sylvester McCoy? Sylvester McCoy was one of the most surprising choices for a Doctor. Even more surprising is the fact that he arguably had more influence on the part than any other actor playing the Doctor in the Classic Series.

Sylvester McCoy was born Percy James Patrick Kent-Smith, adopting his better-known stage name from a play he once starred in, titled *An Evening with Sylveste McCoy* (he added the "r" later). In 1987, he was known mostly for two things: his extreme physical comedy with avant-garde comedian Ken Campbell (McCoy was famous for hammering nails up his nose and stuffing ferrets down his trousers) and his work in children's television, where he played a variety of roles, including a character who lived in a mirror in *Vision On* and an eccentric scientist in *Eureka*. McCoy had excellent theatre credentials (he was performing in a National Theatre production of *The Pied Piper of Hamelin* written especially for him) and, when it came to casting the seventh Doctor, producer John Nathan-Turner wanted McCoy from the outset.

However, thanks to the hiatus and the firing of Colin Baker, the series was now under a more watchful eye, so Nathan-Turner had to audition a number of actors for the role. Fortunately, McCoy passed his audition with flying colours. (McCoy claims the other candidates were ringers designed to fail, despite one of them being *Luther*'s Dermot Crowley.) John Nathan-Turner insisted McCoy wear the hat he wore to their initial meeting to discuss the role. McCoy jokingly says they really wanted the hat and were forced to take him along with it.

While previous actors more or less went along with the direction determined for their costume, McCoy asked for a more understated costume and got it. He added touches such as the umbrella. He also insisted the Doctor wear a paisley scarf, on the grounds that the general public knew the Doctor as someone in a scarf who fights Daleks. And his input wasn't limited to the costume. Script editor Andrew Cartmel was keen to get McCoy's thoughts on the character, allowing him more influence on the role than any other actor. Reflecting on the Doctor's great age, McCoy drew on the sadness he saw in his 100-year-old grandmother. He also asked that stories have their climax based in wit and superior intellect rather than violent action. All this was an against-type shift for an actor who started in oddball comedy.

Decades after he left the role, McCoy was up for the role of Bilbo Baggins in *The Lord of the Rings* (Peter Jackson having been a fan of McCoy's Doctor), narrowly missing out to Ian Holm. Jackson eventually cast McCoy as the wizard Radagast the Brown in the Hobbit trilogy, earning him a new generation of fans in a different genre series — all thanks to his performance as the Doctor.

Top Companion For his final two seasons, the seventh Doctor was paired with Ace, a delinquent teenager with a penchant for explosives. Ace is tomboyish, doesn't scream and gives as good as she gets to practically everyone. While she's outwardly the Doctor's backup, he also engages in tough-love therapy with her, forcing her to face her fears and exorcise her demons. Sometimes this has unexpected consequences, such as Ace revealing the arson in her past in 1989's "Ghost Light." But it can also backfire, as when Ace's faith in the Doctor becomes an impediment in 1989's "The Curse of Fenric," something he has to break in ways that border on cruelty. Ace was a new kind of companion that prefigured the ones from the Modern Series, with a backstory (including a mother with whom she had a tumultuous relationship and a best friend who died in a hate crime) and full-on character growth that was documented onscreen. There was talk of writing out Ace by enrolling her in the Time Lord academy, but viewers never saw how she left the Doctor's company; she's the unfinished symphony of *Doctor Who* companions.

Classic Foe Throughout the seventh Doctor's travels, something plays a long game against him. Ace is transported across time, seemingly at random. Lady Peinforte uses potions and equations to develop time travel in the seventeenth century. And then, in "The Curse of Fenric," we learn that the entity behind these events, Fenric, is a force of evil from the dawn of time, who has been manipulating the Doctor's timeline and those around him. By setting up Fenric as the ultimate evil, the writers ask us to examine whether the Doctor is its obvious counterpart, making their centuries-long battle epic and godlike.

Who is the Doctor? The seventh Doctor is a man of mystery. In a time when it was thought that everything was known about the Doctor, it turns out that he's still a man with a past — one that he desperately doesn't want us to know about.

"Remembrance of the Daleks" (1988) opens this up with the Doctor obliquely suggesting that he might have been a contemporary of Rassilon. This is backed up by the fact that he has voice control of the Hand of Omega, the Gallifreyan superweapon in that story. Lady Peinforte also claims that the Doctor has a dark secret in 1988's "Silver Nemesis," one that we never learn, but one that certainly changed the way the character was seen. Even his future is mysterious, with the revelation in 1989's "Battlefield" that he was — or rather *will* be — Merlin in an alternate universe.

His past means that he carries the weight of the universe on his shoulders; he is capable of acting with great power, but feels the responsibilities weighing heavily. The seventh Doctor does something no other Doctor has done: he shows up in places deliberately, knowing the menace is already there, with a plan in place to stop it. "Remembrance of the Daleks" has him enacting a plan to wipe out the Daleks. (He lays a similar trap for the Cybermen in "Silver Nemesis.") "The Curse of Fenric" has him playing a game of chess with a being who has been controlling events around him for years.

While he's been described as a manipulator, this Doctor is actually a sad clown, an optimist proved wrong too many times. It's no surprise he becomes the most proactive of all the Doctors, steering his TARDIS deliberately, investigating rumours of unrest and bringing down a government in one night, just to flex his muscles (as he does in 1988's "The Happiness Patrol").

He feels a responsibility not only to the universe, but to his companion. As fond as he clearly is of Ace, he nevertheless manipulates her, both physically and emotionally. He forces her to confront her fears, such as those of clowns (1988's "The Greatest Show in the Galaxy") or haunted houses ("Ghost Light") and to confront her own past, including her troubled relationship with her mother ("The Curse of Fenric"). His goal is to build her into someone who's both emotionally stronger and more self-aware, but it can drive a rift between the two, as she often accuses him of keeping secrets or manipulating her. Then again, when the Doctor needs to demonstrate his faith in something to repel vampires, he mutters the names of his companions under his breath — and it works.

Despite all this darkness, he still has flashes of levity. In the midst of battling the embodiment of evil in "The Curse of Fenric," he drops a brick on his foot. Investigating suburban disappearances, he's utterly dotty as he forgets to pay for goods bought in a shop and even crawls along a wall in search of cats in 1989's "Survival." And the final confrontation with the Gods of Ragnarok, enemies the Doctor has fought all through time, is achieved in "The Greatest Show in the Galaxy" via cheap magic tricks and while hanging upside down and struggling to escape from a straitjacket.

This is a Doctor who holds great power but is haunted by the huge choices he has to make. And yet, humans can't comprehend the scale of these decisions in the same way he does. When weighing his decision to destroy Skaro in "Remembrance of the Daleks," he asks John, the café cook, whether he should take sugar in his tea, using the man's responses as a metaphor for his own indecision. The resulting discussion is startling: the Doctor listens to John's thoughts on consequences to help him decide whether or not to go through with an act of genocide, but John has no idea that the conversation he's having will affect the lives of millions.

In the end, the seventh Doctor is a mix of loveable, awkward and terrifying. He's a children's entertainer turned demigod, who brings a smile to your face one moment and obliterates your enemies the next, all the while making it seem as though he never quite gets his hands dirty. You get the sense that if he wanted to change a lightbulb, he'd start by drawing up plans for a thermonuclear-powered lightbulb factory, but he'd also be frighteningly successful at it. And then he'd accidentally trip over the goofy-looking lightbulb-changing superweapon he'd created along the way, partly to distract you from the truth of what he has to do and partly just to make you laugh. Sad clowns are definitely the scariest.

Three Great Moments The thuggish Gavrok is holding the Doctor's companion and an innocent bystander hostage. The Doctor, full of righteous fury, marches past his guards and straight to a head-on confrontation (with, we might note, a man eating raw meat). He then takes everything the villain throws at him and tosses it back effortlessly, condemning him on behalf of life and appealing to justice and law. And then, despite Gavrok's contempt for the Doctor's arguments, he takes his friends, under a white flag of truce, and simply leaves. "Delta and the Bannermen" (1987) is only the third McCoy story, but this is the moment when we see the true seventh Doctor, the small man against the world, begin to emerge.

It's the end of "Remembrance of the Daleks" and the Doctor has just made the ballsiest move we've ever seen him make: he's tricked Davros into activating a weapon that destroys an entire solar system, including the Daleks' home planet and their invading force. But then, for an encore, he finds the last surviving Dalek and calmly walks up to it. Staring death in the face, he tells the black Dalek that its race is gone, its creator is gone, that it has no purpose and no hope. The Dalek, linked to the emotional young girl who's simultaneously threatening Ace, spins around and self-destructs. This is also a story that makes the Daleks scarier than they've been in years. And the Doctor faces one down and talks it to death. As we said in *Who's 50*, holy mother of Rassilon.

"The Happiness Patrol" is a polarizing tale: you either love it or you hate it. But there's one standout scene than even its critics can admire. Two snipers are on a balcony, one glorifying his job and enthusing about weapons, the other unsure. Suddenly, the Doctor appears and turns everything upside down. He goads the gun-lover, tells him to look the Doctor in the eye, pull the trigger, end his life. But the sniper can't do it — and, better yet, he doesn't even know why. McCoy's quiet intensity is magnificent in this scene, especially as he casually tells the other sniper to shut up when he gets distracting, showing his intense focus.

Two Embarrassing Moments In 1987's "Dragonfire," the cliffhanger to the first episode involves . . . the Doctor hanging from a cliff. This should be witty and droll — except that there's absolutely no reason why the Doctor suddenly decides to climb over a railing and hang from his umbrella at that moment. It's made even worse by McCoy's comical gurning and then, if you can believe it, worse again by the resolution, which has him reappearing on the ground with the help of his comrade, dusting himself off as though he just climbed down from a short stepladder, rather than the vertiginous ravine we'd seen in the previous episode.

"THERE WILL BE NO BATTLE HERE!" screams the Doctor in "Battlefield." When Sylvester McCoy is subtle and nuanced, emanating quiet menace with a strategic word or two, he's at his absolute best. When he runs full force into a scene and attempts to shout, he's not. It's even worse when good sense would dictate that the villain should simply decapitate him on the spot. This attempt to make the Doctor a force of nature, able to quell battles with the sheer power of his voice, falls embarrassingly flat.

Wicked? (RS?) Trying to get a handle on the enigma that is the seventh Doctor isn't easy. He spends his time hovering in the background, enacting his plans thoughtfully and methodically. He's the master of a thousand chessboards, who doesn't feel the need to boast about any of them, except as an occasional ploy to wrongfoot his enemies. And often the viewer. He's affectionate and goofy yet commits the most terrible crimes without blinking. In short, he's . . . quiet.

That's not how the Doctor is supposed to be. He's an extrovert, a larger-than-life character, all teeth and curls and bombastic shouting. He's the man who talks villains to death, he's a know-it-all, a name-dropper and insufferably rude. When we think of the Doctor, we think of Tom Baker or Peter Capaldi or Jon Pertwee, Doctors who have a presence and woe betide anyone who gets in their way. Even when it went wrong with the sixth Doctor, you could still see the distorted effect of a loud and grandiloquent man who was deeply insecure on the inside, as most loud people are.

But sometimes, when the wind is right, the Doctor goes in the other direction. It doesn't happen often, but when it does, we get a fascinating take on the character. The seventh Doctor is quiet, but from a place of strength. Even when he's making it up as he goes along, he exudes an air of being in control. The cracks are there, but they don't show very often. Most of the time, you don't doubt for a second that he knows more than he's saying and that behind that calm exterior lies a creature of immense power.

Sylvester McCoy brings an amazing duality to the role. His murmurs are like a threat, warning the villain — and very possibly the companion and the viewer to boot — that they'd better have caught what he said or else things are going to go very badly indeed. He has his share of shouting, but it's mostly there as a front to goad the villains and is used sparingly. However, McCoy adds touches of goofiness, thanks to his past as a slapstick performer, that lighten this dark character in oddball ways that make you smile, in spite of yourself.

But it's McCoy's sadness that really brings the character to life. His moments of levity don't detract from the overall impression that the Doctor is burdened with responsibility. He's like Gandalf, using magic tricks to entertain children while secretly being one of the most powerful entities in existence, cursed with the duty of keeping the plates spinning.

He's also a Doctor who had a significant presence offscreen. The Virgin New Adventures books of the wilderness years went on to define the seventh Doctor as a complex hero for the '90s with a defined character arc: the fall and redemption of the seventh Doctor in the novels is easily my favourite era of *Doctor Who*, bar none. They contain some of the best writing I've ever seen in *Doctor Who* in any medium. Sadly out of print, these books were something of a golden age for *Doctor Who*, despite its absence from our screens.

One of the best things about this era is the sense that it all hangs together. Which is pretty impressive, given that television not only didn't do character arcs back then, it simply couldn't: until transmission, nobody knew in which order the four stories in any McCoy season would air. How do you do a story arc when your stories could be shown in any order? And yet they manage it, with themes and motifs of evolution playing throughout McCoy's final season, while Ace undergoes genuine growth.

Despite having Jon Pertwee as my first Doctor and growing up with Tom Baker, I hit the McCoy era at precisely the right time: I was a disaffected teenager, so this stuff was like catnip. The moral ambiguity was exactly how the world seemed at the time, and I've never felt so old as I did at 19. I remember being absolutely astonished when the Doctor referenced both "Dragonfire" and "Silver Nemesis" in "The Curse of Fenric." Soft continuity had happened before, but here was a master plot, playing out across multiple seasons and multiple timezones, coming together beautifully as Fenric's pawns moved into place, with the Doctor a step ahead.

And the best thing was, while you never quite knew where you stood with this Doctor, you'd follow him anyway. He always had his eye on the big picture, even if there were some casualties along the way. When you can't tell whether the Doctor or the villain is worse — and manage to do that without sacrificing the lead character's likeability in the process — you have a recipe for fascinating drama.

More than any other Doctor, the seventh was a product of his time. His stories embody the late-'80s embracing of complex heroes, seeing the familiar in a new and morally ambiguous light. As a result, if you were there at the time for the wild ride that was the seventh Doctor's run, from the televised output to the written word of the early '90s, you probably adore him. If not, you may be wondering what all the fuss is about. It's fitting, though, that after all this time, the defining feature of the seventh Doctor — as his costume so vividly displays — is still that of an enigma.

Second Opinion (GB) Mostly, what he said.

I pretty much agree with everything my co-author says here. (Okay, maybe a little less of the fetishization of the Virgin New Adventures, many of which were stunning, but a lot of which were not as good as we remember.) There are only three things I really want to add.

The first is to say that pathos is a big part of what makes this Doctor work. Like any good comedian, Sylvester McCoy understands that sadness motivates this Doctor as much as clownishness. There's a moment in "Dragonfire" when Mel is trying to say goodbye to the Doctor, and the Doctor suddenly gets all sad and starts talking about life on a quantum level: "You're going. Been gone for ages. Already gone, still here, just arrived, haven't even met you yet. It all depends on who you are and how you look at it. Strange business, time . . ." It's a scene that Andrew Cartmel originally wrote for McCoy's screen test, a homage to *Watchmen*'s Dr. Manhattan. McCoy utterly nails it because the Doctor is so sad as he says it and then drives it home when he tells Mel, "Think about me when you're living your life one day after another, all in a neat pattern. Think about the homeless traveller and his old police box, with his days like crazy paving."

I love that scene. It's a sign that this is a man with very deep emotions, though he doesn't often let them show.

The second thing is a note of criticism I feel Robert has avoided. There is a big problem at the root of the seventh Doctor era, and that's Sylvester McCoy himself. When he's on, you get scenes like the one above and all the moments stated in the review above mine. But the thing with McCoy is that he isn't always on. There are times when he's actually quite dreadful, r-r-rolling his Rs, overacting, talking too loudly and stabbing the wrong syllables in a speech. I once heard a person who directed him for radio describe him as an actor who went where his mood took him, and the director's job was to consistently point him towards the goal of a scene. And it's for that reason I often blame some of the more inept directors of this era, rather than McCoy himself. Because when McCoy has great direction, he's astonishing.

Lastly, I think what I love most about the seventh Doctor is his relationship with Ace. I think that's one of the most fulfilling relationships in the Classic Series, one where both sides are trying to protect the other, but at the same time the Doctor is trying to teach Ace and help her grow. It's telling in "The Curse of Fenric" that he knows precisely what to say to her to break her faith in him: that she's an "emotional cripple." Because, in his scary way, his relationship with her makes her a better and stronger person. And the obvious affection they have for each other is so beautiful. It helps that Sophie Aldred is an amazing actress.

But, yeah, other than that, what he said. I love the seventh Doctor's era with a passion. *Doctor Who* the Classic Series ended in terrible circumstances, but the seventh Doctor ensured it ended gloriously.

Paradise Towers (1987)

Written by Stephen Wyatt

Directed by Nicholas Mallett

The Big Idea The architectural wonder Paradise Towers has gone to pot, with the survivors turning on each other. But they're being picked off by another force and something is lurking in the basement.

Wicked? (RS?) Where McCoy's debut story was written for a generic Doctor, this is the first script to be tailored specifically for the seventh. He's not yet fully formed (that would come next season), but he's by turns quirky, delightful, cunning and likeable. The contrast with his predecessor couldn't be greater. The highlight is his use of the rule book to bamboozle the overly bureaucratic guards, which is the sort of trick you could imagine just about any of the Doctors pulling off.

The idea is superb: a dysfunctional dystopia among an apartment block, with residents forming into terrifying gangs or turning to cannibalism. I actually prefer the story to *High Rise*, the book on which it's based, which has all of the grimness but none of the fun. The parallels with the Second World War, with a mostly female population left behind, along with a few male guards, is clever, as are the linguistic tricks with the dialogue.

But it also looks cartoonish, in almost every aspect. The Kangs aren't scary youth gone wild, the guards aren't the doddery home-front soldiers they're clearly intended to be, the cleaners aren't able to be taken seriously and Pex isn't the buff hero the story so desperately needs. Then there's the Great Architect, a perfectly fine concept entirely ruined by Richard Briers's performance. Briers is usually a fantastic actor and was a real scoop for the show; shame nobody took him aside and had a word during the fourth episode.

The result is a good idea hidden behind poor execution. Worth it to see the seventh Doctor finding his feet and points for an intelligent script, but a bit of a hot mess otherwise.

Second Opinion (GB) How not to do a *Doctor Who* story well in four easy steps:

1. Set it all in studio except for one sequence, and make it seem so artificial no one ever grasps it. Imagine "Paradise Towers" shot on location in an actual tower block made to look suitably futuristic. Suddenly, many things would work, because the parody is thrown into sharp contrast to the surroundings.
2. Be scattershot in your satire and aim at so many targets that you don't really say anything meaningful or funny about any of them. For instance, picking on modern architecture, the English class system, the Rambo movies, teen gangs, bureaucracy, etc.
3. Let the actors take things too far until it's too arch for words. There is a word that Richard Briers should have been told in 1987. That word is "*No*."
4. Don't veer from the script just because the actor is cute. Or something. Pex was supposed to be built like Sylvester Stallone. Making him someone of ordinary build undercuts everything that's supposed to be funny about his cowardice.

How to do a *Doctor Who* story well in three easy steps:

1. Use interesting wordplay. I adore what "Paradise Towers" does here, right down to the "327 Appendix 3 Subsection 9 Death" and the Kangs' clever *Clockwork Orange*–esque rephrasings of things, like "made unalive." (Side thought: ever wondered what the Kangs called more . . . intimate matters? This has fascinated me for years. Erm. Er, nothing . . .)
2. Use the Doctor in surprising and funny ways, like the scene where he uses the Guards' own rule book to bamboozle his captors into assisting his escape.
3. Cannibalistic old-age pensioners. It's freaking insane, and I still love it. The problem with "Paradise Towers" is it uses both lists. But what's on the good list is ice hot, as the future kids say.

Remembrance of the Daleks (1988)

Written by Ben Aaronovitch

Directed by Andrew Morgan

The Big Idea Two Dalek factions are drawn to Earth in search of the Hand of Omega, a devastating Time Lord weapon. But who set this plot in motion? And just how bad will the consequences be?

Wicked? (GB) In 1990, I went to my first *Doctor Who* event. It was a one-day *Doctor Who* convention held at my university. I had never been among *Doctor Who* fans, so I didn't really talk to them much. What I did do was watch an awful lot of videos. They had missing episodes: I watched the extant episodes of "The Reign of Terror" and "The Web of Fear" with fascination. They had unreleased episodes: I watched the unfinished Tom Baker story "Shada" with delight. But the best was yet to come: they were showing episodes from the latter part of Sylvester McCoy's reign.

I'd never seen those final two seasons — the seasons where *Doctor Who* changed its game in a significant way — because *Doctor Who* stopped being shown on my local public television stations. Instead, it was shown on a cable station in Canada — and I didn't have cable.

I had a major paper due in my Canadian literature class, so I had planned to make a brief appearance and leave. But they were showing "Remembrance of the Daleks" at 7 p.m. It was the seventh Doctor and the Daleks. Everyone was raving about it. So I stayed.

Many years later, I became friends with the people who organized that event. They didn't know me at the time. For many years to them, I was "that guy" who sat in the front row with this ridiculously happy expression on his face having his mind blown while watching "Remembrance."

And I remember why. First, it was the expert way they weaved in the very first *Doctor Who* story, "An Unearthly Child." Then it was the Daleks being fearsome adversaries again (and even climbing stairs!). It was Ace having a genuine character arc with her affections for Mike and his subsequent betrayal. It was the Doctor clearly playing some kind of a deadly game with the Daleks that he wasn't talking about. It was the meta-humour of the BBC continuity announcer nearly introducing *Doctor Who*. It was the incredible ending to episode two. And episode three. It was the Doctor's final confrontation with Davros, which showed a whole new side of him as he gave Davros enough material to work with, then coaxed Davros to destroy Skaro and the Dalek fleet.

Watching "Remembrance of the Daleks" made me happier than I think I've ever been watching *Doctor Who*. My fanboyishness was dazzled by the use of past continuity, but I was equally stunned at how refreshingly different *Doctor Who* seemed.

I handed in my paper a few days later and had my A downgraded to a B for lateness. But, to my mind, getting a B was totally worth it. And I still love "Remembrance of the Daleks" that much.

Second Opinion (RS?) There's a scene we never got to see in "Remembrance of the Daleks," because it was edited out at the last moment. *Doctor Who* has lost scenes before, many of them charming, mostly cut for timing reasons or because the effects weren't up to scratch. But this scene was cut for artistic reasons. It takes place during the final confrontation with Davros, who tells the Doctor that, at the end of the day, he's just another Time Lord. Except the Doctor responds, "Oh no, Davros. I am far more than just another Time Lord."

It's a nice idea and has now appeared in so many documentaries that many people probably think it's part of the original. But I'm glad it was taken out. Because it illustrates one of the great things about *Doctor Who*: that it knows how to play it subtle.

You've got two powerhouses facing each other, with the fate of solar systems in their hands. They're old enemies and each has a tendency to bring out the gloating in the other. So you can see why Davros might provoke the Doctor into revealing something about himself that he may not want to.

But at the end of the day, one thing I love about "Remembrance" is that it underplays its hand. The Doctor manipulates the situation so that he commits an act of genocide . . . but it doesn't quite feel like that, because so many of the moving parts take place just to one side. The arc that runs through McCoy's last two seasons suggests that the Doctor is (and was) something far more powerful than we ever imagined . . . but it does this through subtle shadings and hints, not by ramming it down our throats.

So I'm glad "Remembrance" is the story that was transmitted. As my co-author says, it's one of the all-time greats, perhaps my favourite

Doctor Who story ever, when the wind's blowing in that direction. And a large part of that is due to the fact that there were grownups in charge, keeping the story tight and ensuring that our imaginations did the bulk of the work for us. Because, at the end of the day, that's the whole point of *Doctor Who*.

The Greatest Show in the Galaxy (1988)

Written by Stephen Wyatt

Directed by Alan Wareing

The Big Idea Now welcome folks, I'm sure you'd like to know, we're at the start of one big circus show. There are acts that are cool and acts that amaze. Some acts are scary and some acts will daze. At the Greatest Show in the Galaxy!

Wicked? (GB) It was *Doctor Who*'s 25th anniversary in 1988, and the production team gave us a dazzling season opener with the Daleks that looked to the series' past and a . . . so-so story featuring the Cybermen that was deemed the 25th anniversary story on the grounds that it was called "Silver Nemesis" and the Cybermen were, um, silver.

But neither was really a celebration of 25 years of *Doctor Who*. If you want that, you have "The Greatest Show in the Galaxy." Because the best thing you can do for the 25th anniversary of a long-running series — and one struggling for its life like *Doctor Who* was at the time — is a biting-the-hand-that-feeds-you outright satire of *Doctor Who* and TV itself.

We have Whizzkid standing in for the fan who collects everything but unselfconsciously declares none of it is as interesting as it used to be; the Captain and Mags standing in for the public perception of the Doctor and the companion (and parodying the current status quo of manipulator and manipulated for good measure); and the Psychic Circus itself is a great tweaking of *Doctor Who* on television at this time, as a beleaguered but venerable institution desperately tries to keep things going for a tiny-but-godlike audience that always wants to be amused.

It's delightfully subversive and funny. Like all good satire, there is a variety of interpretations of what the target might be. But it's undergirded by some scary set pieces to make it tense, brilliant direction by Alan Wareing, some thoughtful moments and a stunning performance by Ian Reddington as the Chief Clown. McCoy, guided by Classic *Who*'s last great director, turns in a lovely, nuanced performance.

It's an odd beast, though. It was written as a three-part story and then had a one-part prologue tacked on as the Doctor journeys to the Psychic Circus. He enters the story proper only when he walks into the circus at the start of the second episode. This would be disastrous for most stories, but here the extended prologue gives the story some breathing room by establishing the characters — a perennial problem with the McCoy three-parters (hi there, Suzie Q of "The Happiness Patrol") — and adding more Chief Clown to up the creep factor. On the other hand, it leads to an almost perfunctory first episode. About the only thing we gain that has lasting impact is some backstory to Bellboy.

But if that's the biggest problem with "The Greatest Show in the Galaxy," then we're in pretty good shape. *Doctor Who* concludes its 25th year in style.

Second Opinion (RS?) For me, this might be the ultimate McCoy story. Not necessarily the ultimate seventh Doctor story (we have those elsewhere), but it's a story that showcases McCoy's quirky range. His Doctor is a strange mix of children's entertainer and ruthless demigod — and nowhere is that more obvious than at the end of this story. He spends half of it performing weak magic tricks that barely raise a smile, yet clearly come from the toolkit of McCoy's stage career. And then the other half, he's terrifyingly in control, suddenly having fought the Gods of Ragnarok all through time (even though we'd never heard of them) and then casually strolling out of the blast without so much as a twitch.

It's this last moment that makes me admire Sylvester McCoy all the more. The actor had been told to ignore the small explosion that was going to go off behind him . . . but when they let off the pyrotechnics, the explosion was much, much larger than anyone had realized. And McCoy doesn't flinch. He just marches out, a funny clown with a goofy umbrella, calmly walking away from the destruction of gods. In fact, if you slow down the DVD, you can see that he actually winces for a moment as the explosion occurs — but only for a microsecond.

That, to me, is the mark of a true professional. One who's so committed to making his strange character work that he'll simply ignore something that you or I would have freaked out about. The godlike seventh Doctor finds his roots in the eccentric comedian Sylvester McCoy. And we're all better off for it.

Battlefield (1989)

Written by Ben Aaronovitch

Directed by Michael Kerrigan

The Big Idea UNIT is transporting a nuclear weapon through the countryside. But a war from another dimension has just found its way to ours. And only one man can stop it. The wizard Merlin, otherwise known as the Doctor.

Wicked? (RS?) I freaking love this story. Nobody else does, as you'll doubtless see in the second opinion, but I've never understood why. The story is fantastic, putting the Doctor in the role of Merlin — only he hasn't done it yet, which forces him to improvise madly. Teaming him up with the older Brigadier is superb, and their rapport is simply glorious. Jean Marsh brings class to the role of Morgaine, and the Destroyer is one of the best metaphors for nuclear war I've ever seen. Complaints that it doesn't do much miss the point with a force of megatonnes.

Even better, it's one of the few stories in the Classic Series to realize just how iconic *Doctor Who* is. Just like "Spearhead From Space," it uses the police box as a focal point to show that the Doctor's had an effect. But it takes this further, with Zbrigniev's statement about the Doctor's effect on situations whenever he turns up: "All hell breaks loose."

Introducing a new Brigadier in Bambera takes the show firmly into the '80s — and beyond. The loveable old white guy is replaced by a dynamic woman of colour, while UNIT are, for the first time, genuinely international. And the Doctor's speech to Morgaine at the story's conclusion is tremendous, one of my favourite speeches in all of *Doctor*

Who. Appealing to her sense of honour, he illustrates, using only words, the sheer horror of nuclear weapons ("The child looks up in the sky, his eyes turn to cinders") until she stops the countdown. And then we learn that her feud with King Arthur was born out of love, with another great speech ("The air was like honey").

Yes, there's some bad direction and some bad acting, like many *Doctor Who* stories. But "Battlefield" comes in for a kicking that it simply doesn't deserve. It's the only story in McCoy's final season to be resolutely about the Doctor, and it's a thoroughly entertaining tale, with a perfect final scene of male domesticity. What's not to love?

Second Opinion (GB) "What's not to love?"!? Are you freaking insane, Robert?!?

There's not "some bad direction" in "Battlefield." That's like saying Europe in the Middle Ages had "some Bubonic Plague." It is THE WORST-DIRECTED *DOCTOR WHO* STORY OF ALL TIME. The all caps are entirely deserved. And so is the accusation — and this is a program that endured Chris Clough, Peter Moffatt and 1980s Pennant Roberts. Michael Kerrigan is completely tone-deaf to actors (more on that in a minute) and totally inept at building tension. Worse, in a story that lives and dies by its battle sequences, Kerrigan makes anything involving action look like a first-year film student directed it with some buddies on a weekend.

Aside from Nicholas Courtney, Jean Marsh and Angela Bruce (who all inject a little dignity), every other major role is a train wreck. Sylvester McCoy is back to rrrrrollling and squealing to the point of distraction. His final speech about nuclear armageddon should be quiet and modulated like similar speeches in "Remembrance of the Daleks" and "Ghost Light," but he belts it out like a karaoke version of "Total Eclipse of the Heart." Sophie Aldred is, surprisingly, almost as bad. And don't get me started on Ling Tai as Shou Yuing or the hockey-hair pretty boys playing Arthurian Betty and Veronica.

The design is atrocious. The Destroyer is incredibly impressive, but all the money went into that, leaving the production stranded with terrible effects, some of the most desultory sets ever created in *Who* history and abysmal costume design featuring sci-fi medieval knights that look like something an apathetic cosplayer would wear to a Renaissance Faire. The result of all this is cheap and awful and amateurish. Add in the horrifically dated late-1980s score by Keff McCulloch, and at times it's downright embarrassing to watch.

The idea behind "Battlefield" is incredible: the Doctor arrives in a situation where people know him because of his mythic status — only the Doctor they know is one from the Doctor's own future. It's basically Steven Moffat's timey-wimey version of *Who* about 19 years before that. It's a great idea on paper. (I mean that literally; go find Marc Platt's novelization on eBay.) But ideas only count for so much. On TV, the direction, acting and design make it all look more like a bad fan video than a professionally made television program. Enjoy your padded cell, Dr. Smith?!

The Curse of Fenric (1989)

Written by Ian Briggs

Directed by Nicholas Mallett

The Big Idea In the Second World War, Russian soldiers plan to steal the codebreaking ULTIMA machine from the British. But the game is rigged, and something has been preparing for this moment for a very long time.

Wicked? (RS?) "The Curse of Fenric" is where it all comes together. All the emotional beats of Ace's story have their payoff here as she's forced to confront the contrast between her hatred of her mother and her love for a baby — who turn out to be the same person. The Doctor's manipulations are made flesh as he traps the embodiment of pure evil through a chess game. Subtle clues from the past two seasons, such as the time storm that transported Ace to Iceworld, are played out here.

The result is a story that feels epic, best watched in cinematic glory in the form of the extra-long special edition version found on the DVD. The seventh Doctor is by turns fearless (saving his and Ace's lives by virtue of having crucial information about the deaths of Russian soldiers), clever (deducing that the ancient runes on the wall weren't there that morning), diabolical (calling Ace an emotional cripple, even for the best of reasons, still hurts) and magnificent (his entry onto the base, simply marching up to guards and then signing his own forged documents — ambidextrously — *in front of witnesses*).

And Fenric is a villain that feels worthy of this Doctor. A disembodied entity that plots and plans to outwit his nemesis across time, using people as pawns, could equally be a job description for the seventh Doctor or for the embodiment of evil from the dawn of time.

It's also full of rich characters, from the crippled Judson and the unlikeable Millington to Sorin the sympathetic Russian and Kathleen the ballsy wren. All of them have arcs that take them to places very far removed from where they began, making us care deeply. Only Jean and Phyllis don't really work, but they're relatively minor in the scheme of things.

"The Curse of Fenric" is rightly hailed as one of the all-time greats of Classic *Who*. It's a story that has it all, taking us on an epic journey of plot and emotional peaks and troughs. All that, and dangerous undercurrents.

Second Opinion (GB) Three scenes from "The Curse of Fenric" will always stay with me.

The first is Reverend Wainwright's initial meeting with the Jean and Phyllis vampires. The scene is chilling as they tell him why his faith is no good, with the punchline that the war has done this to him — because the British are bombing German children. It's a beautiful glimpse into one person's abyss.

The second is Ace facing a firing squad, when she suddenly screams, "Mum, I'm sorry!" It's a moment that's a bit sloppily executed because, honestly, it's the whole point of the story right there and there's a perfunctory closeup (that's so fast I honestly thought there wasn't one there for years) and nothing to give it any weight. But Sophie Aldred is acting her heart out, as she is throughout, and the idea of the scene is powerful, even if the scene itself isn't quite there.

The final scene is the Doctor's takedown of Ace's faith in him. McCoy is too often remembered for the over-the-top moments of "Battlefield," rather than the icy matter-of-factness he demonstrates here. What I find so brilliant, and so very disturbing, is how casually and quietly he tells Ace that she's incompetent and a social misfit and he wouldn't waste his time on her unless he had to use her somehow.

It was a sign of how poignant the series could be by this time: this is a Doctor who's willing to say the ugliest things to his companion in order to win the day as part of a grander scheme.

All these show *Doctor Who* going in bold, imaginative and uncomfortable but dramatically incredible places. What a real pity we had to wait 15 years for more of it.

The Eighth Doctor

Brief Romance

(1996, 2013)

Basic Data

First story: "Doctor Who" (a.k.a. the TV Movie, 1996)

Final story: "The Night of the Doctor" (webisode, 2013)

The Changing Face of *Doctor Who* By the 1990s, *Doctor Who* was effectively a dead franchise. For the most part, the BBC had no interest in bringing the show back. This once-beloved series was now seen as a bygone relic that had become an embarrassment.

Hope for its revival came from, of all places, an American television executive named Philip Segal, a British ex-pat who worked in the 1980s and 1990s for Columbia Television, ABC and, latterly, Steven Spielberg's production company, Amblin Entertainment. Amblin had moved into television in the early '90s, scoring a big hit with *ER*. Segal was a production executive on the science-fiction series *SeaQuest DSV*.

Segal was a fan of *Doctor Who* from his boyhood days in Southend in the 1960s. While at Columbia, he worked with the BBC on acquiring the rights to *Doctor Who*, though ultimately nothing came of it. At Amblin, Segal had the opportunity to speak with BBC1 controller Alan Yentob and, through that opportunity, began to work with the BBC and Amblin (working with Universal Television) on co-producing a version of *Doctor Who* for U.S. television. Brokering a deal took tremendous tenacity, but Segal was committed. John Leekley, a writer under contract to Universal, worked on developing a pilot script and series bible. This would have been a complete reboot of the series, providing an origin story for the Doctor as he goes on a quest to find his father, Ulysses, after Gallifrey is invaded by the Master and the Daleks (not quite what they were in the original series).

Segal wanted Michael Crawford for the role of the Doctor (who baulked due to weariness from performing *Phantom of the Opera*) but also liked Liam Cunningham. The BBC's producer Jo Wright favoured Paul McGann. Segal had scouted locations in Utah and then production crashed to a halt. All four U.S. networks passed on the script (though Fox was still interested in *Doctor Who* as a TV movie) and Spielberg lost interest in the project as well. Segal kept the co-production between Universal and the BBC together and worked as an independent. Segal pitched it to Fox as a TV movie (and a possible "backdoor pilot" to a series) using a script by Robert DeLaurentis that all parties hated. Trevor Walton, the head of TV movies at Fox, suggested writer Matthew Jacobs, who came up with a script that was a continuation of the original series. This met with the approval of everyone, and the project was finally green-lit.

The TV Movie (as it came to be known) was made in Vancouver in early 1996. Hopes were high that it would be made into a series . . . but these were dashed by low ratings in the U.S., where it ran against a pivotal sweeps episode of *Roseanne*. The show did well in Britain, but, without the American interest, *Doctor Who* would lay fallow for another nine years.

Who is Paul McGann? When the initial casting call for an American version of *Doctor Who* went out, Paul McGann was one of dozens who read for the part of the Doctor — including Paul's brother Mark McGann. By this point in his career, Paul McGann had starred in a number of critically acclaimed films and TV productions including *Withnail and I*, *The Monocled Mutineer* and *The Hanging Gale* (the latter production with his brothers Stephen, Paul and Mark, actors all of them; in fact, they were briefly a boy band in the late 1980s!).

BBC producer Jo Wright lobbied for McGann to be cast as the Doctor. Executive producer Philip Segal was persuaded after seeing McGann's audition and his work in *The Hanging Gale*. Segal also liked the idea of the Doctor as a Byronic figure with long hair — a hope that was almost dashed when McGann arrived on set with his hair closely cropped after playing a Special Forces operative in *The One That Got Away*. (A wig was quickly procured.)

McGann signed on with an option to play the role for an additional three years should the TV Movie go to series. He even looked at schools in Vancouver for his sons, but one wasn't needed; the TV Movie wasn't picked up. McGann quipped that he was "the George Lazenby of *Doctor Who*," but he did keep an affiliation with the part by reprising the role of the eighth Doctor on audio with Big Finish Productions. Since 2001, the eighth Doctor has had several adventures every year with original companions and monsters old and new. McGann even worked with Weta Workshop (the Visual Effects Company responsible for *Lord of the Rings*) to design a new costume for the character in 2010, deciding he was tired of the same publicity photos from 1996. On TV, McGann's career continued to flourish, with parts in *Horatio Hornblower* and *Luther*.

In 2013, McGann was offered an opportunity to reprise the role of the eighth Doctor onscreen in a prequel to the fiftieth anniversary adventure, "The Day of the Doctor." It was a 10-minute webisode, but it allowed McGann the opportunity to give his Doctor a final adventure and provided the basis for the Doctor's abandonment of his name and his transformation into John Hurt's "War Doctor." The release of this webisode, which had not been publicized, took the internet by storm. Fans subsequently demanded more onscreen appearances of the eighth Doctor, renewing a love for the character that had begun in 1996.

Who is the Doctor? First of all, we need to start with a general note: while the numerous Big Finish audio adventures featuring the eighth Doctor have certainly informed our opinions (and we'd really recommend listening to "The Chimes of Midnight" and "Dark Eyes," to name a couple), we have chosen to base our discussion in this book solely on the onscreen appearances of the character.

We have only two such glimpses of the eighth Doctor — at the start of this incarnation's life and at the end of it — but they offer new facets never before seen in a Doctor.

The first facet is that the Doctor is now capable of kissing someone. The closest the Doctor has had to a romantic dalliance was in 1964's "The Aztecs," where he flirts with an Aztec woman to get the plans to an aqueduct. In the TV Movie, the Doctor has three full-on snogs with Grace Holloway. With this, we suddenly have the first inkling that the Doctor has a sexual side to him, long a subject of debate. Up until this point, the Doctor was largely seen as asexual. (In 1979's "City of Death," he famously said, "You're a very beautiful woman, probably.") While these kisses are remarkably chaste, they show more passion than the previous seven incarnations ever showed — and hint at depths that would be explored with later Doctors.

At the end of his life, we see a very different facet of the Doctor: this is a man who is now willing to break the promise borne by his name. He's become a Doctor willing to abandon his belief in being a good man and helping others, choosing instead to become a warrior. While it's his next incarnation who actually becomes a nameless warrior, the decision was made by the eighth Doctor.

Both these aspects speak to a broader theme with the eighth Doctor. This is a romantic Doctor, in the fullest sense of the word. He is a figure of intense emotions. The same emotions that sweep him into a reverie about growing up on Gallifrey and kissing Grace also take him to the same heights when appreciating a new pair of shoes. He's happy to start travelling with Cass despite having barely met her. In the TV Movie, the Doctor claims that he's half-human on his mother's side. Whether that's a joke (the Doctor says it when he's misdirecting someone while he picks their pocket) or actually true (the Master claims he can see it in the Doctor's retinal patterns), this is a Doctor who seems to be more comfortable with emotions, just as he's more comfortable with idiomatic speech than his predecessors.

He's also dominated by a sense of idealism, which inspires him and others; he refuses to use a weapon on others even when he has it, and it's clear he wants no part of the brewing Time War. However, that idealism also proves to be his downfall as the Time War eventually encroaches and he's forced to see the folly of staying out of the conflict between the Daleks and the Time Lords. His dying act is to forsake himself.

One Great Moment You're watching an American TV movie and there's a moment when a motorcycle cop is about to prevent our heroes from getting where they need to go. And the motorcycle cop discovers that the Doctor has stolen his gun. You're bracing yourself for the moment when the Doctor threatens the cop's life . . . and then you discover the Doctor is pointing the gun at himself, saying, "Now stand back, or I'll shoot myself." That's when you realize it doesn't matter what country produces it: the Doctor is still the Doctor.

One Embarrassing Moment The Doctor's kiss with Grace marks this seismic shift in the perception of the Doctor . . . and it happens in a really hokey scene. The Doctor, having been an amnesiac up until this point, suddenly declares he is the Doctor and kisses Grace . . . and she says, "Good. Now do that again." Old-school *Doctor Who* fans were crying for the loss of their hero's asexuality. Everyone else was rolling their eyes.

Yes, Yes, Yes? (GB) You know what gets me every time I watch Paul McGann as the Doctor? It's the ending of the TV Movie, when Grace tells the Doctor, "I'm going to miss you." And the Doctor says, "How can you miss me? I'm the guy with two hearts." And he smiles, and he and Grace kiss.

If you leave out the kissing part (for the moment, anyway), everything about that scene sums up what I love about the eighth Doctor. It's the fact that he calls himself a "guy." It's this tiny but radical break from the Received Pronunciation, dramatically cogent BBC English the Doctor previously spoke. This is a Doctor who's able to be . . . casual.

Such naturalism is the result of a modern film actor playing the role in a context designed for film and not BBC television, which in the '60s, '70s and '80s relied on theatrical conventions. Watch the scene where McGann's Doctor wistfully reflects upon Puccini: it's something within the skill set of all his predecessors but would never have been done that way when *Doctor Who* was being made at BBC Television Centre and the actors were performing to the back of the theatre. (That said, the eighth Doctor does have some moments like that too, such as when he talks about Gallifrey.) The end result of this is quite pleasing: you have a Doctor who talks and emotes more like us, and it's glorious to watch.

And there's that smile. I'm a heterosexual male, and I'm here to tell you that Paul McGann's smile does it even for me. (He thanked me for an interview I did with him at a convention using that smile. It was on my birthday. Best birthday ever.) I wish we could have seen more of that smile. I can honestly take or leave the eighth Doctor audios. There are some great ones, but, McGann's rich voice aside, he really isn't that great with dramatic acting on audio. His best performances are visual. And he's got charm to spare.

That's probably my main takeaway from the eighth Doctor's less-than-an-era. It's an era full of could-have-should-have-would-haves. You can't take your eyes off him in the Puccini scene or the scene where he talks to Gareth about what questions to take on his mid-term exam or the scene in "The Night of the Doctor" where, when told he has four minutes to live, he says, "Four minutes? That's ages. What if I get bored or need a television, couple of books? Anyone for chess? Bring me knitting." All these things make me wish we could have had five years of him doing things like this onscreen.

But . . . on the other hand, there's the kiss, which time has proven isn't necessarily a bad thing for the Doctor as a character. It's just the terrible dramatic convenience that's employed to bring it about. But that's the TV Movie all over: we can see the potential for the eighth Doctor (even though he doesn't get a lot to do except run around in a big chase sequence), but it's a terrible mishmash of clichés and tropes. I remain convinced it was probably for the best that the TV Movie never went to series, especially given what we did end up getting nine years later. Had we had such a series, it probably would have been a lot of great moments for the Doctor with a lot of tone-deaf material mixed in unpleasantly.

But every time I watch the eighth Doctor, I still sigh because there was such potential for him — and "The Night of the Doctor" proves that, utterly. Because, in the final analysis, the eighth Doctor really does have a gorgeous smile. Sigh.

Second Opinion (RS?)

Eight wonderful things about Paul McGann's Doctor

His casting. The TV Movie did many things wrong. But casting McGann wasn't one of them. He lights up the screen, bringing emotional resonance and sheer joy for life to add depth to something that probably didn't deserve it.

He's a bizarre hybrid between the Classic Series and New. He's half Byronic adventuring hero in a waistcoat and half romantic, sexy guy, kissing his way through the universe. And yet McGann makes it work, against the odds.

"The Night of the Doctor." OMG. You can't imagine just how blown away us long-term fans were when he stepped onscreen, saying, "But probably not the Doctor you were expecting." And then proceeds to be incredible.

He's the standout actor of the TV Movie. Which sounds like a backhanded compliment, but it isn't; Eric Roberts is surprisingly good, Daphne Ashbook holds her own and Sylvester McCoy is quite wonderful. But they can't hold a candle to McGann.

The smile. Well, I take this on hearsay, because it doesn't do a thing for me. I once made the mistake of saying I didn't find McGann attractive in a room full of heterosexual men, my co-author among them. I still have the scars. (Eccleston, on the other hand . . .)

The voice. It's soothing. It's mellow. He could read the telephone book and I'd be basking in its melliferous tones. It's the equivalent of drinking hot cocoa and wearing comfy slippers. Ahhh.

The world-weary intensity he brings to "The Night of the Doctor," a far cry from the life-loving character of the TV Movie — and yet, believable all the same.

Incidentally, my co-author is wrong. A series of unpleasant, tone-deaf material starring Paul McGann as the Doctor might have been quite watchable, actually! Well, wouldn't *you* tune in?

The Warrior

To Light the Flame

(2013)

Basic Data

First appearance: "The Name of the Doctor" (2013)

First story: "The Day of the Doctor" (2013)

The Changing Face of *Doctor Who* For the fiftieth anniversary, producer Steven Moffat had discussed the possible return of the ninth Doctor with Christopher Eccleston, having already secured David Tennant's agreement for the tenth. Eccleston considered it, but ultimately declined. However, the central idea of the anniversary story was revisiting the Time War and its effect on the subsequent Doctors. Originally, the ninth Doctor would have been the one confronted with the decision of whether to use the Moment to destroy the Time Lords and Daleks. However, Moffat also felt that probably wasn't correct, as the Doctor in 2005's "Rose" is clearly still checking his new appearance as though he had recently regenerated. Moffat also felt that Paul McGann's eighth Doctor was unlikely to have been that Doctor either, as he was too heroic.

And so Moffat had a stunning idea: that there could be a "missing" incarnation. Specifically, one who didn't call himself the Doctor (so the numbering doesn't change; Matt Smith still plays the eleventh Doctor) but who committed an act so heinous that the subsequent Doctors kept his existence secret, even from themselves.

Being such a radical concept, Moffat felt that it could only work if an actor with suitable gravitas was cast. This led to the casting of John Hurt, which was a closely guarded secret until its reveal at the end of 2013's "The Name of the Doctor." This warrior made a retroactive appearance in 2013's "The Night of the Doctor," when Paul McGann's eighth Doctor was shown regenerating into him. McGann himself played the body of the warrior seen strapping himself into Cass's bandolier (making McGann the second actor to have played two incarnations of the Time Lord, after Sylvester McCoy doubled for the sixth Doctor in 1987's "Time and the Rani"). Footage of a young John Hurt (taken from the 1975 film *The Ghoul*) was used to show that this regeneration was very long-lived indeed.

Who is John Hurt? Sir John Hurt is easily the biggest name ever cast as the Doctor. His film career goes back decades and includes highlights such as famously being the first victim in *Alien* (a role he reprised in the comedy *Spaceballs*), starring roles in *The Elephant Man*, *Nineteen Eighty-Four*, the Harry Potter films and *V For Vendetta*. Meanwhile, his almost-60-year television career is no less industrious, having played everything from Caligula in *I, Claudius* to the dragon in *Merlin*. He's the only Doctor to have won an acting Oscar before taking on the role.

Hurt is the oldest actor to play the Doctor (at 73, he was a year older than Richard Hurndall had been in 1983's "The Five Doctors") and is the first of the Modern Series Doctors to be older than the show. His first thought when cast was "Brilliant, I'll be a Doctor!" but he had no idea how big the series had become. Hurt claimed the role of the warrior was one of the toughest of his career, saying that he found the scientific jargon difficult to memorize. He took Matt Smith's advice to give his life over to the part while he was playing it, ultimately rating the TV role above his part in *Alien*.

In his final scene, Hurt filmed a regeneration, where he was instructed to stand in the same pose that Christopher Eccleston had at the end of 2005's "The Parting of the Ways," in order to create a seamless regeneration into the ninth Doctor. Hurt said he was wary of meeting *Doctor Who* fans at first, having been signing *Alien*-related autographs since 1979, but found them charming and fun. In recognition of his lengthy career, John Hurt was knighted for services to drama in the 2015 New Year Honours.

Who is the Warrior? Like the eighth Doctor, the warrior's brief appearances give us insights into facets of the Doctor not seen elsewhere. For the first time, this is an incarnation without confidence. He's actually so ashamed of the actions he's forced to take — for a period of close to a hundred years, as he fights the Time War — that he refuses to be called the Doctor (as you can tell, we too have followed his preference). His most climactic action turns out to be negated, but he still spent years as a warrior, not a healer.

And yet, he has a soft side to him as well. When he encounters his future selves, he's primarily a listener, paying attention to what he'll become and using that to inform his decision. Clara notes that his eyes, in particular, betray how young he seems, compared to the tenth and eleventh Doctors. His redemption comes in two ways: the most obvious is that time gets rewritten so that he didn't press the button that caused a double genocide after all. But the other is that the tenth and eleventh Doctors give him his title back, saying that he was the Doctor more than anybody else and that he was the Doctor on the day it wasn't possible to get it right.

What's interesting is that the three Doctors who succeed him — the ones who believe he pressed the button — all adopt quite youthful personas (even the ninth), ashamed of being grownups. However, once the eleventh Doctor comes to terms with the warrior's actions, his next incarnation is that of an older man, played by Peter Capaldi, the third-oldest actor to be cast as the Doctor — and that most definitely counts John Hurt.

One Great Moment The warrior is about to the press the button that will end the Time War, saving billions but sacrificing millions. He comments to the Moment that his replacements were extraordinary. She points out that he's also the Doctor, but he denies it, saying, "Great men are forged in fire. It is the privilege of lesser men to light the flame." This is a beautiful, poetic line, summarizing everything about the warrior that we need to know: it's his shame that keeps him from identifying as the Doctor, and that same shame that will keep his replacements from acknowledging his existence.

One Embarrassing Moment The warrior is introduced via text on the screen, complete with actor credit in the middle of the fiction. It does the job it's supposed to, but flashing "Introducing John Hurt as the Doctor" takes us out of the story altogether. There could have been a thousand better ways to incorporate that information into the narrative. That, and its very existence completely negates the drama of "The Name of the Doctor," because the eleventh Doctor and Clara are trapped inside the Doctor's timestream, which is collapsing in on itself . . . but the onscreen text revelation means we won't worry about how they escaped from that predicament at all.

Oh, for God's Sake? (RS?) It's one of the wildest ideas in the Modern Series. A regeneration we didn't know about? That's a mind-meltingly stupendous concept . . . and one that could so easily have gone very, very wrong. Fortunately, Steven Moffat's instincts were spot-on: if you're going to rock the boat with a retroactive incarnation, then you'd damn well better have one hell of a quality actor to play him.

What's even more surprising than the existence of John Hurt's warrior (which was just one surprise among many during the fiftieth anniversary) is how likeable he is.

The concept of a "dark" Doctor is one that's been floating around since 1986. And the various attempts to make a *Doctor Who* film in the '90s posited actors such as David Hasselhoff and Sylvester Stallone as the Doctor, making it all too easy to imagine a gun-toting, murdering version of the Doctor, substituting violence for wit and consequently ripping the heart out of the character. So there's a very fine line that could easily have been crossed. And it's true that one of the first things we saw him do was take a soldier's gun . . . but then he used it to shoot a message into a wall, and I realized that this too could be my hero.

In fact, the entire storyline of "The Day of the Doctor" is predicated around the idea that the warrior doesn't actually want to commit mass murder but is being forced into a decision with terrible consequences. Despite all the wonderful, wonderful things about that episode, ultimately it's the warrior's story. He's the one grappling with indecision. He's the one who can see the Moment. And he's the one for whom the other two plots are fundamentally illustrations of where his future lies if he presses the button. Because, at the end, as he's about to commit genocide, he's the one who needs hope. He's the one who needs the Doctor. And so the TARDIS lands in the barn, twice over.

However, where the show truly excelled with the warrior was making him funny. He gets all the best lines in "The Day of the Doctor," poking fun at just about every convention of the Modern Series, from the kissing to the weaponizing of the sonic screwdriver to the childlike nature of the modern Doctors. The entire point of the warrior is to provide a link between the Classic and Modern Series, showing how the character has both evolved over the decades and also fundamentally stayed the same. That's an excellent way to celebrate the entirety of *Doctor Who*.

There's a part of me that's sad that we didn't see Christopher Eccleston in the fiftieth anniversary, although I don't think he would have carried the voice of the Classic Series nearly as well. But there's another part of me that's astounded at the sheer audacity of inserting a "lost" incarnation into the timeline. I'm astonished that they made it work so well — and amazed at what a warm and likeable performance John Hurt gave. Yes, the idea of a missing incarnation is a stupendous idea. But isn't that what *Doctor Who* is supposed to be about?

Ladies and gentlemen, despite what you might have heard, John Hurt *is* the Doctor.

Second Opinion (GB) Names are important.

And here's the thing that perturbs me about this incarnation. (Pretty much everything Robert said above, though, I completely agree with.) A year or so after "The Day of the Doctor," the BBC and many fans have taken to using "the War Doctor" to describe this incarnation. But he actually forsakes the name "Doctor." Calling him "the War Doctor" goes against the whole point of that.

My co-author and I had a lengthy debate about this. We could have called this incarnation of the Time Lord what he's called in the BBC branding. But what if . . . we didn't? As near as we can tell, he becomes a man with no name whatsoever, so what if we found a different term to call him, one that had no connection to "the Doctor"?

So we chose to call him "warrior."

Of course, there's a case to be made that he *is* the Doctor regardless: his other incarnations eventually admit it, at least briefly; the Daleks are still calling him "Doctor"; and, while the Gallifreyan War Council is silent on the matter, the Time Lords in "The End of Time" refer to a contemporaneous "Doctor" stealing the Moment, who must have been the warrior.

And yet, that's not what he calls himself. Not how he thinks of himself. And not how his future selves think of him.

We hope that calling him "warrior" pulled you out of your comfort zone, just a little. Made you rethink the fact that this incarnation is, in many ways, *not* the Doctor.

Except, of course, for when he is.

The Ninth Doctor

The Trip of a Lifetime

(2005)

Basic Data

First story: "Rose" (2005)

Final story: "Bad Wolf"/"The Parting of the Ways" (2005)

The Changing Face of *Doctor Who* *Doctor Who* had been away for a very long time. So long, in fact, that the BBC eventually lost track of who had the rights to the property. The 1996 TV Movie had made things complicated with the participation of Universal Studios' television arm and Fox. The attempt by BBC Films and others to make a film (that never worked out) made things even more complicated. By the beginning of the 21st century, BBC executives who wanted to fob off inquisitive fans simply shrugged and said things like "rights issues" and left it at that.

Then, in 2003, for the fortieth anniversary, with the prospect of a live-action version of *Doctor Who* almost nonexistent, the BBC website produced an animated *Doctor Who* webcast called "Scream of the Shalka," which was intended to be a continuation of the show, with a ninth Doctor played by Richard E. Grant. The rights issue came up again, so the *Doctor Who* website team decided to investigate it once and for all, whereupon they discovered that there was no rights issue and, in fact, the BBC had held the rights to *Doctor Who* all along.

Meanwhile, the BBC were interested in poaching Russell T Davies from Channel 4 and ITV. Davies had a series of hits to his name, including *Queer as Folk* and *Bob and Rose*, and was considered a hot property. He was successful enough that he could essentially name his price. Which he did: that he would only make the move if he could bring back *Doctor Who*.

Jane Tranter, controller of drama at the BBC, was already interested in both *Doctor Who* and Davies. The BBC wanted to bring back family entertainment, shows that simultaneously appealed to parents, children and teenagers, rather than servicing demographic subgroups. This type of show hadn't been a mainstay of television since the '80s, so nobody knew whether it would survive in the current market. But ratings had been good on Saturday nights in the mid-1990s for *Lois and Clark: The New Adventures of Superman* and it was thought that this could be built upon. And if ever there was a show that could, that show was *Doctor Who*.

Tranter brokered a deal between Davies and the BBC. She even had a secret weapon: the new BBC facilities in Wales. The BBC wanted to make Cardiff a centre for drama, so it was deemed that *Doctor Who* would spearhead this. And Julie Gardner, a bright producer from ITV, was brought in to be the head of BBC Wales and executive producer on the series.

Davies's involvement with the series was announced in September 2003, which brought the interest of Christopher Eccleston. The new show had its leading man — and a legitimate star, at that. Former pop singer Billie Piper was cast as the companion, fulfilling her own desire to return to acting and simultaneously giving the media something to latch onto. Writers were mostly drawn from the talent pool that had sustained *Doctor Who* throughout the novels and audios of the '90s and early 2000s. Special effects were a mix of practical effects (including hiring Mike Tucker, who had worked on the Classic Series in its dying days) and significant investment in CGI, to bring the show up to date.

And so, in March 2005, everything came together. Without anyone knowing whether it was going to work or not, the show returned to the BBC on Saturday nights, aimed at a family audience. Exactly where it had started. And it was a hit. Again.

Who is Christopher Eccleston? At the time he was cast, Christopher Eccleston was one of the most accomplished actors to have played the Doctor. He had a slew of both film and television credits behind him when he took the role and was critically acclaimed for his performances in *Our Friends in the North*, *Cracker* and *Hillsborough*. He was also the first actor to play the Doctor who was born after the series began: the day after the show's third serial, 1964's "The Edge of Destruction," concluded, in fact.

In 2003, Eccleston appeared in *The Second Coming*, a series written by Russell T Davies. Upon learning that Davies was bringing back *Doctor Who*, Eccleston sent an email expressing his interest in the lead role. For his part, Eccleston was intrigued by the idea of a top-flight dramatic writer working on a children's series. It was a scoop that was too good to resist, with his name adding much-needed gravitas to the show's return.

However, merely four days after the first episode was broadcast, the BBC released a statement attributed to Eccleston, saying that he had decided to leave the show, fearing typecasting. Eccleston denied this and threatened legal action. The BBC recanted, admitting that he'd stated no such thing. And thus we were left with one of the great mysteries of Modern *Doctor Who*. Theories abound as to why Eccleston left, from budgetary considerations (after it was realized *Doctor Who* was a success but that its star was the most expensive aspect) to fraught relationships between the actor and crew.

Eccleston himself moved on, continuing to star in a variety of films and TV. While he didn't make public statements about *Doctor Who* very often, he spoke positively of his time with the show in 2012, leading to some speculation that he might appear in the fiftieth anniversary special; however, after discussions with Steven Moffat, he declined to do so. He thus remains the titular actor who has the most tangential relationship with the series.

Top Companion There's only one choice here — and not because we're necessarily discounting Mickey or Captain Jack. But the ninth Doctor's love story with 19-year-old shopgirl Rose Tyler is one for the ages. He's immensely damaged, suffering from post-traumatic stress disorder. She's at loose ends, unsatisfied with life, but has a heart full of compassion. Together, they each find something in the other that completes them. And they just can't help making starry eyes at one another . . .

Classic Foe The Daleks are back — and this time they're personalized. We not only meet a single Dalek in 2005's "Dalek," we eventually meet a whole fleet of them in the season finale. They're the ninth Doctor's equal and opposite: the enemies who wiped out his people in the Time War, but also a foe to which he's become remarkably similar, whether it be in his willingness to kill the last survivor in "Dalek" or in his almost wiping out the human race in 2005's "The Parting of the Ways" in order to achieve victory. These revitalized Daleks are master manipulators, setting up plans that span decades, but they also know how to push the ninth Doctor's buttons for all they're worth.

Who is the Doctor? With the ninth Doctor, we see an almost violently different take on who the Doctor can be. This Doctor is traumatized and damaged, suffering the after-effects of a great catastrophe. Over the course of his brief tenure, we discover that this took the form of a Time War between the Daleks and the Time Lords and ended with the (apparent) destruction of both races, with the Doctor as not simply the only survivor but the one who ended it.

This gives the Doctor immense survivor's guilt. As a result, he forsakes the usual elaborate fashions of his predecessors, instead cloaking himself in a tough leather jacket, with a shaved head and minimal accoutrements. He has moments of humour, but they all come across as forced, as though he's keeping up appearances, only he's not sure for whom any more. For a man who self-describes as "always moving on," he suffers the shell shock of a tragedy so large he can't move on from it. This means he's a Doctor going through the motions: he'll save humanity, but he doesn't seem clear on why he's bothering. Perhaps because of this, he's looking for that Doctorish quality in others, often inspiring them to act rather than stepping up himself.

He's a Doctor who doesn't speak with the usual dialect, who is equally comfortable discussing reality TV as he is squeeing about Dickens and who can sit down with homeless children stealing food in war-torn London. This makes him much more the everyman than other Doctors, a scrappy streetfighter rather than a master manipulator or aristocratic arbiter of morality. And there's a dangerous edge to this Doctor: when told in 2005's "Bad Wolf" that only a nuclear bomb would get through exoglass, his response is "Don't tempt me."

Furthermore, he's a Doctor with a definite character arc. He changes from someone dismissive and insulting towards humanity to a man who gradually learns how to "dance," in which he rediscovers his ability to relate to others (especially Rose) on both an emotional level and also a sexual one. Faced with the ultimate test in "The Parting of the Ways" — saving humanity by destroying them or choosing cowardice — he chooses "coward, every time," rather than being a killer. Were it not for Rose becoming the Bad Wolf, this would likely have been the end of the Doctor. However, his salvation comes from being more inspiring than he realizes, with Rose stepping up to become a godlike figure and saving him from death before he sacrifices his own life for her.

Three Great Moments In the opening minutes of 2005's "Rose," our titular shopgirl finds herself in a deserted basement where mannequins start coming to life. She thinks it's someone pulling a prank or possibly students. But they don't let up. And then, out of the blue, a hand takes hers, and a stranger utters a single word: "Run!" Two things happen in this moment. The first is an utterly stupendous reintroduction of a hero to a new generation, one who isn't using guns or confronting the threat, but being romantic and running away. The other is that this is a manifesto for *Doctor Who*, as it was in the past and, even better, as it will go on to be. *Doctor Who* is back, but it's like it never went away.

The ninth Doctor is damaged from a traumatic war, is unable to form proper relationships and carries the burden of guilt for so many deaths. So it's no surprise that his one unambiguous moment of joy is when he realizes how to configure some nanogenes to restore those infected by the empty child. And so, at the end of 2005's "The Doctor Dances," he lets forth a triumphant cry: "Just this once, everybody lives!" It's the moment the Time War loses its grip on him, giving him a single instance of pure and total victory.

At the cliffhanger to "Bad Wolf," the Daleks are not only revealed to be the power behind the games, they've captured Rose and are threatening her with extermination if the Doctor doesn't obey. His response? "No." The Daleks query it. He responds, "I said no." They ask what this means. He replies, "It means no." Upon which he tells them what he's going to do: rescue her, save the Earth and wipe out every last stinking Dalek. Which, it turns out, is exactly what happens in the next episode. Even better, the Dalek reaction to this is to point out that he has no plan and no resources. Which the Doctor only sees as a strength. And, just when you think it can't get any better, the Daleks take this as a statement of hostile intent and promptly advance their invasion strategy. Because the Doctor using words, with no weapons and no idea, is just about the scariest thing they can imagine. Anybody else need a cigarette?

Two Embarrassing Moments The Nestenes in "Rose" can possess anything that's plastic. To illustrate this, a wheelie bin swallows Mickey — and burps. It's a moment that's meant to show us that *Doctor Who* is still kid friendly, even as friendly pseudo-companion Mickey has supposedly been eaten, but it makes the mistake of playing the comedy too broad. Even kids would find this embarrassing.

The climax to 2005's "The End of the World" involves the Doctor facing imminent jeopardy: enormous circular fans between him and the switch he needs to reach. It's bad enough that this is set up like some third-rate video-game challenge. What's worse is that, when the fans speed up, the Doctor gets through them by closing his eyes and simply advancing, with no explanation whatsoever. Which leads us to believe that either the writer was entirely out of ideas or this was some sort of appalling pun about cutting through fandom. Either way, it's a terrible end to an otherwise fabulous story.

(What, you thought we were going to choose the farting aliens? Puh-lease.)

Fantastic? (RS?) It's the leather jacket that first did it for me.

I've been a *Doctor Who* fan for a very long time. And I thought I really had a handle on this tricky character. Because one of the things I understood most about the Doctor was that he wasn't a character, he was an archetype. Which is one of the reasons I've loved the show so much. You shuffle the deck, deal out the cards for this incarnation and then play your hand for all it's worth. Until the next regeneration, when everything gets shuffled again. That's a formula for greatness.

But then I saw that leather jacket and my world turned upside down.

I honestly didn't think they could pull it off. One of the best things about the Doctor was that he dazzled you with charm and distractions that made him seem both superficially alien and much more human than you'd think. It's an awesome confidence trick and it usually works. There was no way that stripping the Doctor down to his constituent elements — a madman, a box, a companion and Daleks — could work.

And with the show returning to our screens as a proper TV series, for the first time in decades, I really thought they'd mess it up. I mean, how could they get that balance right? I thought the revived version of *Doctor Who* would do one of two things: either it would appeal to the masses and, in doing so, sell out or it would be exactly the show I wanted, last a single season and about 12 people would watch it. The 12 of us would really, really love it, don't get me wrong, but it wouldn't translate to mass appeal. With the leather jacket, I assumed they were going for the former. They were probably going to have a gun-toting tough guy of an action hero who got all the girls and cracked wise after blasting away at Daleks.

However, there's a third option I hadn't considered. That they'd do both. So when the show returned, it was full of quirky, hard-to-love things that I adored, like farting aliens, media metaphors disguised as meat monsters in the ceiling, space pigs and an alien invasion by fat people. Indeed, if you'd given me that list at the outset, I would have loved this show so hard, sight unseen, but I'd never have predicted that anyone else would.

But here's the other thing I didn't consider: they made the character of the Doctor look and act exactly like what I'd feared — only they plunged him into the world of *Doctor Who* with nary a fundamental change. And so the ninth Doctor runs around looking and speaking tough, kissing people and even pointing an enormous gun at Daleks . . . and it totally works. Why? Not only for this contradiction in tone but also, wonderfully, because of Christopher Eccleston.

I love this man. I never imagined I could be as enthralled as I'd been by Tom Baker when I was 10 years old, but Eccleston stepped into the program for a year and pushed all my fan buttons at once. He's funny, charming, rude, dangerous, awkward, pathetic and magnificent, sometimes all at once. He can scream at a Dalek so hard that there's spittle on his lip, something that would ordinarily be edited out of the story, yet it only enhances his intensity. He can bop away to Soft Cell shortly before shedding a tear at the great loss he's suffered. He can carry off the comedy of a plastic hand as adroitly as he can look into the camera as a hologram and tell Rose to have a fantastic life.

What's more, they did something with the ninth Doctor I never thought they'd do. They gave the Doctor an arc. This Doctor moves from guilt-laden moroseness and grumpiness with humans to facing the aftermath of his trauma, pathetically holding a gun while saying, "I couldn't. I wasn't. Oh, Rose. They're all dead." Then he has an unambiguous win, where — just this once — everybody lives. And so we see the Doctor gradually restored as he lets Rose in and then, for an encore, refuses to repeat the mistake he first made by *not* wiping out two races at once in a bid to destroy the Daleks. Whereupon the TARDIS materializes and he's saved, just as he's usually the one to save others.

There's a behind-the-scenes interview where they ask Eccleston about the Daleks. And he points out that a Dalek is a vulnerable and terrified little creature, coating itself in a hard, armoured exterior. It's a brilliant summation of the Doctor's enemies, unlike anything I'd ever heard before. And it's also a brilliant summation of the ninth Doctor, because he's doing exactly the same thing. That's why the leather jacket works. He's forsaken the trappings of the Doctor because he's scared and broken — and that's a superb arc for the character.

There's a part of me that's incredibly sad we only got one Eccleston season. But there's another part of me that's glad too, because what we got is just about the most perfect season of television ever. And the ninth Doctor's story was so complete that another year or two of adventuring would have diluted that sublime story. I'm only even a little bit sad that he didn't return for the fiftieth anniversary, since we got to have the ultimate stand-in-who-wasn't in John Hurt.

People often ask me who my favourite Doctor is, which is a little like asking who my favourite sibling is. It's a pointless question, because I don't believe in these hierarchies. But Christopher Eccleston holds a special place in my heart, because he did the unimaginable: he brought the Doctor back from the wilderness, he gave him an actual character, and he was good. No, not just good. He was *fantastic*.

Second Opinion (GB) What he said. *Fantastic*.

The End of the World (2005)

Written by Russell T Davies

Directed by Euros Lyn

The Big Idea It's the year five billion and the rich have gathered aboard a space station to watch the destruction of the Earth.

Fantastic? (RS?)

That's great, it starts with a timequake
Spiders, Moxx and Hop Pyleen
And Jabe the Tree is not afraid

Earth when the Sun expands, listen to iPod's songs
Spray serves Cassandra, villain don't teleport
Feed can be reversed.
Big fan no switch
The Filter starts to grill her with a fear of light, sunlight
Repeat in a black sheet, represent adherent memes
A teleport for defeat and a TARDIS flight
Back on Earth and landing in a hurry with the chip smell
breathing down your neck

Gift by gift companion baffled, twigs, breathed on, spat
Look at that ostrich egg!
Fine, then
Uh oh, Gallifrey, revelation, Time Lords gone, but it'll do
Save yourself, serve yourself
War served its own heat,
Listen to your hearts beat
Doctor with the cell phone
And the countdown and the sun flares
You idiotic, semiotic skin, fight, bright light,
Hearing "Tainted Love"

It's the end of the world as she knows it, and Rose feels fine

Earth Death in half an hour
Don't get caught in foreign spaceships
Trees will burn, return,
Listen to the blades turn
Calling home, mobile phoning, mum washing, calm setting
Boe from Silver Devastate
Blue-faced Steward incinerate
Speak a language, speak a strange tongue
Deep South, cheap shots
Watch your home cease, ceased, uh-oh,
This means no tear persevere
Renegade steer clear!
A tournament, a tournament, a tournament of grief
Offer me companions, offer me imperatives and I decline

It's the end of the world as she knows it, and Rose feels fine.

Second Opinion (GB) Let us consider for a moment the splendour that is Raffalo the maintenance worker. This character basically sums up everything that's utterly right with this new *Doctor Who*.

First of all, there's the alien culture who gives us the sense of difference. It's only given through statements that allude to a broader truth. For example, Raffalo has to be given permission to speak by guests on Platform One. Is that something about servants in the far, far future? Is there a caste system? Then there's the fact that she's from Crespallion, which isn't a planet, or, as Raffalo explains, "Crespallion's part of the Jaggit Brocade, affiliated to the Scarlet Junction, Convex 56." All these things hint at a broader culture that we'll never see but we know is there.

Secondly, it's established that Raffalo is actually a plumber, which gives us the sense of similarity. After all, we all need plumbers, whether now or in the year five billion. The similarities make the differences less alarming.

Thirdly, there's the whole reason Raffalo is there: not just to advance the plot — which she'll do when she's killed by the spiders — but, by getting Rose to reflect on the fact that she's just gone into the future with a man she's barely met, to advance the character development, which is totally new territory for *Doctor Who*.

Fourth, there's the casting. Beccy Armory hasn't done a lot of TV, but she was sparkling and charming and sold all of the above even though she was in blue makeup.

Fifth, there's her death scene. Raffalo dies being nice to a robotic life form. Awww . . .

And do you know what's really incredible? The scene with Raffalo was added months after principal photography on the episode, because some CGI sequences with Cassandra had to be dropped and the episode was now underrunning . . . so all this happened out of necessity.

This is *Doctor Who* in its basic essence, boys and girls.

The Empty Child/The Doctor Dances (2005)

Written by Steven Moffat

Directed by James Hawes

The Big Idea A creepy child is stalking wartime London. A con man is selling alien technology to the highest bidder. A young girl is feeding street youth via an ingenious scheme. And the way these events are connected will have profound ramifications for the Doctor.

Fantastic? (RS?) One of the cleverest things they did in the 2005 season was to introduce Captain Jack. He's the perfect counterpoint to the Doctor: a time-travelling hero, but one who's stereotypically handsome, sexy and dashing. In short, one who can dance. And it throws an enormous wrench into the middle of the Doctor and Rose's relationship.

Previously, Rose has been partnered to Mickey, who was a bumbling idiot, and she briefly considered Adam, who was pretty but morally lacking. Both made the Doctor look good in comparison, which wasn't terribly difficult. However, with Captain Jack, suddenly here's a guy who's everything the Doctor appears to be, only he also has a libido. And one hell of a libido at that.

This completely turns our own desires around when it comes to the Doctor. If you're an old-school fan who's unsure about all the flirting and hand-holding that's been going on, the idea of the Doctor as a sexual being is going to be very discomfiting. But what Captain Jack does is show us the alternative — and, rather than make the Doctor look good, he makes the Doctor seem lacking.

The asexuality of the Doctor was always a strength, setting him apart from other heroes like Captain Kirk, who always got the girl. So the Modern Series had the problem of trying to introduce the Doctor's sexuality without making it seem too distant from what had come before. With Captain Jack in the picture — complete with sonic blaster, invisible spaceship and free-flowing champagne — suddenly you're willing the Doctor to step up and, well, *dance* already.

Which he does. And it's adorable. Despite the wartime setting, this is the most optimistic story yet, a symbolic counterpoint to the Time War. The ninth Doctor simultaneously has his one big win, restoring everyone with the nanogenes, and opens himself to Rose fully. So, by the end, even when she's being teleported, Rose doesn't notice. Having been set up as the Doctor-competition figure, Captain Jack eventually takes his place as a companion. And, thanks to this time-travelling con-man from the 51st century, the Doctor remembers how to dance.

Second Opinion (GB) By the time we came to "The Empty Child" and "The Doctor Dances," I thought I had pretty much figured out new *Who*. And then Steven Moffat and James Hawes come round and explain to me politely that no, I hadn't actually figured it out at all.

Basically, it starts with the dialogue. There are jokes. Great jokes (the universal symbol of trouble is a mauve alert, because red is considered camp). There's funny banter about why they keep having to come back to Earth in order to get some milk. And there's even a wry reference to *Star Trek*.

Which brings me to the direction. It's gorgeous. It's cinematic. It looks lush and romantic when it needs to be and threatening when it has to. I wish James Hawes had directed more *Doctor Who*.

There are some great supporting characters (Dr. Constantine and Nancy), a dazzlingly confident romance (flirting via psychic paper is the best) and then, just when you're cozy with all that, it becomes deeply scary — it-will-mess-you-up scary — and it's all because of a child wearing a gas mask.

I thought I had the measure of *Doctor Who* all right until "The

Empty Child"/"The Doctor Dances." Then I realized they could add comedy, horror, romance and cinematic direction to everything I was loving. And the potential became limitless.

Bad Wolf/The Parting of the Ways (2005)

Written by Russell T Davies

Directed by Joe Ahearne

The Big Idea The Game Station has it all. *Big Brother. The Weakest Link. What Not to Wear*. And Daleks. Lots and lots of Daleks.

Fantastic? (GB) There are three moments I will never forget when it comes to "Bad Wolf"/"The Parting of the Ways."

The first moment is just after Rose has been sent back to her own time by the Doctor. Rose is sitting talking to Mickey and then sees "Bad Wolf" written all over the playground and realizes it's a message to her. But she has no way of knowing how to get back to the Doctor. Meanwhile, Daleks are about to invade Satellite Five 200,100 years in the future.

In 2005, watching alone in my apartment, I actually screamed at the television, "I have no idea how this is going to end!"

I honestly didn't. I didn't know how the Bad Wolf mystery was going to be solved. That it turns out to be a message to Rose completely blew my mind. And I'm going on record to say I loved the idea of using the heart of the TARDIS to get Rose back in the fight, mostly because it gave us the frankly incredible scene where Jackie arrives with Rodrigo's truck and Jackie shares a look with Mickey that says they'll help Rose in what might well be a suicide mission.

The second moment is Rose in the TARDIS listening to the hologram of the Doctor delivering the message explaining Emergency Program One. It's a message saying, essentially, the Doctor is about to lose and leave the TARDIS behind. And at the very end of that speech — in which the hologram Doctor is looking straight ahead even though Rose is standing beside the hologram — the Doctor turns to look right at Rose, and he tells her to have a fantastic life. That still gets me.

My final moment is the regeneration. What's amazing to me is the great care taken to reassure an audience who has never seen this before, with the Doctor telling Rose he'll have to change, and this daft old face won't see her again. There's a beautiful melancholy to this scene as the ninth Doctor acknowledges all the places he wished he could have taken Rose and jokes that he might end up with two heads or no head. And the smile the Doctor gives when he says that he was fantastic as well is too adorable for words. It's a moment where you say, "Well done, mate. And thanks." And then he's gone.

"Bad Wolf" and "Parting of the Ways" are full of incredible moments like this (I haven't even talked about the Doctor flirting with Lynda-with-a-Y or Rose on *The Weakest Link* or just about every line Captain Jack says) and it caps off a perfect season of *Doctor Who* full of incredible moments all the same.

Second Opinion (RS?) I have my moment too, but it's not any of the above, as good as they are. It's not the brilliant disorienting direction of the opening scene. It's not the fact that the Doctor makes an announcement to the camera that he's going to get out, find his friends and then come for whomever is behind this (which is precisely what he does). It's not even the "It means no" scene, despite it being one of the standout moments of television history.

For me, the moment is when the ninth Doctor turns to Lynda-with-a-Y and offers her his hand.

I know, it doesn't seem like much. But, despite being a quiet moment, it's one that shows us that the ninth Doctor has finally been healed. Because he's not being angsty or overcompensating, he's simply being the Doctor. Investigating trouble and bringing a smart woman along with him. Eccleston plays it perfectly calm and confident in that moment, giving us the ninth Doctor without the pain for once.

To be sure, it doesn't end well for Lynda-with-a-Y. The ninth Doctor's pain will be back shortly. But, just in that instant, he's complete. Whole. Just for a moment.

The Tenth Doctor

Human League

(2005–2010)

Basic Data

First story: "The Christmas Invasion" (2005)

Final story: "The End of Time" (2009–2010)

Final appearance: "The Day of the Doctor" (2013)

The Changing Face of *Doctor Who* In 2005, *Doctor Who* encountered probably the most important change it ever faced.

We probably won't fully know the reasons for Christopher Eccleston's departure for a while, but one thing is certain: regenerating the Doctor was never a riskier proposition. In the days of the Classic Series, *Doctor Who* was reasonably well established; even in 1966, changing the lead was a novelty designed to extend the life of an off-the-boil series a little further. In 2005, the series had only been back a year. It had huge ratings. And Christopher Eccleston was a bankable star. Changing the lead at this point was potentially dangerous.

The BBC gambled that viewers had signed on for *Doctor Who*, rather than Eccleston's Doctor. That gamble paid off: the series not only survived under David Tennant's tenth Doctor; it thrived.

With the arrival of the new Doctor, Russell T Davies refined the format of the show he'd begun under Eccleston's reign: a season built around "event" episodes (which often featured a classic enemy) with an ongoing story arc, where small clues along the way build to a revelation in the finale. With David Tennant's arrival and, a season later, the departure of Billie Piper, it became apparent that the show gained audience attention with a new cast member. Companions thus tended to stay for only a year but were given season-long character arcs that added to the ongoing drama.

It was a winning format. In 2007, a Christmas special (another innovation) featuring pop superstar Kylie Minogue enabled *Doctor Who* to achieve something its fans couldn't have imagined in 1989: it beat *Coronation Street* in the ratings and was the second-most-watched program in the U.K. that week, with 13.8 million viewers.

Doctor Who also expanded its empire during this time: it spun off two different shows, both created by Russell T Davies. *Torchwood* was intended to be more "adult," with swearing and sex thrown in the mix with alien menaces and an agency led by the Doctor's sometime-companion Captain Jack. At the other end of the spectrum, the BBC's children's channel broadcast *The Sarah Jane Adventures*, a serial for kids featuring the '70s-era companion paired with some smart kids and a whole host of monsters. *Torchwood* ran for four seasons; *The Sarah Jane Adventures* for five. Together, they cemented *Doctor Who* as a franchise. The finale of the fourth season of Modern *Who* featured characters from all the spinoffs — and the second episode of that finale, "Journey's End" (2008), was the number one program in the U.K.

After four seasons, Davies was keen to leave and David Tennant was also interested in taking on new acting challenges, including a Royal Shakespeare Company production of *Hamlet*. But the BBC persuaded both executive producer and star (along with executive producer Julie Gardner) to stay on for a series of specials that would air throughout 2009, giving the show time to develop a story arc to see out the tenth Doctor.

Fans hoped Davies's successor would be the writer whose stories had topped most seasons' best-of lists. He was one of the only writer/executive producers who was as well known a property as Davies.

In May 2008, fans got their wish when it was announced that Steven Moffat would be the new executive producer of *Doctor Who.*

Who is David Tennant? David MacDonald, who took the stage name David Tennant, was something none of his predecessors in the role had been: a full-fledged fan of *Doctor Who* since childhood. While Peter Davison watched the series in its infancy, Tennant read the novelizations and the non-fiction books, watched the videos and DVDs and even wrote an essay in school about how he was obsessed with becoming the Doctor. He was happy to guest-star on a variety of Big Finish's *Doctor Who* ranges. (One of the co-authors of this book — the one without the question mark in his name — proclaimed at the time that they should make Tennant's UNIT commander in the audios a semi-regular character!) He even begged his way into a tiny speaking part in the 2003 webcast cartoon "The Scream of the Shalka," when he discovered it was recording in the studio next to the one where he was performing a radio play.

Tennant was enough of a fan to joke around with Russell T Davies about the Blinovitch Limitation Effect while making Davies's 2005 version of *Casanova.* Already an accomplished stage actor, Tennant's star had risen considerably after appearing in 2003's *Blackpool.* Davies was as impressed with Tennant's talent as he was with his retention of arcane facts.

At some point — the details of precisely when are unclear — Tennant was asked if he would play the role of the Doctor. Tennant's response, apparently, was to joke that he'd like to play the role wearing a long coat. (Perhaps inspired by the trenchcoat-wearing Doctors he grew up with.)

Tennant embraced the part and was celebrated in the role. He went on to continued success in British TV (particularly *Broadchurch,* which even spun off into an American version, *Gracepoint,* in which he also starred). But he kept *Doctor Who* in the family by marrying Georgia Moffett . . . the daughter of Peter Davison.

Top Companion Donna Noble was intended to be a one-off companion in the 2006 Christmas special, "The Runaway Bride." Played by British comedy star Catherine Tate, it was a stunt-cast role perfect for Christmas Day television. Tate played the brash Donna as she went from arrogant bridezilla to someone more enlightened. Tate then surprised everyone by indicating that she'd be willing to come back for a full season with Donna as a proper companion. But that wasn't nearly as surprising as what happened next: audiences fell in love with her. With Donna, the Doctor has found an equal, of sorts — someone just as passionate, someone just as quirky and someone just as lonely. Donna's role, probably more than any other, is to be the human voice, but, unlike her direct predecessors, she isn't in love with the Doctor, which enables her to speak the truth to him in a way that hadn't been seen in the Modern Series. Their relationship is wonderfully nuanced, full of good-natured bickering and disagreement but also full of trust. (Catherine Tate also demonstrates a broad range of dramatic skills in the process.) Donna clearly grows as a person over the course of her relationship, which makes her parting with the Doctor — when he has to remove her memories of him to save her life — all the more devastating.

Classic Foe The Master finally appears in the Modern Series, and the remake of the character is astonishing. First of all, this incarnation is able to use humour and charisma in the same way the Doctor does. But he is more ruthless than ever, turning the joking into total destruction in a moment. While the Master had previously engaged in more small-scaled plots, here he carries out an elaborate plan to take over Earth — becoming the British Prime Minister in the process — and, for once, he succeeds. Key to updating the character was an actual retcon: the Master is now nearly driven mad by the sound of drumming that he always hears in his head, which turns out to be part of a broader Time Lord plot. John Simm brings a manic energy to the part, giving us not just a Doctor turned bad, but one who's just downright wrong — and maniacally so.

Who is the Doctor? If there's one word that sums up the tenth Doctor, it's probably *human*.

This Doctor is passionate and full of emotion. He weeps for the loss of his once-friend and the only other person of his kind when the Master dies, and he cries openly when he has to say a final goodbye to Rose. He apologizes to the people who have died or are about to die because of him. But he also knows the joy of just larking about with a friend somewhere and enjoys saying words for the fun of it. ("I like that, *allons-y*. I should say *allons-y* more often . . . And then, it would be really brilliant if I met someone called Alonso, because then I could say, '*Allons-y*, Alonso.'")

He's a Doctor who's easy to get along with, empathize with and who knows how to flirt. He's the first incarnation who seems utterly comfortable doing the latter (though sometimes he seems vague on what the end result of flirtation can be), and he can be very charming. But he's also the first Doctor who visibly experiences heartbreak, whether that be in fleeting relationships (such as with Madame de Pompadour) or long-term ones (Rose). Even close friendships (Donna) signal the deep well of feeling he has. He can be hurt — he's probably the first Doctor to stop travelling with companions because he's tired of having his hearts broken — and he is emotionally vulnerable in a way unlike other Doctors, as we see with Wilf in the café in 2009's "The End of Time."

The Doctor is aware of his darker aspect since the Time War. In 2005's "The Christmas Invasion," he brings down the British government (led by his friend Harriet Jones) with just six words. In that story, he makes it clear that he doesn't give second chances.

There's an intriguing conflict within this Doctor, where he's accessible, with a high emotional intelligence, and yet he also has an alien perspective. For example, 2008's "The Fires of Pompeii" and 2009's "The Waters of Mars" show the Doctor facing central conflicts the way a Time Lord must view immoveable events, yet with a very human anguish revealing how awful that knowledge must be.

Much of that anguish is survivor guilt. Like his predecessor, the tenth Doctor is still profoundly damaged by the Time War: he grieves his homeworld and even on occasion pretends it hasn't been destroyed. Seeing the Daleks escaping their doom time and again only exacerbates this. He's at his most reckless around them — he repeatedly challenges Daleks to exterminate him in 2007's "Evolution of the Daleks" — and his guilt motivates him to do things he shouldn't, such as saving the crew of Bowie Base One in "The Waters of Mars." He finds some measure of peace in this regard only at the end of his life, when he encounters the Time Lords and realizes that, as a result of the Time War, they are no longer benevolent.

He loves his life in this form. Consequently, he gives up one of his regenerations in 2008's "Journey's End" in order to maintain this body. When the death of this incarnation is prophesied, he tries to avoid it as long as he can; even when dying, he holds back death to say goodbye to everyone he loves. Then, when the time comes, he says perhaps the most human thing the Doctor has ever said in the face of death: "I don't want to go."

Three Great Moments In 2006's "School Reunion," the Doctor confronts the Krillitane leader, who is posing as a school headmaster named Mr. Finch. As they stand by the school pool, the Doctor asks Finch what the Krillitane are planning, telling Finch that if he doesn't like it, he'll stop it. Finch asks him, "Would you declare war on us, Doctor?" and the Doctor replies, "I'm so old now. I used to have so much mercy. You get one warning. That was it." And he means it.

"Blink" (2007) is one of the most lauded *Doctor Who* stories and the Doctor is hardly in it — though his presence is felt all the way through. The centrepiece for this is the Doctor "talking" with Sally Sparrow through responses he gives on a DVD Easter Egg. It's amazing, not only for the payoff that this random series of remarks actually makes up one part of a conversation but also for the way the Doctor describes how space and time work. And for the sheer amount of eccentricity crammed into it, for good measure.

There is probably no climax in the history of *Doctor Who* more emotional than that of 2006's "Doomsday." The Doctor and Rose have been separated forever in parallel universes. But the Doctor has the TARDIS harness the power of a dying sun to transmit himself for one last conversation. At first, they joke around, but eventually the reality that they won't see each other ever again sinks in. Rose admits that she loves the Doctor. And the Doctor, struggling to find the words says, "Rose Tyler, I . . ." before the link is ended. But we see on the Doctor's tear-streaked face what he was about to say. It's breathtaking.

Two Embarrassing Moments The Doctor's whole relationship with Martha Jones is . . . problematic, to put it politely. Martha clearly has a crush on the Doctor, but the Doctor is too busy obsessing about Rose to even notice. Nowhere is this more evident than in 2007's "The

Shakespeare Code" where, right in front of Martha, the Doctor starts musing aloud about what Rose would do in this instance. One thing's for sure, she wouldn't be an outright jerk like you, Doctor.

Throughout 2007's "Daleks in Manhattan"/"Evolution of the Daleks," the Doctor doesn't just react badly to the presence of the Daleks. He pretty much insists that they kill him, screaming at the pepperpots to zap him now. While he's trying to save lives, there's nothing about this that feels noble, and it's not even particularly revealing. It's just shouty and ridiculous.

Brilliant? (GB) It feels weird to admit this, because I've been a fan of *Doctor Who* since 1984, but when the tenth Doctor regenerated in a blaze of TARDIS-trashing glory in the final minutes of "The End of Time," I felt, for the first time ever, that my era of *Doctor Who* had come to a close.

What was it about the tenth Doctor that elicited this loyalty? This excitement? I can tell you the exact moment. It was the final scene of "The Girl in the Fireplace" that did it for me. When Rose asks the Doctor — after discovering Reinette had died having missed him — if he's all right, he says, "I'm always all right," and then fiddles with the TARDIS console, ignoring Rose altogether, living in a world of his own pain. It was an astonishing scene, and David Tennant managed to convey so much just by looking at a prop and absently flicking a switch.

And that's when I realized we were onto something special with the tenth Doctor.

The thing I love about David Tennant is his range. He plays a character with many facets ranging from the comic to the tragic, from the quiet to the totally overblown. And, really, that's the character of the Doctor right from the start of the Russell T Davies era. He has such versatility, from the outright comedic (I love the scene in "Smith and Jones" where he pretends to be a patient in a hospital and can't stop babbling about the cover story he's concocted for himself as a postman with bunions) to the quiet and introspective (I adore the Doctor's quiet conversion from atheist to agnostic as he abseils into the darkness in "The Satan Pit").

I will concede that, for his first season in particular, the garrulous goof was too much in ascendance and there wasn't enough of the moody and introspective. But then "Doomsday" happened. "Doomsday" was, for me, the moment when the tenth Doctor came into his own. Billie Piper is astonishing at capturing the reality of someone whose world suddenly, finally, collapses. David Tennant does that too, but he does it without histrionics, just intense silence, putting his head to a wall. It conveys the emotion, the humanity and the alienness of the Doctor all at once.

The thing about "Doomsday" is that it takes the Doctor to a place we've never seen him before: that precipice where he's brought to tears. Some might have thought it couldn't have been done, given the nature of the Doctor's character as aloof outsider. But David Tennant made it happen and never made it seem out of character. That's what I love about the tenth Doctor: he captures those tensions between being human and being alien. And through him, we find a Doctor with a rich emotional life.

The best of the tenth Doctor's era is when there are emotional stakes for him. "Gridlock" is all about the Doctor not just admitting he's a Time Lord, but recalling his long-dead people. The final scene where he does that is beautiful. "The Waters of Mars" sees the Doctor starting out as his cheery, motor-mouth self and ending in the worst possible place, mentally and spiritually. In "The End of Time," Tennant shows us a man desperate to avoid his end but then takes us to the next place: a man coming to accept his fate.

When I watched "The Day of the Doctor," one of the things I adored most was the mini-episode in the middle of it with the tenth Doctor and Elizabeth and a Zygon and a machine that goes "ding." Because, when it came down to it, the tenth Doctor era was my era of *Doctor Who*.

Second Opinion (RS?) What he sai—

No, wait. I couldn't disagree more.

It's not a popular opinion, but I really, really dislike David Tennant's tenth Doctor. Usually, I find something charming in every Doctor, but the tenth hits me the wrong way. And a large part of that is David Tennant himself.

Don't get me wrong, he's not all bad. But I find that, like Jon Pertwee, he's only good when he's pushed out of his comfort zone. So when he's playing a different character, as in "Human Nature," he's incredible. But so often, his role as the Doctor is just a default: he's a hyperactive child mixing emo with a stock trade in acting tics that don't scream "alien" to me; they scream "actor."

I think the real problem is that there's no "there" there. No real depth. He's a pretty actor, playing to the crowd. And his era has a secondary problem: the show was too successful. In its first year, the show was edgy and dangerous; no one knew if this crazy experiment would work, so they went all out. For the next four years, the show is a victim of its own success, giving us increasingly vanilla stories that feed off their own continuity. "The Stolen Earth" and "Journey's End" each occupied the top spot in the ratings, but the story is so muddled you'd be hard-pressed to explain what's going on, let alone care. It's just a series of crowd-pleasing bangs and flashes.

That, to me, is the Tennant era all over. Sure, it had some moments where it pushed against the vanilla, like the wonderfully angry "Love & Monsters" or the experimental "Blink" or "Human Nature." But too often we got stories like "The Doctor's Daughter" or "The Lazarus Experiment" or "Planet of the Ood" or "Silence in the Library." Stories where "good enough" was the watchword. Stories where boxes get ticked, where everybody pats themselves on the back and moves right along to the next serving of vanilla.

Don't get me wrong, there are some things I like. Martha is criminally underrated. Donna is as fantastic as everyone says. The Series Three arc is very clever. But I find that it's diminishing returns. Yes, even after "Doomsday." And I have a sneaking suspicion that the era isn't going to age very well.

By the time the tenth Doctor is railing at Wilf for needing to be saved, I just want him to go already. Which he does, about 3,000 hours later. But — and I'm fully aware that it's a minority view — for me, it wasn't a moment too soon.

Fortunately, the great thing about *Doctor Who* is that none of this matters a jot. Because if you don't like what's on at the moment, something else will be along presently. And if I loved every era of the show equally, then it wouldn't be trying hard enough. So even in my disliking of the tenth Doctor, I can find something to celebrate. And even vanilla can be tasty, once in a while.

The Girl in the Fireplace (2006)

Written by Steven Moffat

Directed by Euros Lyn

The Big Idea A disabled spaceship in the 51st century is connected to the life of Madame de Pompadour in eighteenth-century France. The Doctor investigates — and falls in love.

Brilliant? (GB) "Human Nature" writer Paul Cornell once told me in an interview about how, back in the days before the Modern Series was even thought up, he used to argue with Steven Moffat about the Doctor falling in love. Cornell felt romance went against the essence of the character; Moffat argued against that.

Guess who won that argument?

When this story first aired almost a decade ago, the idea that the Doctor could be involved in a love story was still genuinely controversial. The Paul McGann movie aside, the Doctor was asexual. Now the Doctor's had a wife he's snogged onscreen (and has allegedly had other wives as well). There's still something of a veil put up around the Doctor and romance (his relationships all seem remarkably chaste), but the idea that the Doctor can flirt and be romantically involved is much more a part of the DNA of the show today than it was in 2005.

Which brings me to "The Girl in the Fireplace." It's true, "The Doctor Dances" tests the ground by asking whether the Doctor . . . dances. And "The Parting of the Ways" gives us the Doctor kissing a companion. (Although he was exsanguinating time vortex energy, but whatever.) But "The Girl in the Fireplace" gives us the Doctor meeting a female throughout her life and, though the veil is drawn somewhat (we're still using dancing as a metaphor), falling in love.

In Reinette, we have the type of girl with whom the Doctor would become besotted. She's witty, forward, intelligent and surprising. She wends her way into the Doctor's heart because she sees things in him most don't; she understands how lonely he is.

She's the one in a trillion who gets in.

The argument against the Doctor being romantic is, in part, that he would become boring and heterosexual and it would be like Captain Kirk having a romance every week. But "The Girl in the Fireplace" is cleverer than that. The Doctor doesn't have a romance every week precisely because it would lead to the situation we see here. His relationships are fleeting by nature and by necessity. The time windows supercondense it, so the Doctor no sooner meets, encounters, saves and comes together with Reinette before discovering she's died. The argument can be made that this is a fling for the Doctor and a guiding relationship for Reinette. But then any relationship the Doctor has with a human will seem like a fling on his side, no matter what.

In the end, the Doctor is always alone.

Second Opinion (RS?) My co-author is married and I'm not, so be aware that we might have different perspectives on this. But I just don't agree that simply because a relationship is short, it's therefore just a fling. As, indeed, I think "The Girl in the Fireplace" proves. One of my most profound relationships lasted only two weeks, and it's not something I'd at all describe as a "fling."

No, I think the real reason the Doctor doesn't have relationships with humans is because it's creepy.

He's a 900-year-old Time Lord, so humans are more like children or pets to him: adorable creatures with much lower IQs and much shorter lifespans. Taking care of them = good. Macking on them = dodgy.

I'm all for romance in *Doctor Who*. Even when it involves the Doctor. But it should be a meeting of equals — River Song, for example. "The Girl in the Fireplace" tries its best to go there, with Reinette being exceptional for a human. But the fact that he meets her as a child ups the ick factor. Remember when Katie Holmes started dating Tom Cruise and gushed about how she'd fantasized about him as a 14-year-old? Or how Céline Dion's husband said he'd been deeply in love with her since she was 13 and he was her manager? Yeah. Like that. Because how different, really, is the child Reinette from the adult Reinette as far as the Doctor is concerned?

Humans falling in love with the Doctor, sure. Hell, my biggest problem with Rose in this story is that she is completely sidelined and her feelings about the Doctor and Reinette are never addressed, which is criminal. But to think that the biggest issue with the Doctor falling in love is that it might hurt *his* feelings, because he'll outlive his paramour, is missing the wood for the trees.

Oh, and there's also the cross-species thing, which I have no particular opinion of except to ask this: would we be shipping this story in the same way if the romance was between the Doctor and Arthur the horse?

Gridlock (2007)

Written by Russell T Davies

Directed by Richard Clark

The Big Idea And you thought your commute was bad: deep under New New York, people live in cars that take years to travel just a few miles.

Brilliant? (RS?) There's a joke in "Gridlock" just for Classic Series fans: the appearance of the Macra. They were giant crabs, last seen in 1967, in a story that no longer exists. "Gridlock" needed a monster in the basement, so it plucked a random creature that most people wouldn't have heard of and threw it in for a throwaway laugh.

Or did it?

The story of "The Macra Terror" might sound somewhat familiar if you've seen this episode. There's a society with a secret that's spoken of in rumours. Announcements from smiling figureheads who appear only on monitors. Collective singing on the part of the populace to keep them content with their otherwise sorry lot. Something hideous lurking deep within the gas.

Except that "Gridlock" takes this starting point and turns it around. Because although the Macra are indeed lurking in the gas, they're not actually responsible for what's happened. Instead, the revelation of the motorway's true function is utterly delicious, overturning every expectation you had and making "Gridlock" into something magnificent.

So if you were an old-school, dyed-in-the-wool fan, you might have watched the first half of "Gridlock" and thought you knew what this story was all about. And then had the rug entirely pulled out from under you, because what we got was far sadder and far cleverer.

Of course, the real genius of this joke is that the audience for it is vanishingly small. "The Macra Terror" is about as obscure a *Doctor Who* story as you can get, hailing from the black-and-white era, with only still photographs and an audio track in existence and no returning monsters. So the number of people to have fallen for that would have been a very select group indeed. Ahem.

And, really, it's the backstory that makes "Gridlock." It has a lot of it, but because we're told so much retroactively, it's rather remarkable. A society that buys moods. The virus wiping out the population. The Senate acting within minutes. This adds a depth that wouldn't be present otherwise.

Some people have complained that what we're being told about sounds far more exciting than what we actually see onscreen, but that's solely because nothing can compete with your imagination. You might read *Lord of the Rings* and wish it were *The Silmarillion* . . . up until the point where you actually attempt to read *The Silmarillion*.

"Gridlock" simultaneously taps into our imaginations and reconfigures a tale from *Doctor Who*'s mythology. It builds on the earlier work to give us something with real depth — and trusts our imaginations to do the rest.

And if that isn't a description of what makes *Doctor Who* great, I don't know what is.

Second Opinion (GB) In all honesty, I cheered when I saw the Macra but didn't get all obsessive like *some* of us did. Ahem.

But then I was probably more distracted by watching Sally Calypso leading all the travellers in the daily contemplation of singing "The Old Rugged Cross." It's a song about the faithful clinging to the symbol of their faith, experiencing humility and receiving a divine reward.

In a scene where the Doctor is desperately trying to get Brannigan and his fellow drivers to realize there is nothing out there, this song should be the *coup de grâce* on what also should be a very on-the-nose critique of religion. But it's not. Because, in a scene where everyone is supposed to be singing a hymn to someone who died five billion years earlier, we have Brannigan saying, "You think you know us so well, Doctor. But we're not abandoned. Not while we have each other."

Singing "The Old Rugged Cross" in this context is about the connection between *people*. The same is true for the beautiful closing scene where the Doctor works through his painful memories and tells

Martha about his destroyed home planet while "Abide with Me" plays. In both cases, the hymns become something that they weren't — or maybe something they already were, but we just didn't know it.

"Gridlock" is one of those stories where, each time you watch it, you get something new from it. It's not just great *Doctor Who*; it's great art.

Human Nature/The Family of Blood (2007)

Written by Paul Cornell

Directed by Charles Palmer

The Big Idea In order to avoid detection by an alien species known only as the Family, the Doctor becomes human and lives life as a schoolteacher named John Smith in 1913. Only it doesn't go according to plan.

Brilliant? (GB) This week's episode of *Mr. Smith* is particularly poignant, though utterly confusing.

The period details of the drama continue to just feel right. From Martha and Jenny having to drink outside the pub and Smith's casual willingness to allow Tim's beating to the dance and the caste system that exists within boys' schools, a genuine attempt is being made to capture a "warts and all" picture of 1913, with a limited number of anachronisms.

It's now quite clear that Martha, his maid, is in love with Smith, but he refuses to acknowledge her (a strong comment on the racial prejudices of the era). And Smith is breaking Martha's heart, because he's started to notice Joan. Watching the romance between Smith and Joan unfold is beautiful. Joan both connives her way into getting a date and shows profound vulnerability at the remembrance of her husband dying in Spion Kop. Smith is hesitant and yet gains confidence the more he interacts with Joan. The two perform a beautiful dance (both figuratively and literally in the episode), around which we have the stories of Martha and Tim circling.

And then it all becomes bloody confusing.

In the midst of this drama, why do we have spaceships and a family that can harvest humans and take them over as puppets?!? This is a beautiful period drama, full of honest emotion, about a history teacher who has strange dreams. Why on earth are there aliens?

Then comes the revelation that Smith is not Smith at all. He's actually the figure he writes about in his book of dreams. He's apparently some incredible, godlike force of nature who can topple civilizations and fight monsters. Smith has to choose to become this man all over again. And I don't know what to make of it all. The whole thing is preposterous. Smith isn't even a particularly courageous man. (He arms children to fight an alien menace!)

That's not to say that it isn't poignant. Hutchison weeping as he fires the Vickers gun while the hymn "He Who Would Valiant Be" is sung in the background causes chills down your spine and a lump in your throat. And Martha — who is apparently some kind of medical student from the future (what?!?) — instructing Joan on the bones of the hand is stirring.

While this finale for *Mr. Smith* goes in an odd direction, Smith's sacrifice in the middle of all this insanity is deeply moving. What Smith does shows the extraordinary courage that scared, frail, ordinary human beings can muster. And it is beautiful.

I hope this "Doctor" is half the man Smith was.

Second Opinion (RS?) There's another version of Paul Cornell's "Human Nature" out there that you might have heard about but may not have experienced. It's very similar: the Doctor hides out as a human in a remote village just before the First World War and has an unlikely romance, while aliens lay siege to a boarding school. It was published in the mid '90s in the New Adventures line of *Doctor Who* novels and, even among the stupendous stories in that series, it's a standout.

However, there are some major differences between the two versions. And I'm not just talking about the fact that one of them is a novel.

The 1995 version stars the seventh Doctor. So, immediately, the romance takes on a different tone, because it's between two middle-aged people, at least one of whom is less than good-looking. Swapping the lead role for someone who looks like David Tennant makes the romance a lot more likely to happen than if it featured a confirmed bachelor in his fifties.

Second, the novel works so well because the Doctor was otherwise asexual back then. Seriously. It's hard to convey just how powerful the idea of the Doctor (or someone with his face) falling in love was. Two reviews above, my co-author mentions Paul Cornell's take on romance in the series; he believes *Doctor Who* should star an asexual Doctor. This novel was his attempt to make it work. And by golly it does.

Unfortunately, the TV version loses something by starring David Tennant, a man the ladies swarm over every other week. Even the subplot has the Doctor's companion pining for him, because that's the house style by this point. Much of the contrast is lost with the TV version.

The other thing that suffers is the ending. When Smith returns to his seventh incarnation in the novel, the reason the Doctor has no interest in Joan is because he isn't wired that way. In the TV version, not a whole lot actually changes once the Doctor is a Time Lord again, so the writers contrive a different reason for Joan not to travel with him and be his girlfriend.

Don't get me wrong, I love the televised "Human Nature" with a passion. See my love letter to it in *Who Is The Doctor*. Or in *Who's 50*. Or note that it's the only story we included here that was in both previous books, because we felt it was that crucial. And many of the other details of the novel (the villains were atrocious) have been smoothed out for the TV version, which is a superb production that never fails to make me cry. It's just a shame that the romance, which is so central, isn't as powerful as it once was.

Partners in Crime (2008)

Written by Russell T Davies

Directed by James Strong

The Big Idea Donna Noble has been searching for the Doctor and finally finds him investigating an alien plot . . . to reproduce through a human weight-loss product.

Brilliant? (GB) You know what I miss? I miss Russell T Davies's season openers. Because they were about showcasing that year's companion in front of a big and sometimes bonkers premise. Here we have weight-loss pills that create creatures from human fat. But let's not look too hard at that.

Instead, let's look at the genius of the first 15 minutes, in which the Doctor and Donna just keep missing each other. The scene with their heads popping up in the sea of cubicles at different times is great farce. Or the laugh-out-loud brilliant scene of the Doctor and Donna's wordless exchange when they finally do meet — which is capped off when it's revealed that Miss Foster is watching them have this increasingly elaborate, mimed conversation.

There's great drama too: Donna stays in the same position as her mother, Sylvia, moves around the room ranting about Donna over what we presume to be a long duration, which says everything about their relationship. And there's Donna's conversation with Wilf where she admits she's been looking for the Doctor; she allows herself a smile and we know the desire of her heart. Miss Foster is a great villain, and the episode has a really fun chase sequence in the middle of it.

Sure, the premise is about as wafer thin as the mint that exploded Mr. Creosote in *Monty Python's Meaning of Life*. But this Russell T Davies season opener is there to make us love Donna Noble, to have the Doctor realize he needs to travel with a companion again and to get us having a good time (and even to start up that year's story arc). God, I've missed these.

Second Opinion (RS?) What he said. I couldn't agree more. I'd just like to add the moment when, Wile E. Coyote–like, Miss Foster hovers briefly in mid-air before plunging to the ground. That's hilarious.

Oh, and the other thing I miss about Russell T Davies's big-band productions is just how nasty they can be, within the comic elements. When Donna visits Stacey and asks if she's going on a date, Stacey, who's a large girl but has recently lost weight, says she's going to do the opposite: she can do better now, so she's going to dump her boyfriend. That's a vicious, but not implausible, indictment of our culture's attitude to body size.

That's what I miss about Russell T Davies. Not just the gonzo ideas and the hilarious comedy, but the way he slips the knife between the ribs just as you're laughing. It hurts, but it's genius.

Midnight (2008)

Written by Russell T Davies

Directed by Alice Troughton

The Big Idea There's something outside the bus, but that's not the Doctor's biggest problem. Inside is something far more dangerous: scared, paranoid humans.

Brilliant? (RS?) Back in *Who's 50*, we had a problem. We tried to include stories from just about every important era of *Doctor Who*. But we missed one: Series Four of the modern show. We missed Donna Noble entirely.

The problem wasn't the lack of good stories. "Turn Left" and "Midnight" are great. But they split up the Doctor and companion, so that neither contains any significant interaction between the two (which was generally a highlight of that season). So we made the difficult decision to leave these out.

Fortunately, since this is a book that's focused on the Doctor as a character, we can turn to "Midnight." One of the *Doctor Who* stories you probably should watch before you die. Because it's utterly superb.

I've complained before that I only like David Tennant when he's pushed out of his comfort zone. Happily, "Midnight" goes all out to do this, and the results are superb. The mirror-speak scene between the Doctor and Sky is just astonishing, in both conception and execution. But it's merely the highlight in a story that has something fundamental to say about the Doctor as a character.

Specifically, this story turns the Doctor upside down. He's someone who can usually swan in, be outrageous and eccentric, blithely skip past the fact that he doesn't even have a name and defeat aliens simply by knowing more than anyone else does. In fact, he does this so effortlessly, you start to assume he must be generating some sort of low-level telepathic field that gets people to trust him. Here, every single one of those things works against him. People simply reject his crap. The issue of his name becomes a serious — and dangerous — sticking point. The fact that he's smarter than everyone else in the room is a liability, not an asset. And his amusing eccentricities at the beginning come back to haunt him.

The result is TV you can't take your eyes off. The characters on the bus are terrifying, not because they're evil (they're not; each has moments of goodness and moments when they're less than perfect) but because they're so achingly human. And if the Doctor ever encountered any such humans in real life, that would be very, very dangerous indeed.

Fortunately, *Doctor Who* is just a TV show.

Second Opinion (GB) I saw "Midnight" for the first time when I was visiting my parents, watching it while my dad was doing something in the adjacent kitchen. My dad doesn't watch *Doctor Who* all that often.

Ten minutes in, he was hovering just outside the room, still watching.

Thirty minutes in, he decided to go upstairs to get something and then sort of sat on the stairs and kept watching.

When it was over, he said, "That was really unsettling."

Which pretty much proves everything my co-author just said. "Midnight" is deeply disturbing . . . but it's television you can't take your eyes off. And I love it for that.

The Eleventh Doctor

Really Old, Really Kind and Alone

(2010–2013)

Basic Data

First story: "The Eleventh Hour" (2010)

Final story: "The Time of the Doctor" (2013)

Final appearance: "Deep Breath" (2014)

The Changing Face of *Doctor Who* Russell T Davies was gone and the era of his successor, Steven Moffat — already an established producer in his own right, with hit shows such as *Press Gang* and *Coupling* under his belt — began with a clear deck: new executive producers working with him, as well as a new Doctor and a new companion.

When it came to casting the Doctor, Moffat was leaning towards someone in his forties when 26-year-old Matt Smith (who'd met Moffat a few weeks earlier when he'd auditioned for the part of Watson on *Sherlock*) walked into the audition room and blew everyone away. The new team had found their new Doctor.

Moffat wanted a darker style for the show, aiming initially for a fairytale-like quality. He also had a free hand to cast the new companion and so dispensed with the revolving door of annual companions, instead bringing Karen Gillan (and then Arthur Darvill) on board for three years. Given the new style, it was also decided that other aspects of the show should be overhauled, meaning a new title sequence, a new TARDIS interior, a new sonic screwdriver and even a St. John's Ambulance badge on the TARDIS door. (That wasn't quite new, but rather a callback to the TARDIS's look with the first Doctor.) In fact, just about the only major player who stayed on between production teams was musician Murray Gold. This meant that the miracle had happened again: *Doctor Who* had regenerated itself, both in front of the camera and behind it.

Moffat's approach was, at first, somewhat similar to Davies's, with story arcs developing around a recurring meme. However, in Series Six, he changed it up by having a season-long mystery surrounding the murder of the Doctor that involved the origins of the Doctor's wife, River Song, and the organization known as the Silence. This resulted in a more novel-like approach to the season, with standalone episodes mixing in with the ongoing story arc. To achieve this, Moffat selected from an impressive pool of writers — past writers from the series, top television writers and showrunners from other series. (The only person who does not fit in any of these categories is Neil Gaiman.)

While the fifth season was broadcast in one uninterrupted block, none of remaining seasons of Matt Smith's tenure were: episodes were shown in partial seasons of six or seven episodes, with extended gaps between them. (There was a nine-month gap between the 2011 Christmas special and the start of the first half of Series Seven.)

Matt Smith announced his departure in the middle of 2013, a few months after production wrapped on the fiftieth anniversary special, which saw David Tennant return to the role (and introduced John Hurt). The 2013 Christmas special would see a new Doctor to welcome the series into its next 50 years . . .

Who is Matt Smith? Only 26 when he was cast, Matt Smith was by far the youngest Doctor to date. His casting was the first big "event" casting for a new actor to play the Doctor, with a special documentary made that teased the audience for some time, before revealing his name partway through. The documentary aired in the middle of the afternoon on January 2, 2009, and pulled in over six million viewers.

Matt Smith originally had his heart set on being a professional footballer, but an injury precluded that. He turned to acting, with his first television appearance a mere three years before being cast as the Time Lord. He had a prominent role in *Party Animals* and even appeared as a client to Billie Piper's sex worker character in *The Secret Diary of a Call Girl*. His lead role as the Doctor was only his seventh role on television.

To prepare for the part, Smith watched episodes of the Classic Series and was particularly taken with Patrick Troughton's performance. Consequently, he decided to play the part as a largely asexual, bumbling professor type. He eschewed the suggestions to dress in hipper garb and settled on a tweed jacket and tie. Steven Moffat — a Classic Series fan from way back — could hardly refuse.

As the Doctor, Smith quickly won both acclaim and awards, including a BAFTA for Best Actor and a National Television Award for Outstanding Drama Performance. After completing his work on *Doctor Who*, Smith followed the call to Hollywood, with parts in *Terminator Genisys* and *Pride and Prejudice and Zombies*. Interestingly, Smith shares a birthday with one of the authors of this volume and the wife of the other. We bet you were just dying to know that.

Top Companion This Doctor met Amelia Pond when she was a child and then spent most of his travelling days with grownup Amy Pond. Sure, he also travelled with Mr. Pond, a.k.a. Rory Williams, and latterly with Clara, but it's Amy who always had his back. She spent her entire youth with the Doctor on her mind, waiting for him for years at a time, but he always came back for her. She was interested in him sexually at first, but they soon morphed into best friends, albeit friends who weren't afraid of snarky comebacks with each other. A married couple as companions was a new trope for *Doctor Who*, although there was a sense that Amy had not one but two "boys." And, at the end of his life, it's fitting that one of the last things the eleventh Doctor sees is a vision of Amy.

Classic Foe The Silence are first mentioned in the eleventh Doctor's debut story. They hover all over his first season. Their confessional priests, the Silents, appear in his second, with the ability to make you forget all about them when you're not looking at them. At first, it seems that they're part of a larger organization, the Silence, which seeks to bring about the Doctor's death, so that his true name won't be spoken on the fields of Trenzalore. To do so, they brainwash River Song into bringing about the Doctor's death as a fixed point. Later, when the Doctor remains on the planet Trenzalore, refusing to reveal his name in order to prevent Gallifrey from coming into this universe and starting a bloody war, it is revealed that the Church of the Silence formed in response to the Doctor's refusal to speak. It turns out that the Doctor was bedevilled at the beginning of his eleventh incarnation by a schism of the organization created near the end of it.

Who is the Doctor? Where the fifth and tenth Doctors were old men stuck in the bodies of young men, the eleventh Doctor is something altogether different. He initially seems like a return to the Classic Doctors of old, wearing a tweed jacket and bow tie and rejecting his companion's amorous advances. But, like everything else about him, it's not so straightforward.

This is a Doctor who starts out in one direction and then twists. He does this on just about every level. For an apparently asexual Doctor, he's something of a ladies man (though an adorably awkward one). For an outwardly old soul, he's also childlike and playful. Even his conversation starts out in one direction and then goes in another midflow, as though he's changing his mind or arguing with himself. For example, in 2010's "The Time of Angels," when River says that looking for a Weeping Angel among statues is like looking for a needle in a haystack, he says, "A needle that looks like hay. A hay-like needle of death. A hay-like needle of death in a haystack of, er, statues. No, yours was fine."

This twisting extends to disobeying the rules. He defines coolness not by fitting in but through sheer force of personality. Bow ties become cool simply because he repeats the mantra enough. Likewise with fezzes and Stetsons. And he avoids his own death, despite it being a fixed point, through a clever, last-minute cheat. Even his own demise, as the final incarnation of the Doctor, breaks the rules as he gets a new regeneration cycle in 2013's "The Time of the Doctor."

He's also a Doctor who bonds heavily with his companions — perhaps more than is healthy. Amy becomes his One True Companion on account of hers being the first face that his eleventh face saw. When Amy is kidnapped by clerics in 2011's "A Good Man Goes to War," the Doctor gets angry enough to assemble an army. He spends most of his time returning to Amy's life, even seeding clues for her to notice while he spends 200 years alone (2011's "The Impossible Astronaut") and then cohabiting with her and Rory in 2012's "The Power of Three." And when Amy and Rory are finally and irrevocably separated from him, he goes into a major depression, removing himself from the world in 2012's "The Snowmen," with only a reference back to Amy (when Clara says, "Pond") able to bring him out of himself. Later, he decides that Clara is only worth investigating because she's the impossible girl and hence the only mystery worth solving. This is a noticeable change from previous Doctors, who were able to move on from companions much more quickly.

On the other hand, he rebuffs Amy's advances in 2010's "Flesh and Stone," because he's seen how this sort of thing can ruin relationships. He brings Rory on board the TARDIS because he genuinely wants Amy and Rory to work out as a couple. He seems to be at his best when larking about the universe with his two best friends, though that may just be a sign of his codependency.

This Doctor not only has companions but also a wife, River Song, who turns out to be Amy and Rory's daughter — but who's had Time Lord qualities imbued in her from being conceived in the TARDIS. (Don't think about it too much.) While the "marriage" between them is dubious (the ceremony was a sham to get River to stop destroying time and involved her marrying a robot facsimile of the Doctor), the Doctor treats it as though it means something to him, even telling River that seeing her after her death would hurt him too much, and she apparently knows the Doctor's real name.

The eleventh Doctor gets something that only two of his previous incarnations had: a chance to die of old age. His final adventure sees him living and growing old over the course of 700 or so years. Perhaps it's no wonder that he lets that youthful aspect go for his next regeneration.

Three Great Moments It's the end of 2010's "The Eleventh Hour," and the Doctor has finally defeated Prisoner Zero, thanks to being very clever. He's saved the planet, won over Amy and made the viewer forget that his predecessor even existed. And then he goes to the hospital rooftop and calls the Atraxi back. In the middle of a costume-change scene! He asks the Atraxi if the Earth poses any threat to them, whereupon they examine scenes of war and nuclear devastation . . . and answer no. Then he tells them that others have come here, so the Atraxi examine scenes of Daleks, Cybermen and so on invading Earth. And, finally, he asks what happened to them. So the Atraxi show scenes of all ten previous incarnations . . . at which point, the eleventh Doctor steps through the bubble, costume complete, and says, "Basically, run." And they do! It's sheer magnificence and it shows us why the eleventh Doctor is here to stay.

The assembled armies of the galaxy have converged on Earth in 2010's "The Pandorica Opens," wanting the greatest weapon in the universe. The Doctor leaps up onto a stone and, talking into a communicator, tells the assembled spaceships to stop whizzing around. He then shouts, "Could you all just stay still a minute because I. Am. Talking!" And they stop! He then makes an amazing speech, one for the ages. Informing his enemies that he has no plan, no backup and nothing to lose, he tells them to do that smart thing: let someone else try first. Whereupon they all back off. You would too, wouldn't you?

It's the climactic moment of 2013's "The Day of the Doctor." The three Doctors — the tenth, eleventh and the warrior — have decided to avoid making the mistake that was made before and instead fly their TARDIS into Gallifrey's lower atmosphere, planning to freeze it in time. The war council objects, saying that the calculations alone would take hundreds of years. To which the Doctors reply that they started a very long time ago — and that they've been doing this all their lives. And suddenly, all the Doctors are there, the first saying words he never said, like "Gallifrey." The Time Lord general notes that all 12 Doctors are present. But his lieutenant points out that there are, in fact, 13. And so Peter Capaldi (or his eyebrows, at any rate) makes his debut appearance in *Doctor Who*, capping off an extraordinary sequence in the fiftieth anniversary, one to please old and new fans alike.

Two Embarrassing Moments "Victory of the Daleks" (2010) has a lot to answer for. We'd like to claim the ridiculous spitfires — in space!!! — as just about the most embarrassing moment in the Modern Series. You've got Second World War pilots who get trained for space flight in ten minutes, plot logic thrown out the window and the absurd visual of spitfires shooting at a Dalek spaceship. Except . . . as goofy as the sequence and the concept are, they're actually nothing compared to the New Paradigm Daleks, which are the real embarrassment. They're lumbering and hunched, come in bathtub-friendly colours and don't look scary in the slightest, undoing decades of the world's coolest design in one fell swoop. Now that's embarrassing.

When the Weeping Angels start possessing existing statues in 2012's "The Angels Take Manhattan," it's scary. The cherubs are frightening because they're half-lit and burble like terrifying babies. But the entire point of the Weeping Angels (hint: it's even in their name) is that they can't move when seen. So the idea that they possess the Statue of Liberty — which isn't even a stone statue but is made of bronze — and take it for a joyride through a harbour, around some streets and up to an apartment block without anyone noticing — in a city that we're explicitly told never sleeps — is nonsensical. Plus, it just looks dumb.

Cool? (RS?)

Dear Matt,

Thank you. No, really, thank you. Thank you for being you.

You see, I was starting to lose the faith. The tenth Doctor never did it for me, so I began to think that maybe I was out of touch with *Doctor Who* for today's generation. But then you burst onto the scene and blew me away. Not only that, but you showed me that the character of the Doctor wasn't just a series of exaggerated acting tics, but could actually be mysterious and eccentric and, well, alien.

I still can't believe you were only 26 when all this started. You carry the wisdom of acting choices far beyond your years. In fact, those choices still boggle my mind. The way you size yourself up to Jeff in "The Eleventh Hour," subtly indicating that you're still "cooking." The way you inflect on "The Doctor will see you n-o-o-o-w!" at the end of that story, taking the climactic moment and making it odd, yet never foolish. The way you perform the "I. Am. Talking!" speech in "The Pandorica Opens" like a man who's had too much to drink at a wedding. Again and again, you make choices that are off the wall, interesting and downright strange . . . but it works.

Oh boy, does it work. You have a physicality that means you're never sitting still, never just a piece of background furniture, but never overdoing it either. I have no idea how you keep that balance, but it works amazingly well. You simultaneously portray the Doctor as childlike, romantic, ancient and bizarre. I'm astonished at how well you shade your performance so that these things work in tandem, often in the same scene. Sometimes even in the same moment.

Look at something like "Let's Kill Hitler," which is really just a comedy existing solely to justify its title. You do madcap zaniness at the beginning, treat the moment with Hitler in the cupboard as sensitively as it's possible to do in such a situation, throw in physical comedy with the top hat and cane — and give us enormous pathos as you lie dying, yet willing the fledgling River to step up to the moral plate. It's an astonishing range that takes a silly story about a time-travel cliché and turns it into something truly great.

Or the way you light up the screen in "Closing Time," giving us laugh-out-loud comedy as you attempt to hold down a job or insult Craig via translations from a baby, as though you're in some sort of improv master class. And then you pull the rug out from under us at the end as you prepare to meet your death, conveying an infinite sadness. That should sit badly at the tail end of a comedic episode, but you make it work.

Perhaps one of my favourite moments is in "The Day of the Doctor," when all three Doctors are about to press the red button in a scene that's shot from above. John Hurt's hand is on the button, while David Tennant simply reaches out for it.

But you don't do that. Instead, your arm hovers, wracked with indecision. You convey so much about where the Doctor's thoughts are in that moment and you do it with only an arm. That's incredible.

When you were first cast, a lot of people were sceptical. They said that you were just a good-looking lead cast to appeal to the youth demographic. Or that we'd never see an older Doctor again. But there were others who'd known that Steven Moffat had been interested in casting older, and who had wondered just what it was about you that had made him change his mind. After we first saw you onscreen, there were no more sceptics.

The comparisons are always made to Patrick Troughton — and for good reason. Not just for the look but because Troughton is the standout actor of the Classic Doctors, the one we point to as having brought something truly special to the role, something far more subtle and nuanced than the show probably deserved. With your tenure as the Doctor, we got to have that again. Most actors who play the Doctor are bringing the sheer force of their personalities to the role, and that's a perfectly fine thing to do. But occasionally, about once in a generation, we get an actor like you, who's bringing so much more.

So I want to say thanks. Thanks for raising the bar on our little show and lending your talents to it. We were probably lucky to get you when we did, because I'm sure you're off to bigger and better things in the future. Frankly, it'll be a sad world if you aren't. But, for a little while, we got to have Matt Smith as our Doctor. And for that, I'll always be incredibly grateful.

Sincerely.
Your greatest fan.
Robert Smith?
(no relation, except for a birthday)

Second Opinion (GB) I should feel too guilty after that outpouring of sentiment to actually criticize the eleventh Doctor and Matt Smith's performance, but my co-author just spent the last entry, after I declared the tenth Doctor's era my era of *Who*, ~~barking at the moon like a lunatic~~ calling the tenth Doctor ultimately forgettable and vanilla. So I'm not going to feel guilty.

Here's the thing about the eleventh Doctor and Matt Smith's performance: when it's on, it's on. When it's off, it's *really* off.

Mostly it's on. And I love the eleventh Doctor when he's there. Every moment Robert mentioned above, yeah, he's pretty much in the zone. And he hasn't mentioned my favourite eleventh Doctor story, "The God Complex," where the Doctor, helpless, has to watch as his friend is claimed by the mania that will eventually kill her. And then later has to quietly break his best friend's faith so it doesn't happen again. Or the brilliant comedic scene when he's discovered by the Secret Service in the Oval Office in "The Impossible Astronaut." Or the staggeringly beautiful scene in "Vincent and the Doctor" where he has to explain to Amy that, even though Vincent killed himself, there's still a pile of good things and a pile of bad things. Or that haunting scene in "The Power of Three" when he gives one of his best speeches: "I'm not running away from things; I am running to them before they flare and fade forever."

When it's working, it really works. I watched all of "The Day of Doctor" and never once thought that the eleventh Doctor was the youngest person in the room. That's amazing. Oh, and huge props to Matt Smith's stylist. Watch the earliest episodes: his hair is so floppy that he looks too young. Someone had the bright idea to slick his hair back, which makes his face look angular, and he reads as much older.

All that is wonderful. The problem is, there's another eleventh Doctor, the one we don't talk about. The one who flaps his arms and moves around awkwardly and thinks that talking louder and sounding alarmed is in any way interesting. He's around in stories like "The Curse of the Black Spot" or "The Doctor, The Widow and the Wardrobe" or the other parts of "The Power of Three" that weren't the speech I mentioned above. Basically, any story Matt Smith is bored with, and, by extension, knows the viewers will be bored with. It's in these stories where Smith inevitably — I'm sorry, Robert, but this is where my truth is gonna hurt you — pulls a series of exaggerated acting tics, instead of being mysterious and eccentric and, well, alien.

Fortunately, however, most of the eleventh Doctor's era is taken with the "good" eleventh Doctor, who modulates the manic shouty bits with quieter, more beautiful scenes. And that's how I choose to remember him.

The Eleventh Hour (2010)

Written by Steven Moffat

Directed by Adam Smith

The Big Idea Prisoner Zero has escaped through a crack in a little girl's bedroom. The Doctor has arrived, but is he too late?

Cool? (GB) On my podcast, *Reality Bomb*, we recently interviewed a bunch of kids about *Doctor Who*, and one of them, an 11-year-old, said his favourite story was "The Eleventh Hour." And my co-author has a torrid love affair with this story that's so passionate I don't even want to get into it. I have several friends who now use it, and not "Rose," as the "gateway" story into the Modern Series for those new to *Who*.

I just like it a lot. And I sort of feel at a disadvantage. But I think I get what it is that causes so many people to love this story passionately.

First of all, there's the astonishing way the new Doctor establishes himself as a character just by eating a bunch of food he doesn't like. His treatment of a plate of bread and butter is comedy gold. Matt Smith is simply amazing playing someone that eccentric.

In fact, Matt Smith is several varieties of awesome throughout this story, culminating in a wonderful speech where he tells the Atraxi to stay away from Earth. (And what kind of geeks would we be if we didn't cheer as the Doctor struts in front of a slideshow of his past incarnations in his new costume, affirming that he is the Doctor?)

But what really makes "The Eleventh Hour" work is the relationship between the Doctor and Amelia. The 12-year jump makes Amy not some random stranger but someone who has already had a relationship with the Doctor, who has expectations of him. That's really clever writing.

Then there are all the charming flourishes, such as the text to Amy's phone saying "duck," followed by the fire engine ladder crashing through a window, and the amazing sequence where we see all the things the Doctor has noticed in the village green. Which is not only really cool in its execution, it's a lovely visual illustration of how observant and clever the Doctor really is.

Hmmm. Thinking about it, I think I might love "The Eleventh Hour" as much as everyone else after all.

Second Opinion (RS?) My co-author is right: I love this story with a passion. And part of the reason for that is the pacing. That's the glue that holds this story together. Just when you've met the wacky fish-fingers-and-custard-eating new Doctor, he blindsides Amelia by telling her that, given how unafraid of everything she is, that must be one hell of a crack in her wall. Which leads into the Doctor's investigation, which leads to him running off in the TARDIS, which leads to the time jump, which . . .

The whole episode is like that. It runs so fast that you barely have time to breathe. What you definitely don't have time for is to wonder if you like this new guy or not. Because it's all moving at such an intense pace that you're caught up in the story and the action and the timey-wimeyness and the characters and the wordplay and the visuals and —

Sorry, where was I?

By the time the Doctor appears on the roof of the hospital, telling off a second group of all-powerful aliens, you want to cheer from the high heavens. I've used this to introduce *Doctor Who* to new fans and non-fans alike. Every single one of them has been swept up from the outset. (The trick, of course, is what to show them next. "The Beast Below" is actually an okay choice, but you can also skip along to "The Time of Angels." Only show people "Victory of the Daleks" if you have a contract written in blood that commits them to watching the entire season.)

"The Eleventh Hour" is a story that starts with a blank slate and becomes the essence of what *Doctor Who* is and can be within an hour. Though, to be honest, it's paced so fast that it feels like 20 minutes.

The God Complex (2011)

Written by Toby Whithouse

Directed by Nick Hurran

The Big Idea A hotel with constantly changing corridors contains rooms with your worst fears and is stalked by a creature that feeds off your faith.

Cool? (RS?) There's an alternate universe where this was Amy and Rory's last story, and the Doctor travelled on with Rita.

And if we lived in that universe, "The God Complex" would have been a fitting end to Amy and Rory's arc. There's a moment, when the Doctor is essentially asking Rita to be his new companion, that he has a realization. He says that if you offer a child a suitcase full of sweets, then they'll take it. Offer them all of time and space and how could they say no? Even as he basically offers the same thing to Rita, he makes the self-aware observation that this is why there should be grownups.

The entire rest of the story sees the Doctor attempting to be a grownup. He's not very good at it, but he's trying.

First, he breaks Amy's faith in him. Not by lying to her, the way the seventh Doctor did to break Ace's faith in "The Curse of Fenric." Instead, he kicks her out of the nest by telling the truth: that he took her on board because he was vain and wanted to be adored. Then he makes a grownup decision to leave Amy and Rory on Earth, only he doesn't really understand how humans work, so he simply buys them a house and a shiny car. Which, as any parent will tell you, is what you'd love to do for your kids . . . only you shouldn't, because it's not healthy.

The story's title, while an amusing pun, is also directly used to describe the Doctor. Likewise, the minotaur's description of the Doctor as "an ancient creature, drenched in the blood of the innocent, drifting in space" indicates that this is a story that's deeply concerned with questioning the way the Doctor operates. Rather than tying into Series Six's plot arc of the Doctor's death, it instead postulates that "for such a creature, death would be a gift." Which is both nasty and powerful.

Of course, in that alternate universe, Rita joins the Doctor — not because she's an adoring child who doesn't know any better, but because she's one of the cleverest people the Doctor's met. And the most self-assured. And possibly has the best smile too. Excuse me, I need a moment . . .

It turns out that there's life in the Amy and Rory arc yet: their near divorce in "Asylum of the Daleks" gives them back some meaty story, while their eventual departure is emotionally satisfying, even if it's a mess, plotwise. But the universe that saw the Doctor be the grownup and walk away from his best friends for good, because that was his way of saving them, is a worthwhile one too. It stars a Doctor who's emotionally healthier than the one we have, and it also features some cracking adventures with Rita, surely the best one-off guest companion the Modern Series has ever produced.

It's a shame we don't live there, actually.

Second Opinion (GB) What he said. I want to live in that alternate universe, actually.

The Snowmen (2012)

Written by Steven Moffat

Directed by Saul Metzstein

The Big Idea Intelligent snow has come to Earth and created deadly snowmen. The Doctor is on hand . . . only he's retired and lives on a cloud.

Cool? (RS?) This is just about the darkest we ever see the Doctor get. Having lost Amy and Rory, he completely abandons any notion of helping save the universe, even forsaking his bow tie for much of the story. The Paternoster Gang (Madame Vastra, Jenny and Strax) try to keep things running in his absence, but we see the Doctor going through a major depression.

And with little wonder, because this is just about the unluckiest story he's ever encountered.

Almost everything that happens causes the Doctor to lose ground. His attempts to remain secluded are ruined by Clara's curiosity. His confrontation with the ice governess causes Clara's death. His attempt to destroy the living snow only results in the creation of the Great Intelligence. He bargains with the universe that he'll return to helping if it lets Clara live . . . but she dies anyway. The only way the plot is resolved is by there being so much sadness that tears wash away the snow.

And so we see the Doctor hurting badly. Worse, he's just recovered from that hurt enough to trust again — and that trust is then deeply broken when Clara falls off the cloud. Just about his only unambiguous victory is the death of Simeon, but a) the Doctor didn't cause that and b) even then, Simeon is back next episode anyway.

The opening scene shows that there's not much daylight between

Simeon the lonely boy, refusing to play with others, and the Doctor, hiding away from his friends on a cloud. And the adult Simeon is what the Doctor could easily become: bitter and lonely, locked away with something out of this world but unable to find the joy in it.

By the end, the only thing sustaining the Doctor is the mystery of Clara. Little wonder he runs away and hides in a monastery in the following episode.

However, there's something larger going on here. Namely, the Doctor is actively allowing himself to mourn. And when he finally steps out of that grief, he'll be able to move on. Where the tenth Doctor ruined his relationship with Martha by not being able to move on from the loss of Rose, here the eleventh Doctor doesn't run from his sadness, but embraces it, feels it and, eventually, heals from it. It's a process he could easily try to skip, by throwing himself into work (i.e., saving the universe) or surrounding himself with friends (e.g., the Gang) or by distracting himself (with travelling). Instead, he's rooted in one place, not interacting with the world but not fleeing it either.

We're only seeing the first half of that story here, but it's the story that eventually leads him to fully embrace a new companion and not live in the shadow of the old one. It's not pretty, but it is healthy.

Second Opinion (GB) My love of Clara Oswald is boundless, as you'll see for the remainder of this book (and probably the next one). But, honestly, there's something about Victorian-era Clara I love even more. It's the secret life she leads as a governess by day, barmaid by night. It's the way that, just when you think she can't be any cleverer, she shows she's even cleverer still. (The scene with the umbrella rocks, by the way.) And, honestly, it's the way she flirts with the Doctor. It's actually really hot.

There's a real confidence about the Victorian version of Clara that's amazing and striking, and that's why her death is such a sucker punch. She's won the audition as a companion.

Don't get me wrong. Contemporary Clara Oswald is great, and she comes into her own with the twelfth Doctor in a way no other companion has. But Victorian Clara is my favourite thing about "The Snowmen." And it's her presence that makes that important transition out of the Doctor's gloomy obsession with Amy and Rory into something healthier. Sort of.

The Bells of Saint John (2013)

Written by Steven Moffat

Directed by Colm McCarthy

The Big Idea Human minds are being uploaded into the wi-fi. Meanwhile, Clara Oswald needs help with her computer, but that help leads her to call a police box in 1207 A.D.

Cool? (RS?) You've got a global threat (something in the wi-fi), the use of media as a storytelling device, mass control of the world's population via an everyday piece of technology, issues of camera surveillance and even the kind of utterly gonzo set piece that makes no sense, but just sounds cool (the plane), complete with reactions no human would have (the pilots shrug and get on with their jobs, as though strangers in the cockpit of an almost-crashing airplane are absolutely nothing to worry about in their line of work). This is a Russell T Davies script in all but name.

And yet, there's also no doubt that this is a Steven Moffat story. There's a catchphrase ("I don't know where I am") that admittedly might be his worst catchphrase yet, but it's unmistakably Moffat. The story starts with the Doctor in disguise in an unlikely location, and there are key developments hidden in plain sight (the woman in the shop) that won't pay off for years.

Then there are the puns on fundamental parts of the series. The episode is titled for the Saint John's Ambulance badge on the TARDIS, for the very good reason that that's what the monks would identify, while Clara invents Oswin as her username partly from "Oswald, for the win" and partly because she'd already heard the Doctor use it.

And yet, instead of a bipolar story that's caught between two styles, "The Bells of Saint John" really comes together with the Davies and Moffat styles complementing one another. The wi-fi is both a piece of global technology we all use without thinking about (Davies) and something ordinary that can easily become terrifying (Moffat). There's a muted and understated romance between the Doctor and his companion that plays to the strengths of each: while the "snogbox" lines are pure Moffat, the scene with Clara leaning out her window to talk to the Doctor is staged like the balcony scene from *Romeo and Juliet*. The former involves a fast-talking, self-aware, independent woman using irony to overcome the fact that she should be completely freaked out (Moffat). The latter is pure kitchen-sink drama and all the lovelier for it (Davies).

Then there's the loopy, punch-the-air set piece of the Doctor riding the anti-grav motorbike (Davies) that's set up by a witty exchange involving wordplay (Moffat), leading directly into the big confrontation with the corporate manager as villain (Davies), but wrapped around a gobsmackingly awesome plot twist (Moffat). Oh, and the coda involves the previously unannounced arrival of an international taskforce (Davies), but with a further plot twist and horrific ending involving a child (Moffat).

The great thing about this melding is that it produces something that exceeds what either style would produce on its own. However, if we're going to pit the two eras against each other, then there's one element where Moffat's has a natural advantage. It's not the plotting, the puns, the companion arcs, the plot twists or the catchphrases. Instead, it's the very first thing Steven Moffat did when he took over the role of executive producer: he had the foresight to cast Matt Smith in the role of the Doctor. And for that, we're forever going to be grateful.

Second Opinion (GB) This is going to seem churlish for me to say because, actually, I really like "The Bells of Saint John." I love it for all the reasons my co-author says, and you can add the sequence where the Doctor takes Clara in the TARDIS to stop a crashing plane, which may be one of my favourite action sequences in *Doctor Who*, ever.

But . . . someone needs to have an intervention with the eleventh Doctor and his creepy stalker nature.

Seriously. With Amy and Rory, it became unnerving when he just couldn't give up travelling with them and let them have a life (telling Amy hers was the first face his new face saw was a bit, um, ick). And then when the Ponds did leave, he threw a massive tantrum and then fell into a funk and for all I know sat in the TARDIS for hours at a time playing Connie Francis records.

Then Clara shows up, and there's a new mystery and, um . . . oh, look what is he doing in the monastery? Painting a picture of her. Then he finds her and goes to her house so he can grin at her while she says, "Doctor who?" a bunch of times. And, after saving her life, he lingers around, answering calls from her family and doing her job for her and . . .

Oh God. This isn't going to go so well, is it?

The Day of the Doctor (2013)

Written by Steven Moffat

Directed by Nick Hurran

The Big Idea The warrior once known as the Doctor is on the brink of ending the Time War. Faced with such a terrible decision, he gets a glimpse into his future from the weapon itself.

Cool? (GB) There was one moment during "The Day of the Doctor" when I audibly gasped and then choked up. For good measure, I did it when I first saw it on broadcast and again in the cinema two days later. It was the scene when Clara asks, "You told me the name you chose was a promise. What was the promise?"

The tenth Doctor says, "Never cruel or cowardly."

The warrior says, "Never give up, never give in."

For those of us who have been around *Doctor Who* for a very long time, this a recognizable quote. It's a description of the Doctor written by Terrance Dicks in his 1976 book *The Making of Doctor Who*. The genius of "The Day of the Doctor" is that it deliberately goes to the heart of those terms to redefine the Doctor.

The central contradiction of the Doctor is between the terrible power that he wields and the decent person that he is. For the past eight years that we've known him, the Doctor's backstory has involved him having been instrumental in the genocide of his own people. We know it was for the greater good. We see the damage the act did to him. And then we learn that, in order to commit it, he regenerated into an incarnation who forsook his own name and was later disowned by his future selves.

The result is a very complex hero — but a hero who is nonetheless defined by an act of genocide. One of the bravest things "The Day of the Doctor" does is finally ask the question that has been skirted for the duration of the Modern Series: were all the people who died on

Gallifrey Time Lords who were embroiled in the Time War? The answer is no. There were innocents. There were children.

Which brings us to the retcon, the changing of history at the climax of the story: Gallifrey isn't destroyed after all, but the Doctor bears the guilt of thinking he destroyed it. It's television's greatest example of having its cake and eating it too. But there's a part of me that thinks this is wonderful. That for the fiftieth anniversary of *Doctor Who*, we had the boldest restatement of the Doctor as someone who does not bow to circumstances, who never gives up, who doesn't take the terrible option.

Or, as Terrance Dicks once wrote, "He never gives in and never gives up, however overwhelming the odds against him. The Doctor believes in good and fights evil. Though often caught up in violent situations, he is a man of peace. He is never cruel or cowardly. In fact, to put it simply, the Doctor is a hero. These days, there aren't so many of them around."

Second Opinion (RS?) There was one moment during "The Day of the Doctor" when I audibly gasped and then choked up. It was the moment Tom freaking Baker appeared onscreen!

I knew almost nothing about the fiftieth anniversary episode going in. There were so many rumours floating around that it all merged into white noise for me, so my spoilerphobic nature meant I was able to fly under the radar. And when the Doctor is about to meet an older man who's been looking for him, I thought I had it pegged: it would be the first Doctor, played by David Bradley from *An Adventure in Space and Time*, returning the cameo favour that Matt Smith had done there.

And then that sonorous voice called out, "You know, I really think you might," and I couldn't hold it in. Embarrassingly, I was in a TV studio at the time. In my defence, I wasn't the only one weeping openly.

Because this was the moment when it all came together. The entire story had been about crashing the old and the new together, with John Hurt's warrior being the voice of the Classic Series, having all the best jokes at the expense of the New. The tenth and eleventh Doctors were there to celebrate what the Modern Series had achieved over a remarkable near-decade. And there were even props to the Classic Series, in the form of clips from all the Doctors, when Gallifrey is saved.

But it was that moment when a man of almost 80 stepped onto

the screen — all short white hair, wrinkles and a limp — that did it for me. Because that took the very essence of my childhood and brought it crashing into the present.

I maintain that "The Day of the Doctor" might be the greatest *Doctor Who* story of all time. Not just because of that cameo, but because every single moving part is working beautifully, turning in conjunction with every other and giving us just about the most consummate story imaginable. But that cameo was the absolute perfect icing on a perfect cake. And it's still delicious, no matter how many times I sample it. Even if I still audibly gasp and choke up whenever I see Tom Baker onscreen.

The Twelfth Doctor

Pain Is a Gift

(2014–)

Basic Data

First appearance: "The Day of the Doctor" (2013)

First story: "Deep Breath" (2014)

The Changing Face of *Doctor Who* In 2013, *Doctor Who* turned 50. The golden anniversary year saw *Doctor Who* hitting new heights of popularity. At the beginning of the Matt Smith era, the Modern Series had finally cracked the U.S. market with the move to BBC America, getting the cable channel's highest-ever ratings and bringing *Doctor Who* into American pop culture in a way it had never been. The series continued to be hugely popular in Canada, Australia and New Zealand as well as non-English-speaking markets and, of course, was also still top rated in Britain. When the fiftieth anniversary episode, "The Day of the Doctor," aired, it was an unprecedented event for a dramatic series, being simulcast with the broadcast in Britain in 90-some-odd countries around the world and also shown in movie theatres in 3D.

The small fly in the ointment was that the incumbent Doctor, Matt Smith, was departing.

In looking for the next Doctor, executive producers Steven Moffat and Brian Minchin wanted to contrast the youthfulness of Smith with an older actor. While several actors (including *Law & Order: UK*'s Ben Daniels) were held in reserve, the original idea of Peter Capaldi stuck.

An older Doctor changed a number of dynamics in the show. Its reliance on a romantic element between the leads, a facet of the series since it was revived in 2005, would change. And, in an era when *Doctor Who* had hewed to the established genre television format of good-looking young male leads, it was — even in a world where older white men being cast in anything isn't news — something of a risk.

Doctor Who went on a charm offensive to sell its new lead, taking its stars on a world tour that included Australia, South Korea, the U.S., Mexico and Brazil, alongside Cardiff and London in the U.K. Following the success of the fiftieth anniversary story, Peter Capaldi's debut episode, "Deep Breath," aired in cinemas worldwide in 2014. Ratings in the U.K. stayed more or less the same (which is more impressive given that *Doctor Who* now aired in the autumn, opposite even stiffer competition) and increased worldwide. *Doctor Who* entered its second half-century with a new Doctor . . . and a new lease on life.

Who is Peter Capaldi? In 1971, Sarah Newman, the production secretary for *Doctor Who* at the time, received repeated requests from a young fan in Glasgow to become the head of the *Doctor Who* fan club (the volunteer position was watched over by the production office). Newman told the fan that the position was filled. Undeterred, the fan continued to lobby for the position and sent other correspondence to the production office, leaving Newman to note that she wished the fan would have a run-in with a Dalek. Not all the correspondence provoked a negative reaction; producer Barry Letts sent the fan the set designs and scripts for the 1972 story "The Mutants."

As you might have guessed, that fan was Peter Capaldi.

In his early teens, Capaldi contributed to fanzines — the mimeographed magazines that were the staple of fan communication in the pre-internet age — before going to art school and knocking about as a musician (he was in a punk band with Craig Ferguson). He eventually settled on acting, writing and directing, winning an Oscar for his 1995 short film *Franz Kafka's It's a Wonderful Life*. As an actor, Capaldi has been acclaimed ever since appearing in 1984's *Local Hero*, but was more recently hugely popular as the acerbic and profane political advisor Malcolm Tucker in the TV series *The Thick of It* (2005–2012) and the film *In the Loop* (2009). In 2008, he was reunited with the show he loved as a youth, *Doctor Who*, when he appeared as a minor character, the Roman father Caecilius, in "The Fires of Pompeii." He followed that up with the major role of John Frobisher in the 2009 miniseries *Torchwood: Children of Earth*.

When Matt Smith departed, Capaldi's name came up as a dark-horse candidate for the role. Most (including one of this book's co-authors in a BBC Radio interview!) discounted Capaldi, because he was 55 and deemed too old for the part. And yet, producer Steven Moffat wanted an older actor. Whereas Matt Smith was part of an open casting call, Capaldi was simply invited to Steven Moffat's home, where they shot footage of him performing a variety of Doctor-ish scenes with Moffat's son in what must be the most high-powered fan video ever made.

The announcement of Capaldi's casting was broadcast live in August 2013 not only on the BBC but in several countries (in a test for what later occurred with the fiftieth anniversary special). Capaldi also made a surprise cameo appearance (shown only in an extreme closeup of his eyes) in 2013's "The Day of the Doctor."

While Capaldi was determined to play the role his own way, he also acknowledged that he was a fan living out his dreams. In the first publicity shot of him in his new costume (which echoes the third Doctor's old capes with its red-satin-lined black jacket), Capaldi struck a pose exactly like that of Jon Pertwee's original publicity photos as the Doctor.

Top Companion To date, the twelfth Doctor has only had one companion. However, even if that weren't the case, Clara Oswald would be the only choice. With the Doctor's regeneration, Clara is left with the question of whether she can trust this apparent stranger. And yet, strangely enough, she is able to get closer to him too, cutting through his bravado, getting him to look at the consequences of his actions and also to understand the tough choices she makes. It's not an easy relationship — it's the first time we see a companion leave the Doctor in anger on television — and, as time goes on, Clara starts to emulate the Doctor: both his good qualities (his bravery, his intelligence) and his bad ones (his tendency to lie, his addiction to adventuring). It's a complex relationship that continues to surprise.

Classic Foe The Master returns, with a long-game strategy to use dead humans as an army of Cybermen. Still psychotic. Still dangerous. Still sort of fancies the Doctor and wants to prove something to him. And she calls herself Missy now. (Short for Mistress; she's a bit old-fashioned when it comes to titles. She even calls herself a Time Lady.)

Yes, we said "she" . . .

Who is the Doctor? The circumstances that created the twelfth Doctor might be a way in to understanding his character. At the time of the eleventh Doctor's death in 2013's "The Time of the Doctor," we learned that he was at the end of his regenerative cycle (it turns out that the tenth Doctor gave up an incarnation in 2008's "Journey's End" and, with the warrior, the Doctor had used all 13 of his lives). The Doctor was facing his final end before the Time Lords gave him a new regenerative cycle.

That may have influenced this new Doctor's way of thinking. He admits in 2014's "Kill the Moon" that he has no idea if he has another 12 lives or if he'll keep regenerating indefinitely. He's now living on "borrowed time," as it were . . . and, perhaps unsurprisingly, he's trying to figure out who he is and what he's doing with his life.

He asks Clara in 2014's "Into the Dalek" if he's a good man. It's an odd question because, throughout the eleventh Doctor's era, the Doctor's self-identification as "a good man" has been repeatedly mentioned. (In 2013's "The Night of the Doctor," it's what the eighth Doctor abandons to regenerate into a warrior.) Which makes this questioning even more puzzling and unsettling. The Doctor is evaluating his life and wondering if he really is the man he thinks he is. His refusal to let himself be called a hero in 2014's "Robot of

Sherwood" and his ongoing qualms with the military also point to a character with an intriguing internal conflict. "Into the Dalek" finds the Doctor trying to show a damaged Dalek the beauty that's out in the universe, but instead he ends up demonstrating the darkness and hatred he keeps at bay within himself. (The Dalek even calls him a "good Dalek.")

Clara eventually answers that she doesn't know if the Doctor is a good man: "I think you try to be and I think that's probably the point." Perhaps that is good enough. By the time of 2014's "Death in Heaven," the Doctor describes himself this way: "I am not a good man. I am not a bad man. I am not a hero . . . Do you know what I am? I am an idiot, with a box and a screwdriver. Just passing through, helping out, learning." It marks an interesting shift in the Doctor's thinking, but one that's more in line with the Doctor of old than the lonely god of his later incarnations.

He's a Doctor who is constantly learning who he is. Instead of making executive decisions, he opts to let humanity, through Clara, choose for themselves what to do with the creature about to hatch within the moon. Perhaps that's why he's also obsessed with resolving past demons, like solving the riddle of sentient life's shared conception of a monster hiding under the bed in 2014's "Listen."

His relationship with Clara also shows the growth made as a result of his eleventh incarnation's final adventure. His 700 years on Trenzalore perhaps made him realize that he couldn't be the pseudo-boyfriend the eleventh Doctor was for Clara. And, as he and Madame Vastra muse in "Deep Breath," perhaps this is why he allowed himself to have an older face this time. But the Doctor and Clara's friendship deepens. It has profound lows — with Clara leaving him in "Kill the Moon" — but there are the moments when the depths of his feelings are revealed, such as when the Doctor is willing to, literally, go to hell to get her boyfriend back even after she's betrayed him in 2014's "Dark Water."

It's a miracle Clara stays with him sometimes. The twelfth Doctor is rude, insulting, mistrustful (he hates hugging because you can't see the face of the other person) and channels his anxieties in misdirected flights of further rudeness and anger. He seems to have the Time Lord–ish Asperger's of his predecessors but even worse. And it's a struggle for him not only to empathize but sometimes to inspire confidence. In "Kill the Moon," the Doctor tries to express his faith that Clara has made the right decision in letting the creature in the moon live — a speech his tenth or eleventh incarnation would have made with utter confidence — but it sounds forced, and Clara calls him on it. He's very much still figuring it out. Twelve Doctors on, and the Doctor is still a mystery — even to himself.

Who is the Doctor? Well, we'll come back to that in a little bit . . .

Three Great Moments At the start of "Into the Dalek," the Doctor rescues soldier Journey Blue, moments before her ship blows up in a Dalek attack, by materializing the TARDIS around her. Journey then holds a gun to the Doctor's head and demands to be taken back to her base. The Doctor is unbothered by this threat and repeatedly barks at her, "Not like that." Eventually, she acquiesces, puts down the gun . . . and asks. And says please. It's a brilliant moment, which immediately establishes the no-nonsense, unsentimental nature of this new Doctor. You don't threaten this man unless you really mean it.

The ending of "Kill the Moon" gives us the moment we thought we'd never see on television: the Doctor has finally pushed the companion too far. Having abandoned Clara to make an impossible decision, the Doctor tries to put forward his view that he did what he did because he felt that humans should make choices for themselves, while Clara is full of righteous fury that he's being patronizing and mean-spirited. As with all good drama, both sides are right and both sides are wrong — and it results in her storming out of the TARDIS, seemingly for good.

Almost exactly the opposite thing happens in "Dark Water." Clara has betrayed the Doctor in a failed attempt to force him to prevent the death of Danny Pink, and she fully expects him to reject her. Instead, he agrees to see if Danny can still be found in some kind of afterlife, saying, "Do you think I care for you so little that betraying me would make a difference?" Excuse us, we might just need a moment . . .

Two Embarrassing Moments The climactic jeopardy of 2014's "In the Forest of the Night" is that the forests being grown overnight are a protective shield from an advancing solar flare (we'll save the discussion of the bizarre science for another time), but the world may destroy them before they can be effective. Which leaves it up to the TARDIS to robocall every phone in the world to deliver a message to stop the deforesting . . . given by a group of kids as a class project. Apparently, no one thought to tell writer Frank Cotrell Boyce to put down his laptop and take three steps back.

There's a dreadful running gag through the first season of the twelfth Doctor that he genuinely can't comprehend that Clara is young and beautiful. It starts in "Into the Dalek" when he tells her she doesn't look like a young woman any more and, when Clara protests, the Doctor says, "Oh, that's right, keep your spirits up." We would honestly forgive Clara if she just kicked the Doctor in the groin and told him to shut up with all the demeaning remarks.

Don't Be Stupid? (GB and RS?) The Doctor is new again. But at the same time, he's also very much the same.

Some aspects of the twelfth Doctor are an amalgamation of his other selves. There's the early fourth Doctor's sense of detachment. There's the first Doctor's crustiness and the sixth Doctor's rudeness, but there's also the vulnerability of the fifth Doctor (in brief flashes) and the signs of woundedness that typify the ninth and tenth incarnations. He has the childlike wonder of the eighth Doctor, the mercurial side of the second, the Time Lord Asperger's of the third, the alienness of the eleventh and bits of the mysteriousness of the seventh.

But he's also blatantly his own Doctor. He operates at a level above us all. Where past Doctors had their moments of rudeness, Capaldi is downright insulting — and he doesn't let up, either. He lies. He doesn't reveal what's going on. He pays little mind to people who die in front of him. His constant observations about Clara's face and body are deeply uncomfortable, but they're meant to be, because this is a Doctor who not only doesn't observe the human niceties, he doesn't even seem to understand them. Previous Doctors bemoaned humans for doing stupid things but then later declared us to be his favourite species. With the twelfth Doctor, you get the sense that he hangs around us because he has nowhere else to be.

The first season of the twelfth Doctor has been a journey for him. He starts off not completely sure of himself, not sure if he's good. This progresses to the point where he declares himself to be nothing more than an idiot who travels, helps people and learns. Between these two points, we see this Doctor figure a lot of things out. We love how in "Into the Dalek" Clara forces him to realize that travelling inside a Dalek to prove that it can't be good is a stupid goal, and he should learn something better. And this first season has a lot of that. Having come to the end of his lives in "The Time of the Doctor," he's starting all over, unsure of who and what he is; not just in a post-regenerative capacity, but in deep and fundamental ways as well. In short, he's the Doctor relearning how to be the Doctor.

A big part of that is his relationship with Clara. It's interesting to note that he starts out the season saying, "She's not my assistant, she's my . . ." and is unable to finish the sentence. By the end of the season, he calls Clara his friend and demonstrates his affection to her by helping her even after she's betrayed him. One of the great things about this Doctor is that we get to see a difficult friendship with real stakes. He rows with her; she rows with him; she leaves him; they get back together. She doesn't get the approbation she deserves from the Doctor . . . but at the same time, she gets moments like the ending of "Mummy on the Orient Express," where she sees how hard it must be inside the Doctor's soul and how difficult it is for him to live with the decisions he's made.

For the first time since the series returned in 2005, we have an asexual Doctor, one who isn't flirting with his companion or indeed anyone (even when Missy kisses him, he looks as uncomfortable as it's possible to be). He not only doesn't "dance," he'd rather you unplugged the iPod and threw it into the river. This is, in some ways, a joyful return to a hero of old: someone who doesn't need to chase skirt to prove how manly he is and who opens a gap for all the kids in the audience who aren't straight, who don't fit into society's norms and who can appreciate friendship for its own sake. And yet, he also has a masculine side, cock-blocking Danny on more than one occasion (mostly unknowingly, although he also revels in the fact that robbing a bank is a much more impressive date than anything a potential suitor could provide).

So many shadings of this character are brought through Peter

Capaldi's incredible performance. No discredit to his immediate predecessors, but Tennant and Smith were relative unknowns; here we get to see the fulfilment of a promise first seen with Christopher Eccleston as the Doctor. This is what happens when a heavyweight actor with a long resumé gets to play a role like this. The physicality of Capaldi's performance should not be underrated; every movement, every smile is perfectly timed and measured — and it's incredible. As is the emotional range he brings to the part; so much is conveyed through Capaldi's looks and gestures. This is a Doctor who's in a codependent relationship with his companion, each of them unable to leave the other even though the relationship is unhealthy. None of that is said out loud, and yet it's very, very clear from the way Capaldi and Coleman portray their characters.

We've only seen the beginning of Peter Capaldi as the Doctor. Just as his first season saw the character discovering himself, so too will his future seasons be a voyage of discovery. And we're very much looking forward to those.

Into the Dalek (2014)

Written by Phil Ford and Steven Moffat

Directed by Ben Wheatley

The Big Idea There's a Dalek that hates all other Daleks. The Doctor and a team of soldiers have to shrink themselves and go inside it to find out why.

Don't Be Stupid? (GB) With so many Doctors, you need to wait until the character's second adventure to really see what they're made of. While "Deep Breath" introduced Doctor number 12, it was too busy trying to rejig the dynamic between the Doctor and Clara and introduce the idea that — shock! — the Doctor could be old and grouchy to really give us much more than that.

We don't have that problem with "Into the Dalek." We have the new Doctor fully established right from the get-go, from the way he literally disarms Journey Blue with nothing more than a stern admonition and a tray of coffees to the vulnerable moment with Clara when he asks her if he's a good man to the surly way he sends up the whole premise of the story. ("Great idea for a movie. Terrible idea for a proctologist.") And that's just the first five minutes.

"*Fantastic Voyage* in a Dalek" is such a brilliant high-concept idea that I'm astounded *Doctor Who* hadn't already done it in 50 years. What makes this so much fun is that it's fully thought through, from the internal anatomy of the Dalek (which has a consistent sense of scale, a bugbear I often have with "shrunk inside something else" stories) to the reasons the Dalek would have to suddenly hate its kind (not just radiation poisoning, but a cosmic, almost religious, experience of beauty). The icing on the cake is the direction by Ben Wheatley, who takes the same care and thought with making interesting visuals for the TARDIS and Daleks as he does directing films like *A Field in England*.

But what really propels this story into the stratosphere for me is watching Clara and the Doctor. The Doctor doesn't honestly do anything different from his predecessors — the tenth or eleventh Doctor might have given Ross the power cell he thinks will save him, which is actually for tracking his remains, but they probably would have said "sorry" — and yet, because he doesn't add any friendly courtesies, he verges on seeming downright cruel. Which makes Clara calling him on being smug all the more powerful. She's encouraging him not to look at the situation like a human would but to use his full potential *as the Doctor*. "What have we learned?" indeed.

The Doctor says at the outset that they're going into darkness. And he does just that as he tries to show the Dalek the beauty of the universe but instead gives it more reasons to hate. It's no wonder the Doctor begins shunning soldiers here, starting with rebuffing Journey Blue's request to travel with him: he comes to realize how much he hates himself and doesn't like seeing it in others. It's into the Doctor as much as it is into the Dalek.

Second Opinion (RS?) As my co-author says, this is a powerful introduction to the character of the twelfth Doctor, wrapped around a sublime idea, with meaty stuff for all the main characters. But if there's one thing it's really about, it's the power of learning.

We have that explicitly, as Clara shows the Doctor that his initial conclusion about the Dalek is the wrong lesson. And it's there in the focus on Coal Hill School. But it's also in Rusty the Dalek's revelation: it saw a star being born. And what impresses the Doctor is that, in doing so, it learned something. We also learn a lot about Danny Pink, in the context of the classroom (his crying at the memory of having killed a civilian), in his personal interactions (the scenes of him conversing with Clara are cut together with scenes of him revising what he should have said) and in his not jumping to conclusions (challenging Clara's assumption that cadets are just about teaching students to shoot people).

Meanwhile, the Doctor is trying to learn about himself. In doing so, he inadvertently learns that he harbours a lot of hatred. Clara's role as a schoolteacher is explicitly questioned early on and proven to be invaluable later. Journey Blue learns that she'd rather be a companion than a soldier, while Gretchen learns that there are things worth dying for. And, in their personal time, both Danny and Clara have mind-expanding hobbies (reading and exploring the universe, respectively).

And you know what I learned? That the final, eyestalk-lingering look that Rusty gives the Doctor might well be one of the most badass things a Dalek has ever done. That'll teach him.

Listen (2014)

Written by Steven Moffat

Directed by Douglas MacKinnon

The Big Idea Is there a reason why everyone in the universe holds the same fear that there is someone watching them when they're not looking? The Doctor thinks so and starts traipsing across Danny Pink's timeline to find out.

Don't Be Stupid? (RS?) "Listen" may be one of the most astonishing episodes in the entire history of *Doctor Who*. What starts out as an investigation of invisible aliens with a B-plot involving Clara and Danny going on a date ends up as a profound investigation into what makes the Doctor tick.

What's particularly clever is the unresolved nature of the threat. The atmosphere is astonishingly effective: like all the best ghost stories, creaks and groans become terrifying, while things that go bang in the night are given pseudo-explanations that everyone believes less and less as time goes on.

But what "Listen" is really about is the nature of fear and the way our minds can amplify our existing anxieties. Which is a perfectly serviceable story to tell under any circumstances . . . but "Listen" becomes iconic by making it fundamentally about the Doctor.

He's the one who starts with a random hypothetical (what if there were creatures perfectly evolved to hide?) and then ramps up the tension again and again with every attempt to solve the unsolvable. If such aliens really were perfectly evolved, then you'd never be able to find them — and you'd probably go mad trying.

One of these madnesses is turning off the TARDIS safeguards, which takes the ship — and the story itself — to dangerous places. Watching Clara inadvertently create Danny the soldier is painful. Forcing Orson to spend another night in the loneliest place in the world is almost cruel. And then the story ends up in the barn.

It's at this point that "Listen" moves from being a very excellent story to something truly magical. It probably shouldn't work — we've never before seen the Doctor as a child, his home or his parents (if that's what they were) — but it does. Partly by keeping crucial details (such as faces) offscreen, but mostly because it ties so perfectly into what's been happening. Things hiding under the bed. The ability of fear to make you strong. The weaponless soldier. All of these come to a head in this scene, and the entire narrative collapses beautifully into a perfect moment as Clara gives a speech that will fundamentally shape who the Doctor is, even quoting a key line from "An Unearthly Child": namely, that "fear makes companions of us all."

But what of the invisible aliens? Was the creature under the bedspread just a child playing a prank? Was the knocking just the metal cooling down? Was the spaceship door turning just an automatic response? I think the answer is actually quite obvious: every single mystery in this episode was, in fact, given a perfectly plausible explanation. It's just that we weren't listening.

Second Opinion (GB) I like "Listen" a lot. But I just don't love it.

I appreciate it as a work of art. I appreciate the bold experiment it's trying to be. Mostly, I appreciate it for the pre-credits sequence that establishes virtually everything as a direct-to-camera monologue, which is a bravura piece of writing, direction and performance.

I think it's remarkable and breathtaking. But when I look at the stories I really love in this first season of Capaldi's Doctor, this story fits in the middle

Why? I don't know. It's not that I have a problem with the ambiguities within the story presented above (quite the contrary). It's not that I have an objection to the fact that apparently it breaks continuity by having the TARDIS go back to what should be a time-locked past for the Doctor. (I was, however, bothered by Orson wearing an anachronistic and incorrect Sanctuary Base 6 spacesuit from "The Impossible Planet." I am that much of a nerd.) And it's not that I'm bothered by the idea that the Doctor, in the end, is just the same scared child millennia later. (I think that's rather cool.)

If had to guess, I'd say I don't rate "Listen" so highly because it's about the Doctor himself, and that becomes ever more self-evident as the story boils away to reveal that it's all about the Doctor projecting his own anxiety on the entire universe. It feels . . . self-important, perhaps? But, on the other hand, when in 51 years has the Doctor merited a character study like this before?

Again, I don't really know why. Maybe my opinion will change by the next book we do about *Doctor Who*. Right now . . . I don't really see it. But I'm listening.

Mummy on the Orient Express (2014)

Written by Jamie Mathieson

Directed by Paul Wilmshurst

The Big Idea If you're travelling on the Orient Express (in space!) and see an ancient mummy, you have 66 seconds left to live.

Don't Be Stupid? (GB) This story begins with Clara ready to leave the Doctor and ends with her enthusiastically embracing the idea of travelling with him anew. And what happens between those two points makes that radical shift seem utterly sensical.

The opening scene is full of heartbreak. The Doctor and Clara are the couple after the ugly break-up when they're only just able to talk to each other. She wants to care for him, knows she can't, but wants the closure. It's one of the most beautiful scenes in Capaldi's short tenure (and probably still will be as his tenure becomes longer) as Clara tries to explain how she feels while the Doctor wants to go back to talking about stars — and the look on his face indicates he doesn't really, but he can't talk about feelings.

Clara doesn't have any reason to trust the Doctor again. She discovers her last hurrah is actually something the Doctor's been meaning to investigate since "The Big Bang," and she's subsequently sidelined through a lot of it (during which time a genuinely scary monster has its way, killing several well-drawn characters while the Doctor tries to solve the problem with panache and gravitas). And then comes the climax, when Clara is told to bring Maisie to him . . . so she can probably die.

Of course, Maisie doesn't die. The Doctor does something heroic and sacrificial and amazing. But that isn't why Clara stays with him in the end. She stays because when she asks him, "So you were pretending to be heartless?" the Doctor doesn't just smile and nod; he says, instead, "Would you like to think that about me? Would that make it easier?" Peter Capaldi is incredible here as the Doctor looks pained, as though he knows he's probably blowing his chance of fixing this friendship by admitting it.

And then the Doctor lets her in on what it's like for him: "There was a good chance that she'd die too. At which point, I would have just moved onto the next and the next until I beat it. Sometimes the only choices you have are bad ones. But you still have to choose." With that, Clara and the viewer learn the awful curse the Doctor has to live with. And Clara, to her credit, asks him if always having to make the impossible choices is like an addiction.

I've focused too much on the beginning and ending of this story. "Mummy on the Orient Express" is my favourite story of Capaldi's first season because of the whole of it. But I do love the fact that Clara stays on at the end . . . simply because this Doctor is unflinchingly honest.

Second Opinion (RS?) I don't love this story nearly as much as my co-author does. It can't hold a candle to "Listen," for instance. (I'm demonstrating great self-restraint in not commenting on what Graeme just said about that.) I'm not sure I'd even put it in the top third of stories in Capaldi's first season — although that really says more about just how good so many of them are than any particular criticism of "Mummy on the Orient Express." It's good; I just wouldn't call it great.

Except for one thing.

I disagree with my co-author that the reason Clara stays is because the Doctor's so heartbreakingly honest. I don't think that's it at all. I think it's because she, like the Doctor, has an addiction problem. And that's a truly fascinating idea.

That the Doctor might be addicted to fighting monsters and saving lives is an interesting take on the character. But the fact that we clearly see that Clara shares his compulsion is what takes this from an above-average adventure story to something truly compelling.

It's there in her initial decision to have one last hurrah with the Doctor. As she tells Maisie, "You can't end on a slammed door." Except that Maisie replies, "Yes, you can, people do it all the time. Except when they can't." It's there in the final scene, when the Doctor says that you can't know if you're addicted to something until you try to give it up — which is precisely what Clara fails to do. And so we see Clara lying to her boyfriend, lying to the Doctor and, really, lying to herself. Because that's what addicts do: they bend reality to support their habit, using any or all justifications at their disposal.

In 50 years of *Doctor Who*, across all its different media, I've never seen this idea floated before. But now I'm amazed that it never was. Because it says something so fundamental about the relationship between the Doctor and Clara that I can't get it out of my head.

But you know the best thing? It's that, after 50 years, *Doctor Who* still continues to surprise me. Oh, how I love this show! I can't wait to see what the future brings . . .

Who is the Doctor? Crotchety old man? Clown? Renaissance man? Bohemian? Lunatic? Vulnerable? Unpleasant? Mysterious chess-player? Romantic? (Disowned?) Wounded? Lonely god? Alien? Codependent traveller? The Doctor is all of these things and none of these things. He can't be pinned down to a few interesting phrases. He's bigger than that. Ultimately, what makes the Doctor so captivating, so wonderful, is that the Doctor is as big as the human imagination. He's bigger on the inside. But we'll keep asking the question:

"Doctor Who?"

The adventures in time and space continue . . .

Appendix 1: *Doctor Who* Episodes

For the first seven Doctors, *Doctor Who* was shown as a serial, with each story taking several 25-minute episodes. From the ninth Doctor onwards, each story was a self-contained 45-minute episode (with occasional two-part stories).

First Doctor: William Hartnell

"An Unearthly Child" (1963) (4 episodes)
"The Daleks" (1963–1964) (7 episodes)
"The Edge of Destruction" (1964) (2 episodes)
"Marco Polo" (1964) (7 episodes)
"The Keys of Marinus" (1964) (6 episodes)
"The Aztecs" (1964) (4 episodes)
"The Sensorites" (1964) (6 episodes)
"The Reign of Terror" (1964) (6 episodes)
"Planet of Giants" (1964) (3 episodes)
"The Dalek Invasion of Earth" (1964) (6 episodes)
"The Rescue" (1965) (2 episodes)
"The Romans" (1965) (4 episodes)
"The Web Planet" (1965) (6 episodes)
"The Crusade" (1965) (4 episodes)
"The Space Museum" (1965) (4 episodes)
"The Chase" (1965) (6 episodes)
"The Time Meddler" (1965) (4 episodes)
"Galaxy 4" (1965) (4 episodes)
"Mission to the Unknown" (1965) (1 episode)
"The Myth Makers" (1965) (4 episodes)
"The Daleks' Master Plan" (1965–1966) (12 episodes)
"The Massacre" (1966) (4 episodes)

"The Ark" (1966) (4 episodes)
"The Celestial Toymaker" (1966) (4 episodes)
"The Gunfighters" (1966) (4 episodes)
"The Savages" (1966) (4 episodes)
"The War Machines" (1966) (4 episodes)
"The Smugglers" (1966) (4 episodes)
"The Tenth Planet" (1966) (4 episodes)

Second Doctor: Patrick Troughton

"The Power of the Daleks" (1966) (6 episodes)
"The Highlanders" (1966–1967) (4 episodes)
"The Underwater Menace" (1967) (4 episodes)
"The Moonbase" (1967) (4 episodes)
"The Macra Terror" (1967) (4 episodes)
"The Faceless Ones" (1967) (6 episodes)
"The Evil of the Daleks" (1967) (7 episodes)
"The Tomb of the Cybermen" (1967) (4 episodes)
"The Abominable Snowmen" (1967) (6 episodes)
"The Ice Warriors" (1967) (6 episodes)
"The Enemy of the World" (1967–1968) (6 episodes)
"The Web of Fear" (1968) (6 episodes)
"Fury from the Deep" (1968) (6 episodes)
"The Wheel in Space" (1968) (6 episodes)
"The Dominators" (1968) (5 episodes)
"The Mind Robber" (1968) (5 episodes)
"The Invasion" (1968) (8 episodes)
"The Krotons" (1968–1969) (4 episodes)
"The Seeds of Death" (1969) (6 episodes)
"The Space Pirates" (1969) (6 episodes)
"The War Games" (1969) (10 episodes)

Third Doctor: Jon Pertwee

"Spearhead From Space" (1970) (4 episodes)
"Doctor Who and the Silurians" (1970) (7 episodes)
"The Ambassadors of Death" (1970) (7 episodes)
"Inferno" (1970) (7 episodes)
"Terror of the Autons" (1971) (4 episodes)
"The Mind of Evil" (1971) (6 episodes)
"The Claws of Axos" (1971) (4 episodes)
"Colony in Space" (1971) (6 episodes)
"The Dæmons" (1971) (5 episodes)

"Day of the Daleks" (1972) (4 episodes)
"The Curse of Peladon" (1972) (4 episodes)
"The Sea Devils" (1972) (6 episodes)
"The Mutants" (1972) (6 episodes)
"The Time Monster" (1972) (6 episodes)
"The Three Doctors" (1972–1973) (4 episodes)
"Carnival of Monsters" (1973) (4 episodes)
"Frontier in Space" (1973) (6 episodes)
"Planet of the Daleks" (1973) (6 episodes)
"The Green Death" (1973) (6 episodes)
"The Time Warrior" (1973–1974) (4 episodes)
"Invasion of the Dinosaurs" (1974) (6 episodes)
"Death to the Daleks" (1974) (4 episodes)
"The Monster of Peladon" (1974) (6 episodes)
"Planet of the Spiders" (1974) (6 episodes)

Fourth Doctor: Tom Baker

"Robot" (1974–1975) (4 episodes)
"The Ark in Space" (1975) (4 episodes)
"The Sontaran Experiment" (1975) (2 episodes)
"Genesis of the Daleks (1975) (6 episodes)
"Revenge of the Cybermen" (1975) (4 episodes)
"Terror of the Zygons" (1975) (4 episodes)
"Planet of Evil" (1975) (4 episodes)
"Pyramids of Mars" (1975) (4 episodes)
"The Android Invasion" (1975) (4 episodes)
"The Brain of Morbius" (1976) (4 episodes)
"The Seeds of Doom" (1976) (6 episodes)
"The Masque of Mandragora" (1976) (4 episodes)
"The Hand of Fear" (1976) (4 episodes)
"The Deadly Assassin" (1976) (4 episodes)
"The Face of Evil" (1977) (4 episodes)
"The Robots of Death" (1977) (4 episodes)
"The Talons of Weng-Chiang" (1977) (6 episodes)
"Horror of Fang Rock" (1977) (4 episodes)
"The Invisible Enemy" (1977) (4 episodes)
"Image of the Fendahl" (1977) (4 episodes)
"The Sun Makers" (1977) (4 episodes)
"Underworld" (1978) (4 episodes)
"The Invasion of Time" (1978) (6 episodes)

"The Ribos Operation" (1978) (4 episodes)
"The Pirate Planet" (1978) (4 episodes)
"The Stones of Blood" (1978) (4 episodes)
"The Androids of Tara" (1978) (4 episodes)
"The Power of Kroll" (1978–1979) (4 episodes)
"The Armageddon Factor" (1979) (6 episodes)
"Destiny of the Daleks" (1979) (4 episodes)
"City of Death" (1979) (4 episodes)
"The Creature From the Pit" (1979) (4 episodes)
"Nightmare of Eden" (1979) (4 episodes)
"The Horns of Nimon" (1979–1980) (4 episodes)
"Shada" (never aired due to a production strike) (6 incomplete episodes)
"The Leisure Hive" (1980) (4 episodes)
"Meglos" (1980) (4 episodes)
"Full Circle" (1980) (4 episodes)
"State of Decay" (1980) (4 episodes)
"Warriors' Gate" (1981) (4 episodes)
"The Keeper of Traken" (1981) (4 episodes)
"Logopolis" (1981) (4 episodes)

Fifth Doctor: Peter Davison

"Castrovalva" (1982) (4 episodes)
"Four to Doomsday" (1982) (4 episodes)
"Kinda" (1982) (4 episodes)
"The Visitation" (1982) (4 episodes)
"Black Orchid" (1982) (2 episodes)
"Earthshock" (1982) (4 episodes)
"Time-Flight" (1982) (4 episodes)
"Arc of Infinity" (1983) (4 episodes)
"Snakedance" (1983) (4 episodes)
"Mawdryn Undead" (1983) (4 episodes)
"Terminus" (1983) (4 episodes)
"Enlightenment" (1983) (4 episodes)
"The King's Demons" (1983) (2 episodes)
"The Five Doctors" (1983) (one 90-minute episode)
"Warriors of the Deep" (1984) (4 episodes)
"The Awakening" (1984) (2 episodes)
"Frontios" (1984) (4 episodes)
"Resurrection of the Daleks" (1984) (two 45-minute episodes)
"Planet of Fire" (1984) (4 episodes)
"The Caves of Androzani" (1984) (4 episodes)

Sixth Doctor: Colin Baker

"The Twin Dilemma" (1984) (4 episodes)
"Attack of the Cybermen" (1985) (two 45-minute episodes)
"Vengeance on Varos" (1985) (two 45-minute episodes)
"The Mark of the Rani" (1985) (two 45-minute episodes)

"The Two Doctors" (1985)
(three 45-minute episodes)
"Timelash" (1985) (two 45-minute episodes)
"Revelation of the Daleks" (1985)
(two 45-minute episodes)
"The Trial of a Time Lord" (1986)
(14 episodes: "The Mysterious Planet," 4 episodes; "Mindwarp," 4 episodes; "Terror of the Vervoids," 4 episodes; "The Ultimate Foe," 2 episodes; titles not shown onscreen)

Seventh Doctor: Sylvester McCoy
"Time and the Rani" (1987)
(4 episodes)
"Paradise Towers" (1987)
(4 episodes)
"Delta and the Bannermen" (1987)
(3 episodes)
"Dragonfire" (1987) (3 episodes)
"Remembrance of the Daleks"
(1988) (4 episodes)
"The Happiness Patrol" (1988)
(3 episodes)
"Silver Nemesis" (1988) (3 episodes)
"The Greatest Show in the Galaxy"
(1988) (4 episodes)
"Battlefield" (1989) (4 episodes)
"Ghost Light" (1989) (4 episodes)
"The Curse of Fenric" (1989)
(3 episodes)
"Survival" (1989) (3 episodes)
"Dimensions in Time" (1993)
(two 7-minute episodes; charity sketch for Children in Need)

Eighth Doctor: Paul McGann
"Doctor Who" (a.k.a. the TV Movie, 1996) (one 90-minute film)
"The Night of the Doctor" (2013)
(10-minute webisode)

Ninth Doctor: Christopher Eccleston
"Rose" (2005)
"The End of the World" (2005)
"The Unquiet Dead" (2005)
"Aliens of London"/
"World War Three" (2005)
"Dalek" (2005)
"The Long Game" (2005)
"Father's Day" (2005)
"The Empty Child"/
"The Doctor Dances" (2005)
"Boom Town" (2005)
"Bad Wolf"/"The Parting of the Ways" (2005)

Tenth Doctor: David Tennant
Untitled Children in Need Special
(2005) (one 7-minute episode)
"The Christmas Invasion" (2005)
"New Earth" (2006)
"Tooth and Claw" (2006)
"School Reunion" (2006)
"The Girl in the Fireplace" (2006)
"Rise of the Cybermen"/"The Age of Steel" (2006)
"The Idiot's Lantern" (2006)
"The Impossible Planet"/
"The Satan Pit" (2006)
"Love & Monsters" (2006)

"Fear Her" (2006)
"Army of Ghosts"/
"Doomsday" (2006)
"The Runaway Bride" (2006)
"Smith and Jones" (2007)
"The Shakespeare Code" (2007)
"Gridlock" (2007)
"Daleks in Manhattan"/
"Evolution of the Daleks" (2007)
"The Lazarus Experiment" (2007)
"42" (2007)
"Human Nature"/
"The Family of Blood" (2007)
"Blink" (2007)
"Utopia" (2007)
"The Sound of Drums"/
"Last of the Time Lords" (2007)
"Time Crash" (2007)
"Voyage of the Damned" (2007)
"Partners in Crime" (2008)
"The Fires of Pompeii" (2008)
"Planet of the Ood" (2008)
"The Sontaran Stratagem"/
"The Poison Sky" (2008)
"The Doctor's Daughter" (2008)
"The Unicorn and the Wasp" (2008)
"Silence in the Library"/
"Forest of the Dead" (2008)
"Midnight" (2008)
"Turn Left" (2008)
"The Stolen Earth"/
"Journey's End" (2008)
"The Next Doctor" (2008)
"Planet of the Dead" (2009)
"The Waters of Mars" (2009)
"The End of Time" (2009–2010) (2 episodes)

Eleventh Doctor: Matt Smith

"The Eleventh Hour" (2010)
"The Beast Below" (2010)
"Victory of the Daleks" (2010)
"The Time of Angels"/
"Flesh and Stone" (2010)
"The Vampires of Venice" (2010)
"Amy's Choice" (2010)
"The Hungry Earth"/
"Cold Blood" (2010)
"Vincent and the Doctor" (2010)
"The Lodger" (2010)
"The Pandorica Opens"/
"The Big Bang" (2010)
"A Christmas Carol" (2010)
"Space"/"Time" (2011) (two 3-minute episodes, broadcast as part of *Comic Relief*)
"The Impossible Astronaut"/
"Day of the Moon" (2011)
"The Curse of the Black Spot" (2011)
"The Doctor's Wife" (2011)
"The Rebel Flesh"/
"The Almost People" (2011)
"A Good Man Goes to War" (2011)
"Let's Kill Hitler" (2011)
"Night Terrors" (2011)
"The Girl Who Waited" (2011)
"The God Complex" (2011)
"Closing Time" (2011)
"The Wedding of River Song" (2011)
"The Doctor, The Widow and the Wardrobe" (2011)

"Asylum of the Daleks" (2012)
"Dinosaurs on a Spaceship" (2012)
"A Town Called Mercy" (2012)
"The Power of Three" (2012)
"The Angels Take Manhattan" (2012)
"The Snowmen" (2012)
"The Bells of Saint John" (2013)
"The Rings of Akhaten" (2013)
"Cold War" (2013)
"Hide" (2013)
"Journey to the Centre of the TARDIS" (2013)
"The Crimson Horror" (2013)
"Nightmare in Silver" (2013)
"The Name of the Doctor" (2013)
"The Day of the Doctor" (2013)
"The Time of the Doctor" (2013)

Twelfth Doctor: Peter Capaldi

"Deep Breath" (2014)
"Into the Dalek" (2014)
"Robot of Sherwood" (2014)
"Listen" (2014)
"Time Heist" (2014)
"The Caretaker" (2014)
"Kill the Moon" (2014)
"Mummy on the Orient Express" (2014)
"Flatline" (2014)
"In the Forest of the Night" (2014)
"Dark Water"/"Death in Heaven" (2014)
"Last Christmas" (2014)

Appendix 2: *Doctor Who* Companions

Note: Determining what makes a companion is a subject for heated debate. At what point is Mickey no longer a recurring character but a companion? Are the regulars of UNIT companions? What you see here expresses no consensus but that of the co-authors'.

First Doctor: William Hartnell

Susan Foreman (Carole Ann Ford) (1963–1964)
Barbara Wright (Jacqueline Hill) (1963–1965)
Ian Chesterton (William Russell) (1963–1965)
Vicki (Maureen O'Brien) (1965)
Steven Taylor (Peter Purves) (1965–1966)
Katarina (Adrienne Hill) (1965)
Sara Kingdom (Jean Marsh) (1965–1966)
Dodo Chaplet (Jackie Lane) (1966)
Ben Jackson (Michael Craze) (1966)
Polly (Anneke Wills) (1966)

Second Doctor: Patrick Troughton

Ben Jackson (Michael Craze) (1966–1967)
Polly (Anneke Wills) (1966–1967)
Jamie McCrimmon (Frazer Hines) (1966–1969)
Victoria Waterfield (Deborah Watling) (1967–1968)
Zoe Heriot (Wendy Padbury) (1968–1969)

Third Doctor: Jon Pertwee

Liz Shaw (Caroline John) (1970)
Jo Grant (Katy Manning) (1971–1973)
Sarah Jane Smith (Elisabeth Sladen) (1973–1974)
Brigadier Alistair Gordon

Lethbridge-Stewart (Nicholas Courtney) (recurring character, 1970–1974)
Sergeant John Benton (John Levene) (recurring character, 1970–1974)
Captain Mike Yates (Richard Franklin) (recurring character, 1971–1974)

Fourth Doctor: Tom Baker
Sarah Jane Smith (Elisabeth Sladen) (1974–1976)
Harry Sullivan (Ian Marter) (1974–1975)
Brigadier Alistair Gordon Lethbridge-Stewart (Nicholas Courtney) (recurring character, 1974–1975)
Sergeant John Benton (John Levene) (recurring character, 1974–1975)
Leela (Louise Jameson) (1977–1978)
K9 (voice of John Leeson, David Brierley) (1977–1981)
Romana I (Mary Tamm) (1978–1979)
Romana II (Lalla Ward) (1979–1981)
Adric (Matthew Waterhouse (1980–1981)
Nyssa (Sarah Sutton) (1981)
Tegan Jovanka (Janet Fielding) (1981)

Fifth Doctor: Peter Davison
Adric (Matthew Waterhouse) (1981–1982)
Nyssa (Sarah Sutton) (1981–1983)
Tegan Jovanka (Janet Fielding) (1981–1984)
Turlough (Mark Strickson) (1983–1984)
Kamelion (voice of Gerard Flood) (1983–1984)
Peri Brown (Nicola Bryant) (1984)

Sixth Doctor: Colin Baker
Peri Brown (Nicola Bryant) (1984–1986)
Mel Bush (Bonnie Langford) (1986)

Seventh Doctor: Sylvester McCoy
Mel Bush (Bonnie Langford) (1987)
Ace (Sophie Aldred) (1987–1989)

Eighth Doctor: Paul McGann
Grace Holloway (Daphne Ashbrook) (1996)

Ninth Doctor: Christopher Eccleston
Rose Tyler (Billie Piper) (2005)
Mickey Smith (Noel Clarke) (recurring character, 2005)
Adam Mitchell (Bruno Langley) (2005)
Captain Jack Harkness (John Barrowman) (2005)

Tenth Doctor: David Tennant
Rose Tyler (Billie Piper) (2006)
Mickey Smith (Noel Clarke) (2006)
Martha Jones (Freema Agyeman) (2007; recurring character, 2008–2010)

Captain Jack Harkness (John Barrowman) (recurring character, 2007–2008)
Donna Noble (Catherine Tate) (2006, 2008)
Wilfred Mott (Bernard Cribbins) (recurring character, 2008–2010)

Eleventh Doctor: Matt Smith
Amy Pond (Karen Gillan) (2010–2012)
Rory Williams (Arthur Darvill) (2010–2012)
Clara Oswald (Jenna Louise Coleman) (2012–2013)

Twelfth Doctor: Peter Capaldi
Clara Oswald (Jenna Coleman) (2014–)

Appendix 3: Multi-Doctor Stories

One incarnation can be a handful, so what happens when there are multiple Doctors? Here's a listing of all the stories featuring more than one incarnation of the Doctor.

"The Three Doctors" (1972)

Starring Jon Pertwee, Patrick Troughton and William Hartnell

This story celebrated the tenth anniversary of *Doctor Who* as the Time Lords dispatched the Doctor's previous incarnations to help the third Doctor stop the threat of the renegade Time Lord Omega. Patrick Troughton was happy to return as the second Doctor but, after initially agreeing, William Hartnell was too infirm from arteriosclerosis to return to acting. The first Doctor only made brief appearances on a television screen, Hartnell reading his lines from cue cards.

"The Five Doctors" (1983)

Starring Peter Davison, Tom Baker, Jon Pertwee, Patrick Troughton, Richard Hurndall and William Hartnell

When the twentieth anniversary came around, another multi-Doctor revival seemed inevitable. By this point, William Hartnell was dead, so Richard Hurndall was cast to play the first Doctor (a clip with Hartnell saying farewell to Susan from "The Dalek Invasion of Earth" was used as a pre-credits sequence). This story also brought back past companions and menaces as the Doctors were brought to the Death Zone on Gallifrey to find the secret of Rassilon's Tomb. The one problem was that Tom Baker decided not to participate late in the game, so clips from the unfinished (and unbroadcast) 1980 story "Shada" were used at the opening and closing to represent his Doctor.

"The Two Doctors" (1985)

Starring Colin Baker and Patrick Troughton

Patrick Troughton apparently had a great time making "The Five Doctors" and asked if he could come back for more. Producer John Nathan-Turner leapt at the opportunity and quickly commissioned a script involving Troughton and the new sixth Doctor, Colin Baker. Unusually, rather than take past Doctor out of their own timestream, this story decided to try and fit into what Troughton's Doctor would have been doing way back in the '60s. Unfortunately, the author got a little muddled and had the second Doctor able to steer the TARDIS and on a mission for the Time Lords, which, by virtue of being wrong, has caused no end of issues with fans.

"Dimensions in Time" (1993)

Starring Sylvester McCoy, Colin Baker, Peter Davison, Tom Baker and Jon Pertwee

This was a charity crossover featuring all the living Doctors, most of the companions and the cast of *EastEnders*, and it was even made in 3D. All in 13 minutes. Rights issues means that it will never be released commercially, but it's easily discoverable on YouTube. It's not particularly good, but as a piece of loveable kitsch, it's never been bested.

"Time Crash" (2007)

Starring David Tennant and Peter Davison

Writer Steven Moffat was a friend of Peter Davison and convinced him to come back for a seven-minute special shown as part of the BBC Children in Need appeal. It's all set in the console room of the current Doctor and has the tenth and fifth Doctors sorting out what to do when it seems both of their TARDISes have crashed into each other. It also has the useful explanation of why the younger Doctors always seem older when they meet the current Doctor: the time differential is shorted out between them, and the younger Doctor takes on the added years!

"The Day of the Doctor" (2013)

Starring Matt Smith, David Tennant, John Hurt and Tom Baker

For the fiftieth anniversary, a multi-Doctor team-up was inevitable. What was surprising was that one of those Doctors had never been heard of! Steven Moffat had introduced the idea of the warrior only seven months earlier, so this multi-Doctor story is really from his perspective, as he looks at two of his future incarnations to see what the consequences of the Time War will be. David Tennant was happy to reprise his role as the tenth Doctor, while the cameo appearance of Tom Baker, linking the newer Doctors to the past, was a well-kept secret.

Recommended Resources

"It's always different. The library goes on forever."

— Little Girl, "Silence in the Library"

You're reading a book about *Doctor Who* right now. And you know what? There are even more books about *Doctor Who* to read. Because the great thing about *Doctor Who* is that it has really smart fans who want to know everything about their favourite show. And so they've written a great deal about it, or recorded things worth knowing. Here are just a few of them.

The Classic Series

For the past three books, we've been telling you that the best books to read on the Classic Series include David J. Howe, Mark Stammers and Stephen James Walker's *Doctor Who: The Sixties* (Virgin Publishing, 1992), *Doctor Who: The Seventies* (Virgin Publishing, 1994) and *Doctor Who: The Eighties* (Virgin Publishing, 1996), alongside Philip Segal and Gary Russell's book about the making of the 1996 TV Movie, *Doctor Who: Regeneration* (HarperCollins, 2000). They still are. Howe, Stammers and Walker's books on the making of the Classic Series by decade have a staggering amount of archival research and interviews. *Regeneration* is a remarkably detailed recounting of the six-year odyssey to put the TV Movie onscreen. Sadly, all these books are out of print, but they're still available on eBay or AbeBooks.com.

Have you ever heard of VAM? Value Added Material is what makes the *Doctor Who* Classic Series DVD range so incredible. Just about every DVD has some sort of a making-of featurette, along with commentaries (text and audio) and a wealth of information. Oh, and they have the actual stories to watch as well!

As you can tell, the missing episodes are a big part of 1960s *Who*. If you want to better understand how these episodes went missing and how they're being found, we'd highly recommend Richard Molesworth's *Wiped! Doctor Who's Missing Episodes* (Telos Publishing, revised 2012). While the recent discoveries of "The Enemy of the World" and "The Web of Fear" are absent, it's still an unputdownable book for geeks interested in how these miraculous recoveries of lost 1960s episodes were made.

One of the best books to come out of *Doctor Who*'s fiftieth anniversary was *The Doctor Who Vault: Treasures From the First 50 Years* by Marcus Hearn (Harper Design, 2013), which collects a treasure trove of photos, documents and details from behind the scenes of *Doctor Who* over the past five decades.

The Modern Series

One of the finest documentaries on how the Modern Series came together is "The Unquiet Dead," a documentary that is (oddly) on the special edition DVD for "The Green Death." In it, Jane Tranter, Russell T Davies and other key people explain how *Doctor Who* began the process of returning to our screens back in the dark days of 2003 . . .

One of the best glimpses into making New *Who* has to be *Doctor Who: The Writer's Tale* (BBC Books, 2008) and its semi-sequel *Doctor Who: The Writer's Tale — The Final Chapter* (BBC Books 2010) by Russell T Davies and *Doctor Who Magazine* contributor Benjamin Cook. It's a series of detailed emails between Davies and Cook that tracks the making of Series Four (and, in the sequel, the final David Tennant specials) from its earliest concepts through to production. Included are scripts-in-progress for several episodes; the discussion about them is a master class in TV script-writing.

An event every season is reading Andrew Pixley's in-depth companion volumes, which are published by *Doctor Who Magazine*. Pixley is *Doctor Who*'s most eminent historian, and you can see his brilliance at making all the behind-the-scenes details eminently fascinating.

The Worlds of *Doctor Who*

If the fictional universe is more your thing, your best bet is still *Doctor Who: The Encyclopedia* by Gary Russell (BBC Books, 2011), which captures just about everything ever mentioned in *Doctor Who*; it's been updated for the iPad. We're also huge fans of the recent *The Official Quotable Doctor Who* by Cavan Scott (Harper Design, 2014), which has a wealth of great zingers from the series, and *Doctor Who: The Doctor's Lives and Times* by James Goss and Steve Tribe (Harper Design, 2013), which deftly mixes fiction and non-fiction to provide a lively tour through the Doctor's 50-year career.

General Resources and Analysis

We're deeply indebted to Paul Cornell, Martin Day and Keith Topping's *Doctor Who: The Discontinuity Guide* (Virgin Publishing, 1994; reprinted by Gollancz, 2013), which includes thoughtful and irreverent analysis and reviews of all the Classic Series stories. It was hugely influential to us as authors. For a long time, the beloved standard of episode guides for the Classic Series was *The Programme Guide* by Jean-Marc Lofficier (Target Books, 1981), sadly out of print but worth looking for on eBay. The Modern Series is well represented by Shaun Lyon's *Back to the Vortex* (Telos Publishing, 2005) and *Who Is The Doctor: A Guide to Doctor Who — The New Series* (ECW Press, 2012), which provides reviews for the first six seasons of New *Who*, written by some guys named Burk and Smith? (We followed it up with a book called *Who's 50: The 50 Doctor Who Stories to Watch Before You Die.*)

Shannon Patrick Sullivan's site *A Brief History of Time (Travel)* (shannonsullivan.com/drwho) continues to be the best source of history on the Classic Series by story. The *Doctor Who News Page* (doctorwhonews.com) continues to be essential for up-to-date news on what's happening in the world of *Who*.

For a great read about gender politics in *Who*, look no further than *Chicks Unravel Time: Women Journey Through Every Season of Doctor*

Who, edited by Deborah Stanish and L.M. Myles (Mad Norwegian Press, 2012), which features essays by women about every season of the show.

The co-author with the question mark has edited a series of books where every *Doctor Who* story is reviewed by different fans. The first volume, *Outside In: 160 New Perspectives on 160 Classic Doctor Who Stories by 160 Writers* (ATB Publishing, 2012), does exactly what it says in the title. The same is true for its sequel, *Outside In 2: 125 Unique Perspectives on 125 Modern Doctor Who Stories by 125 Writers* (ATB Publishing, 2015).

Three and a half decades after starting as a Marvel comic, *Doctor Who Magazine* has turned into the best source for *Doctor Who* news. Published 14 times a year, it delivers brilliantly written behind-the-scenes features and interviews, as well as intensively researched pieces on *Doctor Who*'s rich history. Plus, it features a regular column by the executive producer, which is always entertaining.

Podcasts

Podcasting is increasingly becoming the thing that fans do to discuss and build communities around *Doctor Who*. There are so many *Who* podcasts to choose from that we couldn't name them all, but we'll recommend four: *Radio Free Skaro* (radiofreeskaro.com) is the most popular *Doctor Who* podcast and for good reason: every episode is full of lively and quirky discussion you want to argue with while listening to it. The *Verity!* podcast (veritypodcast.wordpress.com) was one of the first all-women *Doctor Who* podcasts; it's also the smartest, and it offers a thoughtful cross-section of the diaspora of *Doctor Who* fandom. We also recommend *Two-Minute Time Lord* (twominutetimelord.com), which (mostly) does what it says, providing always-fascinating commentary in a short amount of time. And, finally, we recommend *Reality Bomb* (realitybombpodcast.com), which is a magazine-style show that's more like current-affairs radio. Admittedly, it's hosted by that Graeme Burk guy, so we're a little biased . . .

Fandom

Meeting up with *Doctor Who* fans either online, in print or in person is always a great thing to do. Online, we recommend Gallifrey Base (gallifreybase.com) for discussion forums and *The Doctor Who*

Ratings Guide (pagefillers.com/dwrg, edited by that question-mark guy) for reviews. In terms of conventions, we love Gallifrey One in Los Angeles in February (gallifreyone.com), Console Room in Minneapolis in May (console-room.mpls.cx) and Chicago TARDIS in November (chicagotardis.com).

If you're looking for fan community in Canada, there's the Doctor Who Society of Canada (doctorwhosociety.com), which has fantastic social events and a great community. The Doctor Who Information Network (dwin.org), also based in Canada, is North America's oldest and largest *Doctor Who* fan club. They too have social events (often hosted by Who Party Toronto; whopartytoronto.org) as well as a fanzine, *Enlightenment*, to which each of this book's co-authors contributes.

Acknowledgements

"Let's write a book about the Doctors," we said. "It'll be easy," we said. We were wrong.

Nonetheless, this book would have been a lot harder without the help of a lot of great people. First and foremost is our editor, Jen Hale, who has our backs even when we don't know it. One of our favourite things about writing these books has been working with Jen, who has been an amazing friend as well. She even used a "Talons of Weng-Chiang" reference in casual conversation recently. We're so proud.

We also enjoy the opportunity to work with ECW Press's managing editor, Crissy Calhoun, who provides Robert with many great opportunities to argue about points of sentence construction that Graeme has long given up understanding. Crissy has been a big supporter of our work, and we're grateful to her. We're also thrilled to be working again with sales and marketing director Erin Creasey and with ECW's wonderful publishers, David Caron and Jack David.

We had help on this book from some really smart people who not only zeroed in on some laughable mistakes but gave us some fun collegial arguments as well. So let's hear it for Shannon Patrick Sullivan,

Jon Arnold, Jon Preddle, Anthony Wilson and Jim Sangster. Deborah Stanish and Scot Clarke gave helpful assistance at other key junctures. There are probably some mistakes we haven't found yet in this book, but that's not their fault at all.

Much of this book has been shaped through many, many smart and interesting conversations with friends and *Doctor Who* fans in pubs, at conventions, on podcasts and online. We're very grateful for the support of many, many people including Erika Ensign (our number one fan), Mark Askwith, Alex Kennard, Shaun Lyon, Dennis and Christine Turner, Lori Steuart, Katie Moon, Felicity Brown, Cadence Gillard, Hindy Bradley, Paul Cornell, Steven Schapansky, Christopher Burgess, Warren Frey, Chip Sudderth, Sean Homrig, Cameron Dixon, Arnold T. Blumberg, Nick Abadzis, Simon Fraser, Phil Ford, Richard Dinnick, Rob Shearman, Lars Pearson, Christa Dickson, Barnaby Edwards, Daniel Changer, Steve Traylen, Jason A. Miller, Felicity Kuzinitz, Greg McElhatton, Kim Rogers, Sage Young, Taylor Deatherage, Bill Evenson, Eva Monaghan, Laura Gerald, Andy Wixon, Dallas Jones, Tony Cooke, Paul Deuis, Dave King, Henry Yau, Lauren Davis, Michael Arndell, Paul Scoones, Jennifer Adams Kelley, Liz Myles, Sam Maggs, Teddy Wilson, Rob Jones, Robin Careless, Rod Mammitzsch, Mike and Nina Doran, Gian-Luca Di Rocco, Ari Lipsey, Andrew Flint, Kenyon Wallace, Colleen Hillerup, Heather Murray, Ryan Piekenbrock and pretty much the entirety of the Toronto *Doctor Who* Tavern (first Thursday of every month at Pauper's at Bloor and Bathurst).

Extra-special thanks to Julie Hopkins and Kate Fleming for support and care above and beyond the call of anything. Thanks also to Laura Collishaw for moral support.

This book was put together in Australia, Austria, Brazil, Denmark, Haiti, India (twice), Japan, Namibia, Senegal and, in Canada and the United States, in Ottawa, Toronto, Montreal, Windsor, Sherbrooke, Lakeview, Quebec City, Oakville, Wellesley, Hamilton, Sudbury, Chicago, Minneapolis, Ronkonkoma, Los Angeles and a hotel room in Lombard, Illinois. We're grateful for the invention of the wi-fi router, especially in hotels.

And, as ever, thank you, dear reader, for sticking with us through 12 or so Doctors. If you want to ask us questions, give feedback or just ask why Robert loves acrostics, feel free to send us an email at whoisthedoctor@gemgeekorrarebug.com.

We said in our first book, *Who Is The Doctor*, that we're here because we think *Doctor Who* is the greatest television show ever. We still think that. And we think the Doctor is the best hero on television as well. We hope you do too.

GRAEME BURK (right) is a writer and *Doctor Who* fan. He is the the co-author (with Robert Smith?) of the best-selling and award-winning books *Who Is The Doctor: The Unofficial Guide to Doctor Who — The New Series* and *Who's 50: The 50 Doctor Who Stories You Should Watch Before You Die* (ECW Press, 2012 and 2013). He is host and co-producer of the *Doctor Who* podcast *Reality Bomb* (realitybomb-podcast.com). By day, he works as director of communications for a non-governmental organization; his short fiction and non-fiction have been published in North America and Britain, and he currently has a screenplay in development. Toronto is still home to him, but Ottawa is where he lives. His website is gemgeekorrarebug.com; follow him on Twitter @graemeburk.

ROBERT SMITH? (left) is a) a Guinness World Record holder, thanks to his efforts to model a zombie invasion, b) a bona fide ambassador of mathematics, c) editor extraordinaire of the Outside In series of utterly gonzo reviews of *Doctor Who*, d) inventor of an entire academic sub-discipline, e) on first-name terms with Morgan Freeman, f) the person who pioneered the application of impulsive differential equations for infectious diseases, and g) precisely the same age, to the day, as one of the Doctors. Only one of these statements is false.

Published by ECW Press
665 Gerrard Street East
Toronto, ON M4M 1Y2
416-694-3348 / info@ecwpress.com

Editor for the press: Jennifer Hale
Cover design and illustrations:
Risa Rodil / risarodil.com
Author photo: Lisa MacDonald

LIBRARY AND ARCHIVES CANADA
CATALOGUING IN PUBLICATION

Burk, Graeme, 1969–, author
The Doctors are in : the essential and unofficial guide to Doctor Who's greatest time lord / written by Graeme Burk and Robert Smith.

Issued in print and electronic formats.
ISBN 978-1-77041-254-5 (pbk)
ISBN 978-1-77090-781-2 (pdf)
ISBN 978-1-77090-782-9 (epub)

1. Doctor Who (Television program).
I. Smith?, Robert J. (Robert Joseph), 1972–, author
II. Title. III. Title: Essential and unofficial guide to Doctor Who's greatest time lord.

PN1992.77.D63B86 2015 791.45'72
C2015-902814-0 C2015-902815-9

We acknowledge the financial support of the Government of Canada through the Canada Book Fund for our publishing activities, and the contribution of the Government of Ontario through the Ontario Book Publishing Tax Credit and the Ontario Media Development Corporation.

Canada

Printed and bound in Canada

Printing: Norecob 1 2 3 4 5